The ULTIMATE SIDE HUSTLE BOOK

450 *Moneymaking Ideas for the Gig Economy*

ELANA VARON

Adams Media

New York   London   Toronto   Sydney   New Delhi

For my parents, Judy and Dan.

Aadamsmedia

Adams Media
An Imprint of Simon & Schuster, Inc.
57 Littlefield Street
Avon, Massachusetts 02322

First Adams Media trade paperback edition December 2018

ADAMS MEDIA and colophon are trademarks of Simon & Schuster.

For information about special discounts for bulk purchases, please contact Simon & Schuster Special Sales at 1-866-506-1949 or business@simonandschuster.com.

The Simon & Schuster Speakers Bureau can bring authors to your live event. For more information or to book an event contact the Simon & Schuster Speakers Bureau at 1-866-248-3049 or visit our website at www.simonspeakers.com.

Interior design by Katrina Machado
Interior images © 123RF/Victoriia Parnikova

10 9 8 7 6 5 4 3 2 1

Library of Congress Cataloging-in-Publication Data
Varon, Elana, author.
The ultimate side hustle book / Elana Varon.
Avon, Massachusetts: Adams Media, 2018.
Includes index.
LCCN 2018031998 (print) | LCCN 2018034731 (ebook) | ISBN 9781507209226 (pb) | ISBN 9781507209233 (ebook)
Subjects: LCSH: Supplementary employment. | Part-time self-employment.
Classification: LCC HD5854.5 (ebook) | LCC HD5854.5 .V37 2018 (print) | DDC 658.1/141--dc23
LC record available at https://lccn.loc.gov/2018031998

ISBN 978-1-5072-0922-6
ISBN 978-1-5072-0923-3 (ebook)

Contents

Acknowledgments

The career advice that has served me best has little to do with any specific job I sought or the path I've wandered. First, that your opportunities involve some luck, they don't. You find opportunities because you've worked to put yourself in the right place. Second, the "right" job isn't about the title or any rung on the career ladder: it's about working with people you like, and respect, and enjoy spending time with every day.

With that in mind, I am grateful to the family, friends, and colleagues without whom I would not have written this book.

Michael Goldberg, who is both a friend and colleague, introduced me to Cate Prato at Adams Media. Proof, if I still needed it, of the first lesson. Cate is enthusiastic even in an email, and she kept me on track. Peter Archer picked over every side hustle, questioned my assumptions, and found the holes I needed to fill—he also asked for kitten pictures.

Nancer Ballard, Monty Brower, Tammy Byrne, Beau Dure, Fawn Fitter, Bela Gorman, Melanie Hardy, Shirley Hartley Chinn, Bettye Kearse, Sharron Kahn Luttrell, Jen Kettell, John Klossner, Christopher Koch, Mark Lowenstein, Naomi Mansbach, Larry Marion, Chris McLennan, David Rosenbaum, Irena Roman, Lisa Rosowsky, Esther Schindler, Steve Ulfedler, Dave Varon, and Cheryl Umana brainstormed with me, connected me with sources, shared their own side hustle experiences, gave advice and moral support, and provided a reality check. Thank you not only for your help, but also for sharing my excitement about this project.

Andy, Ari, and Mira Eschtruth were unwavering during the weeks that I looked up from my laptop only for meals. I love you.

Introduction

Today the economy—like practically everything else—is changing fast. More and more, people are working several jobs at once: a main job and something on the side. In what's been called the "gig economy," many people augment their incomes with side hustles.

Maybe you are one of 78 million people in the United States who earned money from a side hustle in 2017. If so, you supplemented your regular paycheck with work that ranges from traditional gigs such as babysitting and selling crafts to ridesharing and renting out your house through an app. Or maybe you've never done it before but you want to start—anything from teaching part time at a community college to starting a snow removal service in the winter.

Although side hustles are hardly a new phenomenon, the room for opportunity is growing. Increasingly people are earning extra money by working for themselves rather than from part-time jobs with other employers. Within the next decade, the majority of US adults could be bringing in at least some of their income from self-employment, up from about a third who do so today.

Such side hustles can provide additional income to pay bills, fulfill dreams, or save for retirement. There's a tremendous variety to these hustles; often they draw on skills, qualifications, and interests that aren't part of your main job. That's one of the great things about side hustles: they can focus your energy on your passion. Another important feature of your side hustle is that it offers flexibility.

Whatever the reason for your side hustle, this book can help. Whether you are a student, a stay-at-home parent, an office or shift worker, or a retiree, there are opportunities for you to explore. Many books document gig economy trends or explore why government policies and business practices should change to support independent workers. Read this one to find practical ideas to help you choose a side hustle that works for you depending on your experience, your goals, and your financial needs.

Part I has advice about how to succeed as a modern side hustler, including identifying the skills and abilities you can put to work, defining your goals, looking for jobs, and staying organized. Even if you pursue your side hustle infrequently, it pays to think of yourself as running a small business. You'll get insight into managing your finances, protecting your rights, and keeping your work legal.

Part II contains more than 450 side hustles arranged in twelve categories, collected from interviews with side hustlers and research into dozens of on-demand platforms, classified listings, and other resources about informal and freelance work. Side hustlers share their tips about making the most from their side hustles and pitfalls to watch for.

For each side hustle, you'll learn about what's involved and where to find leads. This key will tell you at a glance how much skill and experience you need, equipment requirements, and how much the work pays:

- Skills and experience needed: + (none or minimal); ++ (some special skills/experience); +++ (specialized training or experience preferred); ++++ (high level of experience)
- Special equipment: ★ (none or minimal); ★★ (some special equipment needed); ★★★ (special equipment required)
- Pay range: $ (starts at $12 or less per hour/gig); $$ (starts at $12.01–$20 per hour/gig); $$$ (starts at $20.01–$35 per hour/gig); $$$$ ($35.01–$100 per hour/gig, or more)

Use this book as a reference to discover work you can start right away, get ideas for the future, and pick up again when you want or need to try something new.

PART I

Making the Most of Your Side Hustle

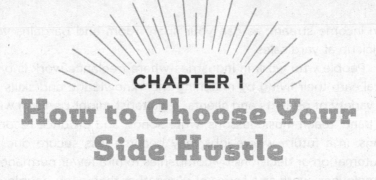

CHAPTER 1
How to Choose Your Side Hustle

When you searched for your current job, you probably had a plan. You figured out the types of work you were interested in and qualified for based on your training and education. You had wage or salary goals and some idea about how this job could lead to your next one or shape your career path. Then you searched for openings, networked with your friends and colleagues, and interviewed until someone hired you. The same principles apply to your side hustle. In this chapter, you'll learn what goes into choosing a good one. Learn to identify your saleable skills; you'll find you have more of them than you may think. Read about how to fit your side hustle to your circumstances so you can reach your earnings targets as well as any goals beyond making money to supplement your income. Get information to help you create a strategy for finding your side hustle. You'll also hear from a graduate student, a former air force officer transitioning to a new career, a retired systems engineer, and a yoga instructor, who offer their insights about choosing and finding a side hustle.

TURNING WORK INTO A HUSTLE

Nearly any work that people do can be turned into a side hustle, whether low-skilled tasks such as running errands and cleaning houses or high-skilled trade and professional services like electrical work, nursing, and accounting. Your artistic ability, cooking prowess, or fluency in a foreign language can be turned into an income stream, as can your spare room and bargains you pick up at yard sales.

People who work in industries where freelance work is typical earn their living by matching their knowledge and skills to a variety of projects and clients. A guitarist might perform with a band, teach music lessons, write songs, and produce recordings. In a future where jobs may become less secure due to automation or decisions by companies to hire fewer permanent employees, work as a series of gigs rather than a job people go to every day for years could become more common. Millennials, whose expectations about work were shaped by the Great Recession, have taken this idea to heart. They are more likely to freelance at least part time—one way to describe a side hustle—than workers from previous generations.

Many university students, in fact, anticipate a career full of side hustles. "Even if I do get a 'real job' I may have a side hustle of a blog, or teach on the side, so I have freedom to do what I want with my time and not choose one kind of career path," says Jeanelle Horcasitas, a graduate student. The side hustle isn't only about getting some quick money by walking dogs or cleaning houses. Students are applying their classroom and laboratory training to gigs with potential to become independent businesses.

That's a good model for any side hustler. Entrepreneurs—whether their business is a tech startup or a garden design service—succeed by identifying a product or a skill they have to offer that fills a need. Doing work you are good at will help you to maximize your earnings. As you gain experience and increase your expertise, you'll be able to get more work—and potentially higher-skilled work, enabling you to earn higher rates. You'll also be building your resume. With experience, your side hustle could provide you with more options for work should your career interests or employment status change.

LET YOUR SKILLS AND INTERESTS GUIDE YOUR CHOICES

Everyone has saleable skills. With online platforms to match work with people who want to do it, even the most basic tasks have value. You don't need formal work experience to wait in a line, but if you have patience (and books to read or smartphone games to play), you can make $25 per hour or more as a line waiter.

Think about everything you do in a typical day at work and at home. If you focus on tasks or activities where you excel or that you especially enjoy, you'll come up with a list of skills and expertise that you can turn into a side hustle. These might align with your education or your primary job, but they may just as easily relate to a way you think, a hobby, a household task you've mastered, or your family responsibilities.

Tune in to what your friends and colleagues admire about you, or the areas where they rely on your advice or experience.

- If people ask you for help with their presentations, you might be able to create a side hustle crafting slide decks, critiquing presentation delivery, or selling an online course that teaches others how to improve.
- If your wardrobe is full of thrift store purchases that you have tailored, embellished, or otherwise altered, you might be able to provide mending and alterations, or sew clothes to order.
- If you have an abundant garden, you might help others choose plants, give advice about garden feeding and maintenance, or help with outdoor chores.

Don't forget about making money from things you own or that you can easily and cheaply acquire. Your eye for bargains or love of yard sales can become a resale business or provide raw materials you can use to create and sell upcycled goods.

MATCH YOUR SIDE HUSTLE TO YOUR CIRCUMSTANCES

Whatever your reason for starting a side hustle, setting goals will help you to choose the best work to fit your skills, your location, and your time—and maximize your earnings. If it takes you two hours to put together a coffee table, and you're also fluent in Spanish, tutoring two students in the same amount of time could potentially earn you more than assembling furniture for a flat fee.

For most people, their side hustle contributes a small amount to their household finances. The supplemental income may be essential, helping to cover regular expenses. It may pay for family fun, like vacations and summer camp for kids, or fund a home renovation. Or it may provide a financial cushion. "I'm past having security. Now it's about options," explains Jim. While serving in the US Air Force, he actively invested his own funds in stocks, bonds, mutual funds, and real estate.

How fast you need the money may be a factor in the side hustle you choose. Some side hustles enable you to work for an hour, or a few, and get paid right away. If you're selling your homemade soaps, you will have to buy supplies, spend time making your products, and market them before you see any return. With experience, you may find that some side hustles aren't for you, and you'll become more strategic in what you seek out.

You may also have goals beyond making money: to fund a hobby or otherwise get paid to do something you enjoy; to get entry-level job experience or practice a skill you need for the future; or to have a flexible source of funds for when you can't work full time due to caregiving responsibilities, have a reduction in salary or wages, or experience a layoff.

For people who are working in industries that are shrinking, or where jobs will be lost to automation, having a side hustle offers a way to ease the transition by updating their skills or learning a new field. The same is true for anyone facing a career change or retirement. If you're retired, a side hustle can help you to stay busy and connected to people in your community in addition to picking up extra income.

Whether you're starting your career or starting over, a relevant side hustle while you're still employed offers a way to make contacts and gain the skills you need to get a job in a new industry or start your own business. You will also be able to learn which aspects of the work you enjoy the most, figure out how to deal with any challenges you may face, and explore different ways your business can grow.

Be aware that some side hustles—particularly in healthcare, education, law, personal finance, food service, and any work that directly impacts public or individual health and safety, such as electrical work—may require you to be licensed, certified, or otherwise trained. In some fields where credentials are not required, having them can make it easier to find work or earn higher rates.

As side hustles, jobs that require an academic degree or formal training are best for people who already have the qualifications or who are looking for a long-term career change that makes the time and expense a good investment. When I talked to Jim, the retired air force officer, he had qualified as a tax preparer and was in the process of becoming accredited as a financial counselor so he could start a part-time business.

But you can train quickly for other side hustle jobs. Learning to referee grade school soccer takes only a few hours. Tutors, like Steven, a retired systems engineer in Houston who teaches math and science, can easily add a new subject to their repertoire. When he took on a student who needed help with advanced calculus, he filled the gaps in his knowledge of the subject by watching online lectures.

COMBINE TIME-TESTED AND NEW METHODS TO FIND WORK

When you have ideas about the type of work you want to do, and you know your goals, you can create a strategy to find work. The time-tested ways, such as networking with personal and professional contacts, and getting referrals from customers, serve most side hustlers well. Social media extends that network. On-demand and freelancing services platforms are emerging as another source of work.

Most freelancers find work through their family, friends, or professional colleagues. Every industry has conferences, meetups, and other gatherings where you can meet people who may hire you for side work. People who know you can provide references and referrals even when they don't have work to give you. Meanwhile, if you are starting a side hustle doing work that is unrelated to your regular work, your friends could become your first customers. Because they already know and trust you, they will likely be more confident in your skills and abilities than a stranger, and these early jobs will help you build your reputation.

You may also be able to find part-time work through online classified ads, and by cold calling organizations you would like to work for. When Andrea, a social worker who teaches yoga on the side, wanted to offer a class for retirees, she introduced herself to local community recreation directors, which led to a short-term gig.

Social media platforms are also an important source of connections and help to expand your network beyond people you know. *Facebook* and other social networks such as *Nextdoor* support community-based groups, where members often ask their neighbors to recommend home improvement contractors, tutors, housecleaners, and a wide variety of other service providers. These platforms also provide ways for people offering services to advertise their availability and interact with potential customers. Meanwhile, business networks—*LinkedIn* as well as industry-focused platforms—provide a venue for making connections with professional colleagues who may hire you for your side hustle.

If you haven't tried to find work using an online freelance marketplace or on-demand service for independent work, such as *Uber* or *Lyft* for driving, *TaskRabbit* for household tasks, *Catalant* for professional services, *GigSalad* for event planning and entertainment, or *Thumbtack* for a wide range of personal and home services, you're not alone. As of mid-2018, most independent workers have not joined these platforms. However, it's wise to become familiar with how they operate because they have potential to play a larger role in finding gig work in the future.

On-demand and freelance platforms are supposed to make finding gigs easier: once you join and set up your profile, the platforms generate opportunities for you based on customers' requests. This happens in one of several ways:

- The platform matches you to customers' criteria and presents you with gig offers. Ridesharing, delivery services, and household task services work this way.
- Your profile is presented to customers as the first step in a hiring process. Platforms for hiring nannies, tutors, home improvement contractors, and professional consultants tend to work like this.
- You can search for available gigs and bid on them, similar to searching and applying for a conventional job.

Regardless of the process for matching you with tasks or projects, you have access to a wider range of customers and opportunities than you would be able to find by yourself. These platforms also facilitate finding work you may not think to market yourself for, but for which you are qualified.

Though on-demand and professional services platforms are still new to many people, most people who sell things have been doing so online for more than twenty years: *eBay* launched in 1995. Peer-to-peer rental platforms, such as *Airbnb* for home rentals, are newer but gaining popularity. You can list your rentals on *craigslist* or other online classified sites the traditional way, but you can also find peer-to-peer rental platforms covering many types of property—from boats to RVs to your driveway.

Meanwhile, if your side hustle is selling stuff, *eBay* is just one option. For example, *Facebook* has its Marketplace and numerous yard sale groups, while *Nextdoor* has For Sale and Free sections. And there are platforms that specialize in specific types of products, like *Etsy* for art and crafts. If you want to set up an independent online store, there are tools for that as well.

With a clear idea about what you can do, goals for what you want to accomplish, and a strategy to find work, you're ready to side hustle.

Where People Find Freelance Work

- Friends and family: 43 percent
- Professional contacts: 38 percent
- Social media: 37 percent
- Online ad/classified: 27 percent
- Previous employer as a freelancer: 24 percent

Source: Edelman Intelligence/Upwork and Freelancers Union, September 2017

CHAPTER 2
How to Manage Your Time and Money

Even if you don't think of your side hustle as a business, treating it like one will help it succeed. Just like a business, your side hustle needs customers, and you have to define your work and your pay. There may be equipment to maintain, and you have to have revenue goals. Laws and regulations may affect your operations. You have to protect yourself from risk and pay taxes. In this chapter, you'll learn how to keep your side hustle in the black by managing your time and expenses wisely. Find out how to structure your time. Learn why you need to keep track of your expenses and get ideas for thinking about how to set prices for your products or services or decide what an acceptable wage is. Read about why getting legal advice and buying insurance can protect you from losses due to lawsuits, accident, or injury, and about investments you can make to help you to earn more money.

Your side hustle may be a part-time job on an employer's payroll, a series of gigs through an on-demand platform, or a freelance business—or you may have multiple side hustles.

FIRST, MAKE IT PROFITABLE

Whatever the work and how much of it you do, you need to manage your time and your money to make your side hustle profitable.

Even if you don't think of your side hustle as a business, it makes sense to treat it like one. To get work, you have to market yourself and your services or products—even if all you do is set up an online profile. Expenses can eat up your earnings if you don't pay attention to them. In addition, you may need to take steps to protect yourself and your assets in case of an accident, an injury, or a lawsuit.

Consider these aspects of running any business that also pertain to your side hustle:

CUSTOMERS

You are either selling your time, by providing a service, or you are selling a product. Either way, you need to invest some effort in finding people who will pay you. That includes taking the time to craft a professional online profile, including a photo. Independent business owners typically have websites. They may also advertise in local newspapers and online, distribute postcards and flyers, write a blog, or devise other ways to help clients or customers to discover them and learn more about their products or services. For example, an artist, photographer, videographer, or graphic designer will need a portfolio.

CONTRACTS

Depending on the work, you may need formal contracts with your customers or clients. If you work for an online platform, you agree to its terms and conditions, including the cut it will take of your earnings. Though they obviously vary according to the type of work, contracts will define what you will do, what you have to deliver, how much time you allot, and what your customer owes you. Even a job with a paycheck carries expectations about your work, its quality, your compensation, and your employer's obligations.

EQUIPMENT

Any of your own equipment you use for your side hustle has to be maintained in good condition, and you need a plan for covering repairs or replacing it when necessary. Many of the jobs in this book require a computer or a smartphone, as well as a reliable broadband Internet connection. You may find you need to upgrade your laptop, phone, Internet, or data service to perform your work successfully.

REVENUES AND EXPENSES

Whatever you are working toward—paying bills, taking a vacation, buying a new car—you have a target for how much money you want or need to make. Having a budget for your side hustle will enable you to see how much money you need to make—and thus how much you need to work—to cover your materials and any other expenses and still earn enough to reach your goals. If your side hustle is a step toward running your own business full time or gaining experience to change careers, it may be worth it to take a loss temporarily. But without a plan, you won't know how any decision you make will affect your income.

LAWS AND REGULATIONS

Some types of work may require you to be licensed or certified, or to comply with health, safety, or business regulations. Side hustles involving driving require a valid driver's license. If you're selling baked goods, you are subject to regulations concerning food safety and sanitation. You may need a permit to hold classes in your house, perform, or set up a booth in a public place.

RISK

If you are an employee, laws concerning pay, workplace conditions, accident or injury, disability, and liability cover you. But if your side hustle is your own (even if you get your work through an online platform or service), you need measures in place, such as insurance, to shield yourself from losses, medical bills, or legal bills without going bankrupt or losing your house.

TAXES

Money you earn from self-employment is taxable, but you may be able to deduct your expenses.

Do research, talk to others in your area of work, check with relevant state or local government agencies, and consult qualified professionals for advice and answers to your questions about taxes, licensing, insurance, and the laws that may affect you. The rest of this chapter offers suggestions for using your time wisely and safeguarding your earnings.

TIME TO HUSTLE

You can devote a lot of time to your side hustle or a little. Your success depends on how you use it.

First, you have to be realistic about the time you have available. If you work in an office full time, it's likely your side hustle will be limited to evenings and weekends. If you are taking care of family members, you will have to work your side hustle around those responsibilities.

When you know how much time you are able to commit to your side hustle, it's easier to stay focused on work opportunities that will contribute the most to your financial, career, or personal goals.

BUILD A SCHEDULE

Next, you need a schedule. The more control you have over when you work, the more decisive you have to be about doing it. Without a schedule, you may end up not working as much as you need to, or you may take on more than you can manage.

However much you decide to work, you'll want to take into account when there is demand for what you do. May through October is the busiest period for weddings—important if your side hustle is wedding photographer. If you teach music lessons to middle and high school students, you will probably need weekday afternoons or evenings available during the academic year. If your side hustle is on call, like decorating cakes, you will need to know how much time it takes you to complete an order so you accept only as many as you can realistically deliver.

Although low-skilled on-demand work such as ridesharing, making deliveries, or performing household tasks is available almost anytime through online platforms, the people who make the most money at this work choose regular shifts at times when there is high demand (such as Friday and Saturday nights for ridesharing drivers) and devise strategies for reducing their time waiting between gigs.

While researching on-demand work, Jen Curry at Samaschool did a *Postmates* delivery that took forty-five minutes and netted her less than minimum wage. "You have to know where to position yourself during busy times, take advantage of the bonuses, and stack jobs by picking up and delivering along the same route," she advises.

For any side hustle in which you are self-employed, you need to ensure you are earning enough to cover the time you spend doing the work. If you already have experience, you will have some idea of how much you should pay yourself; if not, we give you some estimates for what each side hustle in this book typically pays. Take that knowledge and research what people in your community with your expertise usually earn, and you'll be able to determine a fair rate. Don't forget to cover your overhead—the expenses you incur to support your business. Time you spend traveling to see clients, packaging up orders, buying supplies, and maintaining your equipment all adds up.

MIND YOUR MONEY

By tracking your time and all of your expenses, you will be able to set prices that cover your costs and may also help to offset any taxes you have to pay on your earnings. If you are losing money to car expenses, equipment, materials, and the IRS, it might make sense for you to try something else.

Beyond what you pay for things such as gasoline, art supplies, and computer software, it may be prudent, depending on your work, to invest in training courses. You may need legal advice, tax advice, and insurance. Even if training isn't required to operate your side hustle, it may be hard to get hired without it. In addition, having credentials in fields where they're available may enable you to charge more and attract more customers.

A lawyer can advise you about licensing laws and other regulations you have to comply with, as well as review your contracts to make sure they protect you if clients don't pay, or if you're sued. An accountant can advise you about eligible business deductions and help you set aside enough money to pay your taxes. Insurance protects you if you do end up in court, or if you suffer an accident or injury on the job.

Darline Turner began a side hustle as a doula, providing support to women with high-risk pregnancies, after her son was born. At first, she was helping friends, and friends of friends. When she started to get paid, her relationship to her clients and the work had to change: "Especially in birth work, if something goes wrong, everyone present is at fault," she says. Liability insurance became essential, along with having a properly registered business.

It's clear why a lot of people resist such expenses: after all, it's just a side source of income, and the more money you put into it, it seems, the less there is for you at the end of the day. That's more reason to think carefully about all your costs, and to account for any legal and financial risks, when choosing your side hustle.

Darline became a certified doula and now runs a private practice in Austin. Because many side hustlers envision their work as a test run for a business, or a step toward a new career, the investment in certifications or licenses, or in a new skill that will help you get more work and charge higher rates, will often become worthwhile in the long run. So can buying a piece of equipment or investing in materials to test out a new product design. Some of these investments may be expenses you can deduct from your taxes.

A lot of side hustlers are surprised to learn they owe taxes at all. In fact, earnings of $600 or more from any source have to be reported to the IRS, and if you expect to owe at least $1,000, you may have to pay quarterly estimated taxes.

In 2016, Caroline Bruckner of American University surveyed members of the National Association of the Self-Employed about their income from on-demand and sharing platforms such as *Uber*, *Lyft*, and *Airbnb*. Among those who said they participated, about a third didn't know they had to make quarterly tax payments on those earnings. Half didn't know which expenses they could write off or the deductions or credits they were eligible for.

These were people, Bruckner points out, who ran their own businesses and were more likely than the average person to know the rules. They were confused, she concludes, because they did not earn enough to receive a Form 1099, the form that companies use to report payments to independent contractors.

"Once you become aware, you get with the program, file any back taxes owed, and you get organized. Or you've already missed so many payments, and what you owe is so overwhelming, that many people walk away and don't file. I've had that analysis confirmed anecdotally by the IRS and CPAs who specialize in advising," Bruckner says. Meanwhile, some people, though they know they will need to pay taxes, aren't organized enough managing their expenses and end up in debt when the bills come due.

When you have a handle on all your expenses, you can determine how much you want or need to earn in order to cover your costs and your time, while turning a profit.

Melissa Dinwiddie runs workshops for companies that use games, improvisational theater, and other play-based techniques to teach employees skills that improve communication, collaboration, and managing conflict. It's a full-time business, and she is a serial entrepreneur. Several of the companies she has run over the past twenty years started as side hustles. "I've always thought more in terms of streams of income," she says. "I haven't gotten a paycheck since I was twenty-three and worked at a nursery school."

At first, she thought about pricing in terms of whether she would be paid enough to justify her time. But during one of her early ventures, as a calligrapher making hand-lettered books and artwork, she learned to charge based on how much money she wanted to make from the work. If the customer balked at the price, she would suggest an alternative product rather than cut her rate.

She also learned that customers were not paying her for her time, but for the value of the art she created. "In some cases, I would estimate a book would take twenty hours and it only took me ten, and I would think I should collect less money." Her epiphany came when delivering to a client who lived in a mansion. "The amount of money was insignificant to her."

Like Melissa, self-employed side hustlers who sell their products or services independently have control over what they charge. That's not so much the case for side hustlers who work through online marketplaces and on-demand platforms, which may set your rate for each gig. Even if you are able to set your rate, the platform takes a cut. It may be worth it, if you're still getting a wage you think is fair (without costing you) and you would not have the work otherwise because it was too difficult or time consuming to find.

You may make other tradeoffs. Matt, a public school teacher in New Jersey, tutors high school students studying for the SAT. He has tutored privately and worked for test prep centers. Private tutors can charge $75 per hour in his area, but have to find their own clients and put time into creating lesson plans. He earns less when he teaches at the test prep centers, but the work—and thus the income—is more predictable. "The lower wage of the learning center is often made up for by the regularly scheduled work," he says, and he doesn't have to deal with cancellations. There are other advantages. With full-time teaching responsibilities in his day job, "It's a great relief to have lesson plans provided."

The bottom line: you want your side hustle to succeed on your terms. And for that, you have to be vigilant about your time and your money.

Top Five Industries for Independent Contractors, Consultants, and Freelancers (Percentage of Workers in 2014)

- Personal Services: 39 percent
- Construction: 35 percent
- Agriculture and Mining: 34 percent
- Finance: 22 percent
- Professional and Business Services: 22 percent

Source: Aspen Institute, American Action Forum, January 2017

PART II

Side Hustles

CHAPTER 3

Drive

When Megan, a single mother living near Boston with two teenagers, needed a new car, she signed up with *Uber* to fund it. She drives for the ridesharing service a few mornings a week, shuttling fellow suburbanites either to Logan Airport or to work or school nearby—before she heads to her day job as a writer for a market research company.

"My mother sends me every horror story," she says. The Internet brims with tales about drunk, disorderly, destructive passengers—and worse. "But I drive early in the morning and I don't do the bar crowds." She nets enough to make her car payment and pay for gas every month. "And if I need to make more money quickly for a vacation or something, I can do that."

NEW OPPORTUNITIES FOR DRIVERS

Driving a taxi has long been a go-to gig for people who want to make spare cash. During the past decade, *Uber* and its main competitor, *Lyft*, have created the same opportunities for anyone with a newish car and a smartphone. The same kind of software—an app that matches drivers and people who need help with tasks requiring transportation—has also spawned services for delivering packages and groceries and running errands. If you're free on Saturday mornings or you have a couple of hours between classes, you can log in and pick up some extra cash. In some cases, if you don't have a car, you can use your bicycle.

Driving or cycling gigs with app-fueled, on-demand services are available mainly in large cities, university towns, and popular travel destinations. Meanwhile, businesses everywhere continue to depend on part-time workers to drive buses or shuttles, make deliveries, and park cars. These jobs sometimes require special training or licenses. Delivery van, truck, and bus drivers, for example, need commercial driver's licenses. Your driving or cycling skills may net you some unique work too—such as pedicabbing (see entry in this chapter).

Drivers who are part-time employees, as opposed to on-demand freelancers, have defined shifts, although employers may let workers choose them. By definition, the part-time jobs are less flexible, but the income may be more predictable. Ridesharing or on-demand delivery drivers may work anytime, but those who drive often, who work when rides are in high demand, and who are able to minimize their downtime between passengers or delivery orders earn the most. It's best to set modest goals and surpass them. As time goes on, you'll be better able to judge how much time you want to spend as well as the money you want to earn.

If you use your own vehicle, keep in mind that you will usually have to cover your expenses—not just gas, but also repairs that may be more frequent due to extra wear and tear. On-demand services may provide limited insurance, but only when you're making the trip; if you get into an accident while you're driving home after dropping off your customer, you're on the hook. In addition, the more you drive your car, the faster it loses value. If you plan to sell the car or trade it in when it is no longer eligible to be used for work, the added mileage will affect how much you can get for it.

SIDE HUSTLES USING YOUR CAR OR BICYCLE

AUTO ADVERTISING

SERVICE PROVIDED Display advertisements wrapped around your car.

SKILLS AND EXPERIENCE NEEDED + | You don't need experience, but you need a newish passenger vehicle, and you have to be able to drive in the area targeted by each advertising campaign. Some local laws may require you to register your car as a commercial vehicle, and you may have to comply with city or homeowners' association parking rules. If you drive with a ridesharing company, check whether their rules allow you to wrap your car.

SPECIAL EQUIPMENT ★ | Your own vehicle and provided advertising materials.

WHERE TO FIND LEADS Sign up with a car-wrapping company. Beware of scams: legitimate companies will not ask you for money up front, to deposit a check and wire money, or send you messages asking for personal information. You may not get many opportunities unless you live in an urban area.

PAY RANGE $ | It depends on the ad campaign, when you drive, and where. For a typical campaign, drivers earn around $100 per month.

CAR DELIVERY

SERVICE PROVIDED Drive cars between locations for an individual, dealership, fleet service, or car rental company. Some jobs offer the opportunity to drive long distances.

SKILLS AND EXPERIENCE NEEDED ★★ | Meet eligibility criteria. You need to know how to drive and have a valid driver's license and clean driving record. You may need a commercial license in some states.

SPECIAL EQUIPMENT ★ | Cars.

WHERE TO FIND LEADS Car dealerships, rental car agencies, fleet services, and car relocation delivery services all hire drivers. You may find openings advertised in online classifieds.

PAY RANGE $$ | Pay varies based on the type of company you're driving for. Earnings of $10–$25 per hour are common.

COURIER

SERVICE PROVIDED Deliver documents, small packages, food, liquor, lab specimens, business supplies, and other items.

SKILLS AND EXPERIENCE NEEDED ++ | Depending on the work and location, you will need to know how to drive and have a valid license or be able to ride a bicycle. Some courier jobs require experience with deliveries or with handling sensitive materials.

SPECIAL EQUIPMENT ★ | Your own car, bicycle, motorcycle, or scooter.

WHERE TO FIND LEADS On-demand services match couriers with tasks posted by customers. Courier agencies, as well as some banks, pharmacies, healthcare providers, and medical laboratories advertise on job websites.

PAY RANGE $$ | Couriers earn an average of $18 per hour, but pay rates vary widely—anywhere from minimum wage to $30 per hour or more.

FORKLIFT OPERATOR

SERVICE PROVIDED Operate a forklift in a warehouse.

SKILLS AND EXPERIENCE NEEDED ++ | You need to be trained to operate the type of forklift you drive.

SPECIAL EQUIPMENT ★ ★ ★ ★ | Your employer's forklift.

WHERE TO FIND LEADS Manufacturing companies, logistics companies, retail distribution centers, and dockyards typically need forklift operators. Network with people you know who work for these companies. Join task-on-demand platforms and look for advertised openings in the online classifieds to learn about opportunities.

PAY RANGE $$ | Most forklift operators earn at least $15 per hour.

GROCERY DELIVERY

SERVICE PROVIDED Bring groceries to people's homes.

SKILLS AND EXPERIENCE NEEDED ++ | Know how to drive and have a valid license and insurance. Be able to lift heavy bags. If you work for an on-demand service, you may have to do the shopping, too, so you should know kale from mustard greens.

SPECIAL EQUIPMENT ★★ | On-demand services like *Instacart* or *Shipt* require you to use your own vehicle. You'll also need a smartphone to access the app. Supermarket-operated delivery services may provide a company van.

WHERE TO FIND LEADS On-demand services generally operate in urban areas. You have to join and download an app to see work opportunities. Find supermarket jobs through help wanted websites.

PAY RANGE $$ | Grocery delivery drivers typically earn $15–$25 per order for on-demand services, plus tips. You have to complete jobs quickly to maximize your hourly rate. Supermarket chains pay delivery drivers around $20 an hour.

HAYRIDES DRIVER

SERVICE PROVIDED Provide recreational hayrides.

SKILLS OR EXPERIENCE NEEDED ++ | Know how to operate a tractor or Jeep while pulling a wagon. Be fit for heavy lifting.

SPECIAL EQUIPMENT ★★★ | Tractor or Jeep and wagon.

WHERE TO FIND LEADS Local parks and recreation departments and farms.

PAY RANGE $ | Hayride drivers earn on average $10 per hour, which is around the minimum wage in some states.

MEAL DELIVERY

SERVICE PROVIDED Bring meals to people in their homes or offices.

SKILLS AND EXPERIENCE NEEDED ✦✦ | Know how to drive and have a valid license. In urban areas you may be able to use a bicycle, in which case you need to be physically fit and comfortable cycling fast in traffic. You'll be lifting heavy packages too.

SPECIAL EQUIPMENT ★ | Your own car or bicycle. Smartphone to access delivery requests, get directions, and manage transactions. You may need your own insurance.

WHERE TO FIND LEADS On-demand services including *Uber Eats*, *DoorDash*, *Seamless*, and *Grubhub* operate mainly in urban areas. You have to join and download the app to see job opportunities. Search for postings by restaurants such as Domino's or Panera that hire their own drivers.

PAY RANGE $ | Meal delivery jobs typically pay $5–$6 per delivery from on-demand platforms. Restaurants that hire their own drivers pay an hourly base rate (a starting rate of $5 an hour is typical). If you're using your own vehicle, make sure you're getting reimbursed for mileage. As with server jobs in restaurants, you'll be expected to boost your per-delivery or hourly rate from tips.

Similar Jobs

Meals on Wheels delivery: while volunteers often fill these jobs, occasionally the position is paid.

MOVING SERVICE

SERVICE PROVIDED Transport furniture and household items. Possibly work with a team of packers (see Chapter 10).

SKILLS AND EXPERIENCE NEEDED ✦✦ | Have experience driving trucks, including those supplied by rental companies. Moving truck drivers typically need a commercial driver's license. Be fit enough to lift heavy boxes if required.

SPECIAL EQUIPMENT ★★ | If you are offering a complete moving service, you will need your own truck.

WHERE TO FIND LEADS Moving companies hire drivers. You can also find work by joining task-on-demand platforms, including services that specialize in helping people move. Some companies supply drivers to drive customers' rented trucks. Community-focused social media groups may be a source of work; members ask for recommendations when they need help.

PAY RANGE $$ | Moving services drivers earn around $13 per hour.

NEWSPAPER DELIVERY

SERVICE PROVIDED Deliver newspapers to subscribers' homes or businesses.

SKILLS AND EXPERIENCE NEEDED ★★ | Know how to drive and have a valid license. Be able to lift stacks of newspapers.

SPECIAL EQUIPMENT ★ | Your own vehicle.

WHERE TO FIND LEADS Newspaper distribution companies, advertised openings.

PAY RANGE $ | Most newspaper delivery drivers earn $10–$18 per hour.

PACKAGE DELIVERY

SERVICE PROVIDED Deliver packages to residences and businesses.

SKILLS AND EXPERIENCE NEEDED ★★ | Know how to drive, and have a valid license. You may need a commercial driver's license. Because you're lifting and carrying packages that may be heavy, you need to be fit enough for the work.

SPECIAL EQUIPMENT ★ | Depends on the employer or service. You may need your own vehicle and insurance, as well as a smartphone to access work requests and routes.

WHERE TO FIND LEADS Established logistics companies such as UPS and FedEx, as well as many businesses that deliver supplies or equipment to customers, advertise part-time positions. If you join an on-demand platform such as *Amazon Flex* or *Task-Rabbit*, you have more flexibility to set your hours, and you'll see opportunities via their smartphone app.

PAY RANGE $$ | Pay depends on your location and the nature of the job. If you work regular shifts for one single company, you'll be paid an hourly or weekly rate. Many of these jobs pay more than minimum wage. On-demand services—which generally operate in major cities and let you work when you want—advertise that drivers can earn $18 an hour or more.

PEER-TO-PEER DELIVERY

SERVICE PROVIDED Transport items for individuals locally or long-distance.

SKILLS AND EXPERIENCE NEEDED ✦ | Know how to drive and have a valid license. If you're transporting heavy objects, you need to be physically fit.

SPECIAL EQUIPMENT ★★ | Your own car, van, or pickup truck.

WHERE TO FIND LEADS As with moving services, you may find work by joining task-on-demand platforms and community groups on social media. In some cities, peer-to-peer delivery platforms specialize in matching people who have an item to transport with someone who is going to the same place.

PAY RANGE $$ | Depending on the job and the distance traveled, peer-to-peer delivery drivers can earn anywhere from a few dollars delivering locally to several hundred dollars for an interstate trip.

PEDICAB DRIVER

SERVICE PROVIDED Transport people, give tours.

SKILLS AND EXPERIENCE NEEDED ++ | You must be physically fit enough to pedal a big tricycle in traffic while pulling a cab and passengers: total weight may exceed 500 pounds. Knowledge of local history and landmarks helps if you want to pedal for a tour company or you pick up fares from tourists. Sometimes pedicab shops provide training.

SPECIAL EQUIPMENT ★ ★ ★ | Typically pedicabbers rent their vehicles. Some pedicabs are electric-assisted.

WHERE TO FIND LEADS Most of these jobs are in cities with a lot of tourists and at resorts. You may find openings advertised on help wanted sites or by contacting pedicab shops and companies that give pedicab tours.

PAY RANGE $ | Pedicabbers typically charge by the mile or by the minute and get tips, earning anywhere from $10 to $60 per hour.

RACE CAR PIT CREW

SERVICE PROVIDED Work on racing pit crews and test the cars.

SKILLS AND EXPERIENCE NEEDED +++ | Knowledge and curiosity about cars and how to optimize their racing performance. You can attend a training program, but you also need real-world experience working on cars. If you want to race, working with a team is a common way to get exposure to the sport and develop relationships that can lead to competitive opportunities.

SPECIAL EQUIPMENT ★ ★ ★ | A racing car and tools.

WHERE TO FIND LEADS Your local track.

PAY RANGE $$ | Professional pit crew team members can earn upward of $100,000 per year. At the local track, under $20 per hour is more common.

RIDESHARING

SERVICE PROVIDED Transport people.

SKILLS AND EXPERIENCE NEEDED ++ | Know how to drive and have a valid driver's license and insurance. As with driving a taxi (keep reading), good conversation skills help you earn tips.

SPECIAL EQUIPMENT ★★ | You need your own car, and it has to comply with the ridesharing service guidelines for age and condition (your 2002 hatchback with a broken seatbelt is a no go). You need a smartphone to receive ride requests, access directions via GPS, and manage transactions.

WHERE TO FIND LEADS Large urban areas are best. Once you qualify on a ridesharing platform, you'll use their app to access ride requests.

PAY RANGE $$ | Per trip rates vary widely and depend on many factors, including local demand, the type of car you drive (newer, bigger, and higher-end vehicles earn more), and when and how often you drive. Drivers may also get tips. According to the website *Rideshare Central*, drivers for *Uber* and *Lyft* earned an average of $15.50–$17.50 an hour in 2017 before accounting for gas and other expenses, although some drivers can earn $25 an hour or more.

ROAD TEST OR DRIVER'S LICENSE EXAMINER

SERVICE PROVIDED Administer road tests to people applying for a driver's license.

SKILLS AND EXPERIENCE NEEDED +++ | Know how to drive, and have a valid driver's license for the type of vehicle you are testing. You need a clean driving record and to complete training programs and other requirements as determined by state law.

SPECIAL EQUIPMENT ★ | No special equipment needed.

WHERE TO FIND LEADS State licensing agencies, driving schools, word of mouth, advertised openings.

PAY RANGE $$$ | Road test examiners earn an average of $21 per hour.

RUNNING ERRANDS

SERVICE PROVIDED Take packages to the post office; drop off and pick up dry cleaning; bring prescriptions to the pharmacy; buy cards, snacks, or household items; get the car washed; and other routine tasks.

SKILLS AND EXPERIENCE NEEDED ++ | Know how to drive and have a valid license or be able to ride a bicycle. You may find yourself spending a lot of time in checkout lines and traffic, so don't do this if idle minutes make you impatient.

SPECIAL EQUIPMENT * | Car or bicycle. If you join an on-demand service, you'll need a smartphone to access the necessary apps.

WHERE TO FIND LEADS On-demand services such as *TaskRabbit*. In addition, people sometimes post requests for help with errands to local groups on social networking sites—especially worth checking out if there are no on-demand services in your area. You may be able to post your availability on those sites too. But check the group rules first (some consider it advertising and don't allow It).

PAY RANGE $$$ | It varies by the job, but *HomeAdvisor* suggests errand runners be paid $25–$30 per hour or more for driving errands. *TaskRabbit* enables its "taskers" to set their own rates and matches them to customers who are willing to pay those rates.

SCHOOL BUS DRIVER

SERVICE PROVIDED Transport children to and from school, day care, after-school programs, and camp.

SKILLS AND EXPERIENCE NEEDED +++ | Experience driving, a commercial driver's license, and other training or certifications required by law. Have a good rapport with children of all ages. Be able to think quickly and stay calm during an emergency or if kids get out of control.

SPECIAL EQUIPMENT ★★★★ | School bus supplied by the school district.

WHERE TO FIND LEADS Sources of jobs include bus companies, school districts, summer camps, and other programs that use buses to transport children. You may find openings advertised on job classified sites.

PAY RANGE $ | School bus drivers typically earn $11–$20 per hour, depending on where they live.

> ### *Similar Jobs*
>
> Shuttle bus/van driver, adult day-care/assisted-living driver, medical van driver, wheelchair van driver, chauffeur/limousine driver: drive a shuttle bus, van, or limousine. Work includes transporting people and groups between hotels and airports, around a corporate or an academic campus, to events (such as weddings, proms, or nights out), or taking elderly adults and people with disabilities to and from medical appointments and recreational programs. For the latter, you may need First Aid/CPR certification.

TAXI DRIVER

SERVICE PROVIDED Transport people.

SKILLS AND EXPERIENCE NEEDED +++ | Know how to drive, have a valid driver's license and a taxi (or hackney) license. Good conversation skills help earn tips.

SPECIAL EQUIPMENT ★★ | Taxi drivers either own their own vehicles or rent them from a fleet company.

WHERE TO FIND LEADS Fleet companies advertise online, or you may hear about work from friends or colleagues.

PAY RANGE $ | Fares, which are composed of a base rate plus a rate per mile, are regulated locally. Typical fares range from an estimated $2 to $12 for a mile trip and $14 to $63 for 10 miles. Taxi drivers typically earn around $11 per hour.

TRUCK DRIVER

SERVICE PROVIDED Transport goods and make deliveries.

SKILLS AND EXPERIENCE NEEDED ++ | Know how to drive a truck, have a valid commercial driver's license and meet other eligibility criteria. For example, you need a hazmat license to transport hazardous materials.

SPECIAL EQUIPMENT ★★★ | If you offer your services independently, you need your own truck.

WHERE TO FIND LEADS Trucking companies, package delivery companies, and peer-to-peer delivery or task-on-demand platforms can be sources of work, as can any company with a fleet of trucks or products to haul. Openings may be advertised in the online classifieds. You may also learn of opportunities from your friends and colleagues, including through social media.

PAY RANGE $$ | Drivers of heavy trucks and tractor-trailers usually get paid by the mile, most earn more than $20 per hour. Light truck and delivery truck drivers typically earn around $17 per hour.

TOW TRUCK DRIVER

SERVICE PROVIDED Assist motorists when their vehicles are disabled or tow cars that are violating parking laws.

SKILLS AND EXPERIENCE NEEDED ++ | Have a valid driver's license and meet other criteria required by state law. You may need a commercial driver's license. Most tow truck drivers learn on the job, though some employers prefer to hire people with experience.

SPECIAL EQUIPMENT ★★ | Tow truck and equipment for charging batteries and changing tires.

WHERE TO FIND LEADS Local car repair shops, gas stations, and roadside assistance services may have openings for tow truck drivers. You may find opportunities listed in the online classifieds or hear about them from your friends and colleagues.

PAY RANGE $$ | Tow truck drivers typically make around $13 per hour, although drivers of heavy duty rigs can earn more. Some drivers also earn a commission on their calls.

VALET ATTENDANT

SERVICE PROVIDED Park cars at restaurants, event venues, airports, hotels, or private parties.

SKILLS AND EXPERIENCE NEEDED ++ | Know how to drive and have a valid license. You may need to know how to work a standard transmission. If you work for a valet service, you may need at least a year or two of previous valet, driving, or delivery experience. You should also be physically fit: this work requires a lot of walking, standing, and sometimes running if you need to get to a customer's car quickly.

SPECIAL EQUIPMENT ⋆ | No special equipment needed.

WHERE TO FIND LEADS Agencies advertise online. Networking in your community may help you find work parking cars for local events or private parties.

PAY RANGE $ | Like restaurant servers, valets are expected to get tips, which means they can be paid a lower minimum wage than workers who don't receive tips. That accounts in part for the wide pay range anywhere from $5 (below the federal minimum wage of $7.25) to $25 per hour depending on the location.

"I would say set modest goals for how much time you want to spend and how much money you want to make."
—Megan, *Uber* driver

CHAPTER 4
Teach

Most people know a side hustler who teaches. The painter who taught your watercolor class. Your Zumba teacher at the gym. The tutor who helped your kid to an A in Spanish. If you're an expert at something and you are good at explaining it to others, teaching or tutoring is a flexible gig that can sometimes pay well. Today, thanks to web-based platforms that help people create and sell their own courses, it's even possible—though not necessarily easy—to create a course once and sell it repeatedly.

PICK THE APPROACH THAT SUITS YOU

Teachers who prefer to work with students directly can choose an approach that suits them: one-on-one tutoring, private group classes, and getting work through a school, club, community center, or other sponsoring organization.

Steven, a retired systems engineer in Houston, has tutored high schoolers in math and science for more than forty years. When he started, he was looking for an antidote to his day job helping to improve the performance of optical systems used in satellites and telescopes. "I was working all the time," he recalls.

When he and his wife bought a house in eastern Massachusetts, he signed up with the local school district to tutor math, physics, and chemistry. "I appreciated getting paid for tutoring, because I wasn't being paid for doing all that extra work in my job."

After moving to Houston, however, Steven had to make adjustments. "All their tutors are certified teachers," he recounts.

Substitute teaching doesn't require teaching credentials (he had done this back in Massachusetts when he first retired), so he works several days a week and tutors privately.

The qualifications for working within a public school department are often set by law. Health clubs and other venues that hire fitness instructors may want them to be certified for another reason: liability. Generally you need to be certified, and, depending on what you're teaching, you may have to carry malpractice insurance.

Some people teach colleagues during their lunch hour. Others teach privately in their homes or, in the case of physical activities such as yoga, at nearby health clubs and studios. Still others teach school-age children and their teachers in local schools or teach community-sponsored classes for seniors. For some types of classes, such as yoga, private students pay best; when classes are offered to the public, the venue takes a cut.

TEACHING SIDE HUSTLES

ADULT EDUCATION TEACHER

SERVICE PROVIDED Teach classes for nondegree personal enrichment, skill development, or continuing education to groups of adults in person.

SKILLS AND EXPERIENCE NEEDED +++ | Students will want you to be an expert in the subject you're teaching. For your course to be accepted as part of a formal program—such as at a community college or vocational school, you may need an academic degree in that subject, professional certification or a teaching certificate, some years of practical work experience, or all of these.

SPECIAL EQUIPMENT ★ ★ | Equipment needed depends on the course. The facility where you are teaching may have it available.

WHERE TO FIND LEADS Colleges, community colleges, vocational schools, and community organizations may advertise openings and respond to inquiries. Some programs may accept proposals from teachers who want to offer a course. You may be able to give your course independently if you have a place to meet.

PAY RANGE $$ | Teachers of enrichment courses typically earn around $18 per hour. Teaching technical or professional subjects, such as computer training, earns the most: if you offer vocational training, you could earn more than $25 per hour.

AEROBICS INSTRUCTOR

SERVICE PROVIDED Lead aerobics classes.

SKILLS AND EXPERIENCE NEEDED +++ | Be physically fit, enthusiastic, and knowledgeable about creating aerobics routines. Health clubs may prefer to hire instructors who have a group exercise certification.

SPECIAL EQUIPMENT ★★ | If you teach at a health club or other facility where exercise classes are offered, they will likely have the equipment you need.

WHERE TO FIND LEADS Facilities that offer fitness classes may advertise for instructors, or you can pitch your services to them. If you belong to a health club, you may learn of opportunities there or at other places by word of mouth. You may also be able to find work by signing up for an on-demand platform that matches instructors with clients.

PAY RANGE $$ | Group exercise instructors earned an average of around $20 per hour. If you teach at a health club, membership may be part of your compensation.

Similar Jobs
Water aerobics, group fitness classes using cardio equipment: you may need additional certification to teach water aerobics.

AFTER-SCHOOL AIDE

SERVICE PROVIDED Help to supervise school-age children, lead activities, and assist with homework in an after-school childcare program.

SKILLS AND EXPERIENCE NEEDED ++ | Requirements vary by state and by program and may depend on whether the program is publicly or privately operated. You can work as an after-school caregiver with a high school diploma, although some programs prefer aides who are working toward an education or related degree or have some training or experience. You may have to be certified in First Aid and CPR.

SPECIAL EQUIPMENT ★ | Kids will do homework, make crafts, or play board games. The equipment you need will depend on which of these activities they take part in. If you work for an after-school program, they may provide all the necessary supplies.

WHERE TO FIND LEADS After-school programs post jobs online, or you may learn of openings from your school or people in your community.

PAY RANGE $ | Teacher assistants earn $13 per hour on average.

ART OR CRAFTS TEACHER

SERVICE PROVIDED Teach art or craft classes or workshops to adults or children.

SKILLS AND EXPERIENCE NEEDED +++ | You should have experience with the medium or methods you plan to teach. If you are teaching at a school, you may also need a teaching degree or certification, a fine arts degree, teaching experience, or all three.

SPECIAL EQUIPMENT ★★ | You and your students will need the appropriate tools and materials to execute your lessons. Teachers typically charge students for materials, but in some cases, such as photography, students may need to supply their own equipment.

WHERE TO FIND LEADS If you are offering lessons privately to groups or individuals, registering with an online platform may help you find clients. You can also promote your lessons on social media. Art schools, adult education programs, or enrichment programs for children may advertise for instructors or consider a proposal from you.

PAY RANGE $$ | Art teachers typically charge per student. For private in-person instruction, rates of $60 or more for an hour lesson are common, but as with any business, your earnings will depend on what is left after your expenses.

ATHLETIC COACH

SERVICE PROVIDED Coach youth or high school team sports, or teach athletic skills.

SKILLS AND EXPERIENCE NEEDED ++ | Skills and experience vary depending on the ages of the athletes, the level of play, and the sponsoring organization. Enthusiasm for the sport and some experience playing it may be enough to teach children basic skills. Some programs and private clients may require prior coaching experience, certification, or time playing at the college- or semipro-level.

SPECIAL EQUIPMENT ★ ★ ★ | Depending on who you are coaching, and whether you are doing it independently, you may need to supply some of the equipment needed for lessons or practices.

WHERE TO FIND LEADS Coaching jobs for school-affiliated teams are usually available to teachers in their school district. Local recreation leagues or independent sports programs may advertise for coaches, or you may hear of these jobs by word of mouth. Online platforms can connect you with private clients.

PAY RANGE $$ | Rates vary widely depending on the ages and level of the athletes, the league or sponsoring organization, and the experience required. A weekend job coaching soccer for children under ten in Des Moines, Iowa, recently paid $14 per hour, while private football coaches in San Diego may charge $30 per hour or more.

BRIDGE INSTRUCTOR

SERVICE PROVIDED Teach the card game.

SKILLS AND EXPERIENCE NEEDED ++++ | The American Contract Bridge League (ACBL) and the American Bridge Teachers Association (ABTA) offer certifications and a teaching curriculum.

SPECIAL EQUIPMENT ★★★ | Cards and teaching materials.

WHERE TO FIND LEADS Both the ACBL and the ABTA offer online lists of teachers for people who want to hire one. You may find students by networking with community organizations, local bridge clubs, schools, and assisted living residences.

PAY RANGE $$ | For teachers who earn $150 or less for teaching classes of eight or more students, the ACBL will add a $350 stipend. For private instruction, teachers may charge $45–$75 per hour.

CAMP COUNSELOR

SERVICE PROVIDED Supervise and teach children at summer camp.

SKILLS AND EXPERIENCE NEEDED ++ | Enthusiasm for working with children, singing silly songs, and spending time outdoors is essential. Some programs may look for counselors who can teach arts and crafts, drama, sports, computer software, or other skills. Counselor-in-Training experience and First Aid/CPR certification may help you get hired.

SPECIAL EQUIPMENT ★ | Camps typically provide the equipment needed for the activities they offer.

WHERE TO FIND LEADS Networking with people who work at a camp you have attended is a good way to learn about openings. Summer camps and programs, as well as local parks and recreation departments, may advertise.

PAY RANGE $ | Recreation workers, which include camp counselors, earn an average of $13. However, many entry-level camp counselors earn minimum wage.

COLLEGE INSTRUCTOR

SERVICE PROVIDED Teach adults in a degree or continuing education program.

SKILLS AND EXPERIENCE NEEDED ++++ | An academic degree (usually at least a master's) and professional experience as a teacher or practitioner in your subject area is essential.

SPECIAL EQUIPMENT ⋆ | You need access to any equipment needed to teach your course.

WHERE TO FIND LEADS Colleges and community colleges may advertise when they need instructors. Networking with colleagues in your field may also help you learn of opportunities.

PAY RANGE $ | Although pay varies depending on your field and highest degree, adjunct college instructors—who are contractors—typically earn $2,000–$3,000 per course. When the time for lesson planning, teaching, grading, and meeting with students is taken into account, many instructors net less than minimum wage.

COOKING TEACHER

SERVICE PROVIDED Teach adults or children how to cook.

SKILLS AND EXPERIENCE NEEDED +++ | You should be an expert at cooking the type of food you are teaching people to make. You will need to obtain any licenses and certifications pertaining to handling, processing, and serving food that are required by law.

SPECIAL EQUIPMENT ⋆ ⋆ ⋆ | Cooking tools and equipment for yourself—and, if it is a hands-on course, for your students—as well as enough dishes and cutlery for serving. Depending on local regulations, you may have to use a commercial kitchen or have your home kitchen certified as complying with food safety and storage rules. These regulations usually do not apply to teaching a private class to someone in their home.

WHERE TO FIND LEADS Online platforms can match you with students. By joining local community groups on social media, you can meet potential clients or people who will provide referrals. You can also offer your class to local recreation departments, other cooking-related businesses, and adult education programs. If you are a professional chef, you may be able to teach at a cooking school or interest locals in taking a class at your restaurant.

PAY RANGE $$ | Cooking teachers and chefs charge a wide range of prices depending on whether they are teaching adults or children, the number of students in a class, their location, the venue where the lessons are held, and the teacher's expertise. A common price for a private, hour-long cooking lesson is $60. A company providing cooking lessons to children after school in Columbia, Maryland, recently offered $210 to teach a six-session course—around $20 per hour.

DANCE TEACHER

SERVICE PROVIDED Teach dance to children or adults.

SKILLS AND EXPERIENCE NEEDED +++ | In addition to your dance expertise, you may need teaching experience to work at a dance school or in a recreation program, or to attract students to your own classes.

SPECIAL EQUIPMENT ★ ★ | Depending on the type of dance you teach, your students, and their level, you may need studio space.

WHERE TO FIND LEADS Online platforms may be able to match you with private clients. Dance schools and recreation programs may advertise openings. You can promote your classes and network with people in your area in person, with flyers and business cards, and on social media.

PAY RANGE $$ | Dance instructors teaching classes in a school earn $20 per hour on average. If you are teaching private lessons, as part of a fitness program, or to students with specific goals, such as learning choreography or preparing for a wedding, you may be able to charge more.

DAY-CARE TEACHER

SERVICE PROVIDED Provide childcare to babies, toddlers, and preschoolers.

SKILLS AND EXPERIENCE NEEDED ++ | Training and education requirements vary by state. States also have regulations that govern home childcare businesses.

SPECIAL EQUIPMENT ★ ★ ★ | If you provide day-care services from your home you will need toys, food, and equipment required to run your program and comply with state and local regulations.

WHERE TO FIND LEADS Online platforms may connect you with parents who need day care for their children or day-care centers that are hiring part-time teachers.

PAY RANGE $ | Childcare workers earn an average of $11 per hour, which is the minimum wage in some states. Preschool teachers typically earn more: an average of $16 per hour.

DRAMA/ACTING TEACHER

SERVICE PROVIDED Teach theater skills.

SKILLS AND EXPERIENCE NEEDED +++ | If you have theater experience, you could teach acting to children or adults. A school-sponsored enrichment program may require you to have teaching experience or an academic degree in a related field.

SPECIAL EQUIPMENT ★ ★ | Depending on the focus of the instruction and the venue where you are teaching, you may need to help with props, costumes, or other materials.

WHERE TO FIND LEADS Local school districts, independent enrichment programs, universities, and theaters hire part-time instructors. You may learn about openings from friends and colleagues, or from advertisements in online classifieds. You can promote your expertise on social media.

PAY RANGE $$$ | Drama teachers typically earn around $20–$30 per hour.

DRIVING INSTRUCTOR

SERVICE PROVIDED Teach people how to drive a motor vehicle.

SKILLS AND EXPERIENCE NEEDED ++++ | Driving instructors must take a training course (some driving schools may sponsor your training) and meet other state-mandated qualifications, such as a license for, and experience driving, the type of vehicle you will be teaching. Good communication skills and patience are critical.

SPECIAL EQUIPMENT ★★★ | You need access to a dual-control vehicle.

WHERE TO FIND LEADS Driving schools hire part-time instructors.

PAY RANGE $$ | Driving instructors earn about $15 per hour for teaching students to drive passenger vehicles. You may be able to earn more for teaching commercial vehicles.

ENGLISH LANGUAGE TUTOR

SERVICE PROVIDED Help non-native speakers learn English.

SKILLS AND EXPERIENCE NEEDED ++ | If you are a fluent English speaker or writer, non-native speakers may hire you for conversation practice, studying help, or writing advice. However, teaching experience and English as a Second Language (ESL) certification are preferred and often needed to get work tutoring students learning formal English. Familiarity with your students' native language or career field may help you get work.

SPECIAL EQUIPMENT ★ | If you are working with students online, you will need to be proficient using video chat software (for example, Skype or FaceTime) for your meetings.

WHERE TO FIND LEADS Online platforms can connect tutors with students around the world. Schools and private companies may advertise for tutors. You can also use social media to promote your services.

PAY RANGE $ | Rates depend on your location, experience, and the format of your lessons. Online tutoring generally pays less than if you meet with students in person. Some English language tutors earn less than $10 per hour, which is the minimum wage in some states. However, adult literacy teachers, the category that includes certified ESL teachers, typically earn around $27 per hour.

FARM EDUCATOR

SERVICE PROVIDED Teach children about farming and farm animals.

SKILLS AND EXPERIENCE NEEDED +++ | Usually farm educators need a degree in agriculture or a related field and experience working with children, but some jobs may not have a specific education or training requirement.

SPECIAL EQUIPMENT ★ ★ ★ | Use farm equipment as appropriate for the program.

WHERE TO FIND LEADS Agricultural extension programs and community farms hire educators to teach their programs. You can learn about openings from friends and colleagues, social media, and online classified listings. These may be seasonal positions.

PAY RANGE $$ | Farm educators earn an average of about $16 per hour.

FLIGHT INSTRUCTOR

SERVICE PROVIDED Teach people how to fly airplanes.

SKILLS AND EXPERIENCE NEEDED ++++ | Hold a commercial pilot or airline transport pilot certificate, become certified as a flight instructor, and complete training with an experienced instructor.

SPECIAL EQUIPMENT ★ ★ ★ | An airplane.

WHERE TO FIND LEADS Offer your services to local flight schools. Your friends and colleagues may be aware of open teaching slots, and you may find some jobs listed in the online classifieds.

PAY RANGE $$ | Flight instructors earn $15–$50 per hour. Independent flight instructors generally charge more than people working for flight schools, but work may be harder to find.

FOREIGN LANGUAGE TUTOR

SERVICE PROVIDED Tutor native English speakers in a foreign language.

SKILLS AND EXPERIENCE NEEDED +++ | Fluency in the language you are teaching is important. Students may prefer a tutor with formal credentials (such as a related degree or teaching certification), and schools may require that you have credentials in order to refer you to their students.

SPECIAL EQUIPMENT ★ | If you are tutoring online, you will need to be proficient using video chat software (for example, Skype or FaceTime).

WHERE TO FIND LEADS Use online platforms and social media to find students. You may be able to get referrals from colleges or local school districts.

PAY RANGE $$ | Rates start at under $20 per hour, but some tutors charge as high as $80 per hour depending on their location, experience, and the format of their lessons. Online tutoring generally pays less than in-person, and native speakers may be able to charge a premium.

GYMNASTICS INSTRUCTOR

SERVICE PROVIDED Teach gymnastics to children.

SKILLS AND EXPERIENCE NEEDED ++ | Instructor certification, competition experience, coaching experience, or all three may be preferred or required by gyms and private clients. Some recreational programs will hire people without certification who have experience in gymnastics or related sports, such as cheerleading.

SPECIAL EQUIPMENT ★ ★ ★ | Gymnastics equipment.

WHERE TO FIND LEADS Join an online platform and use social media to connect with private students. Gyms and recreation programs advertise job openings.

PAY RANGE $$ | Coaches generally earn an average $20 per hour. However, private coaches may charge significantly more: a gymnastics coach in Athens, Georgia, charged clients $63 per session in April 2018.

LESSON PLAN CREATOR

SERVICE PROVIDED Sell your lesson plans and teaching materials to other teachers.

SKILLS AND EXPERIENCE NEEDED +++ | Be a K–12 teacher. Research whether your school district owns your materials. If so, it owns the copyright and you may not be allowed to publish and earn money from them yourself.

SPECIAL EQUIPMENT ★ | No special equipment needed.

WHERE TO FIND LEADS Post your materials to online marketplaces where teachers sell lesson plans and materials. These sites may offer marketing tools to help you promote your work to other teachers.

PAY RANGE $$ | You can set your own rates for your materials: you may have to pay a membership fee, and sites usually take a cut. Prices range from less than $1 to $15 or more.

MEDITATION TEACHER

SERVICE PROVIDED Guide people in meditation.

SKILLS AND EXPERIENCE NEEDED +++ | Meditation teachers can earn a variety of certifications depending on the type of practice they offer. Many meditation teachers also teach yoga, tai chi, or other so-called "healing arts."

SPECIAL EQUIPMENT ★ | You need a teaching space.

WHERE TO FIND LEADS Find open teaching slots at yoga and meditation studios, or give private classes to your friends and colleagues. You can list your profile in professional directories to help clients find you, and promote your services on social media.

PAY RANGE $$$ | Meditation teachers may charge anywhere from $30 to $180 or more for an hour session.

MUSIC TEACHER

SERVICE PROVIDED Provide private instruction to students learning a musical instrument.

SKILLS AND EXPERIENCE NEEDED +++ | You need to be proficient to expert in the instrument you're teaching. Usually musical instrument teachers have had some formal training as well as performance experience.

SPECIAL EQUIPMENT ★ ★ ★ | You need your instrument.

WHERE TO FIND LEADS You may be able to get referrals from local school districts, instrument sellers, and current or past students. Online platforms may be able to match you with students, and you can promote your services on social media.

PAY RANGE $$$ | Rates vary from $30 per hour to more than $100 per hour depending on your instrument, location, training, and professional credentials. Students typically begin with half-hour lessons.

ONLINE INSTRUCTOR

SERVICE PROVIDED Present an online class about a subject in which you are expert.

SKILLS AND EXPERIENCE NEEDED +++ | In addition to your subject matter expertise, you need good presentation skills. You should be comfortable with learning and using online tools to create and package your course content and interact with students.

SPECIAL EQUIPMENT ★ | You need a computer and Internet connection sufficient to access and interact with the online platform that will host your course, as well as to create your lesson materials and communicate with students.

WHERE TO FIND LEADS Multiple online platforms host courses and provide resources for instructors to create and manage their content. Once you choose a platform and create your course, you will have to promote it online and gain reviews to attract students.

PAY RANGE $$ | Instructors usually set their own rates for their courses and pay the hosting site a cut or a fee. On *Udemy*, a course about decluttering a home cost $19.99, while a beginning Java software development course cost $194.99.

OUTDOOR EDUCATOR

SERVICE PROVIDED Teach about the environment and outdoor survival skills.

SKILLS AND EXPERIENCE NEEDED +++ | The training you need depends on the type of programs you're teaching. You may need to take an outdoor education course for some positions, as well as obtain CPR, safety, and Wilderness First Responder certification.

SPECIAL EQUIPMENT ★ ★ | Gear and tools appropriate to the program you're teaching.

WHERE TO FIND LEADS You can work in recreation programs and summer camps, for outdoor gear outfitters, at parks, and in schools. Get referrals from friends and colleagues, and promote your work on social media. Outdoor educator jobs may be seasonal.

PAY RANGE $$ | Depending on the job, outdoor educators typically earn $12–$17 per hour.

PARAPROFESSIONAL EDUCATOR

SERVICE PROVIDED Assist classroom teachers.

SKILLS AND EXPERIENCE NEEDED ++ | Depending on the state where you work, you may need some college or an associate's degree and certification.

SPECIAL EQUIPMENT ★ | You need teaching materials, which may be supplied by the school where you work.

WHERE TO FIND LEADS Find jobs in local school districts or private schools. You may hear of openings from friends and colleagues or find them advertised in online classifieds.

PAY RANGE $ | Most paraprofessional educators earn $11–$16 per hour.

PERSONAL TRAINER

SERVICE PROVIDED Provide one-on-one physical fitness instruction. Some personal trainers also run group fitness classes.

SKILLS AND EXPERIENCE NEEDED +++ | Be physically fit and knowledgeable about kinesiology, health, and fitness. You may need certification to work at a health club, and having training may help you get private clients. Some states are considering requiring personal trainers to be licensed.

SPECIAL EQUIPMENT ★★ | Exercise and training equipment appropriate to the training you do, and a place to meet with clients.

WHERE TO FIND LEADS You may be able to offer training to clients at a health club where you are a member, or at other clubs. You can also offer private sessions. Your friends and colleagues can provide referrals, and you can promote your services on social media. Joining an online platform that provides referrals for personal services may help you connect with potential clients.

PAY RANGE $$$ | Personal trainers typically make around $25 per hour, but as a private trainer you may be able to charge $80 or more. Pay varies depending on location; personal trainers in in large urban areas tend to earn the most.

PILATES INSTRUCTOR

SERVICE PROVIDED Teach people how to practice Pilates.

SKILLS AND EXPERIENCE NEEDED +++ | Train as a Pilates instructor, practice, and get teaching experience. Most health clubs require teachers to obtain a group fitness certification.

SPECIAL EQUIPMENT ★ ★ ★ | You must have Pilates equipment at the studio where you teach.

WHERE TO FIND LEADS As with other fitness instructors, you may be able to teach classes at the gym or studio where you are a member, as well as at other studios. Social media, personal and professional contacts, and word-of-mouth referrals can help you attract students.

PAY RANGE $$$ | Part-time Pilates instructors typically earn around $27 per hour.

RELIGIOUS SCHOOL TEACHER

SERVICE PROVIDED Teach students about religious beliefs and practices.

SKILLS AND EXPERIENCE NEEDED ++ | Be a practitioner of the faith you're teaching. Some congregations may want you to have teaching experience.

SPECIAL EQUIPMENT ★ ★ | You need teaching materials.

WHERE TO FIND LEADS Houses of worship in your area (especially your own). Your friends and colleagues may be able to refer you. You may also hear of openings on social media or find them in the online classifieds.

PAY RANGE $$$ | Religious educators typically earn around $25 per hour.

SAT/ACT TUTOR

SERVICE PROVIDED Help students study for college readiness tests and improve their scores.

SKILLS AND EXPERIENCE NEEDED ++ | Start with having a high score on the exam you are tutoring. Familiarity with test taking strategies is useful, but if you work for a test prep company or a learning center, you may get training. Some companies require teacher certification.

SPECIAL EQUIPMENT ★ | Test prep companies supply a curriculum and teaching materials. If you tutor privately, you'll need your own lesson plans.

WHERE TO FIND LEADS Test prep companies may advertise openings. Joining an online platform can help you to connect with private clients.

PAY RANGE $$ | Rates for tutors in learning centers start at about $14 per hour, though some positions pay $20 per hour or more. Private tutors with experience can get $50 and up.

Similar Jobs
Tutor for GED, MCAT, LSAT, GRE, and GMAT: students studying for other standardized tests for high school equivalency and graduate or professional school admissions also hire tutors or take test prep courses.

SKI INSTRUCTOR

SERVICE PROVIDED Teach people how to ski.

SKILLS AND EXPERIENCE NEEDED +++ | Be a good skier with patience and endurance. Some resorts may want you to have instructor training and certification.

SPECIAL EQUIPMENT ★ ★ ★ | You need skiing gear.

WHERE TO FIND LEADS Most ski mountains offer instruction. Get to know people on the staff, and you will be able to learn about opportunities to teach.

PAY RANGE $ | Ski instructors make an average of around $11 per hour, which is minimum wage in some states.

SUBSTITUTE TEACHER

SERVICE PROVIDED Fill in for classroom teachers when they are absent.

SKILLS AND EXPERIENCE NEEDED +++ | Requirements vary by state and sometimes by school district. You may need an academic degree and teaching credentials in some states, but others have minimal or no degree requirements.

SPECIAL EQUIPMENT ★ | Classrooms will be equipped with what you need.

WHERE TO FIND LEADS School districts may advertise openings, or you may be able to learn about available jobs by contacting school departments in your area. Once a school district accepts you for substitute work, you may have the ability to choose your assignments.

PAY RANGE $$ | Substitute teachers earn an average of $15 per hour. Usually, substitutes are paid a daily rate.

SWIMMING TEACHER

SERVICE PROVIDED Teach people how to swim.

SKILLS AND EXPERIENCE NEEDED ✦✦✦✦ | Swim instructors must be certified according to state law in the state where they teach. You may need other teaching experience.

SPECIAL EQUIPMENT ★★ | You need kickboards, floatation devices, and other equipment to help students learn swimming skills, as well as safety equipment as required by law.

WHERE TO FIND LEADS Health clubs, community pools, and beaches may advertise for instructors. Online platforms may connect you with students who want lessons in their backyard pools.

PAY RANGE $ | Hourly rates for swim instructors start at around minimum wage, though some earn $20 per hour teaching at a club or public pool. Private instructors may be able to charge significantly more depending on where they live.

TECHNOLOGY TRAINER

SERVICE PROVIDED Teach people, often seniors, how to use their digital devices or smart home technology.

SKILLS AND EXPERIENCE NEEDED ✦✦ | Know how to set up consumer devices such as laptops, smartphones, and tablets, and instruct users in how to use their basic functions. You can also help people learn to use popular apps.

SPECIAL EQUIPMENT ★ | No special equipment needed.

WHERE TO FIND LEADS You can find a job with a computer support service or offer help independently. If you work solo, tap your friends and colleagues and join community-focused groups on social media to find potential clients and generate referrals.

PAY RANGE $$$$ | Retailers charge customers anywhere from $0 to $40 to perform basic setup in the store. A house call can cost

$70 or more. You can figure out a price that offers a better value to customers who are willing to pay something for the service.

TEST PROCTOR

SERVICE PROVIDED Verify students' identities and supervise them during tests to ensure they don't cheat.

SKILLS AND EXPERIENCE NEEDED + | Test proctors usually do not need special skills, although some schools and organizations prefer to hire people who have academic degrees or related experience.

SPECIAL EQUIPMENT ★ | No special equipment needed.

WHERE TO FIND LEADS Schools and test centers may advertise. Jobs may also be offered internally to employees or students who are qualified. Test prep companies hire proctors to supervise practice SAT, ACT, and similar exams.

PAY RANGE $ | Pay rates range from near $10 per hour, which is the minimum wage in some states, to more than $20, depending on the location, type of test, and the hiring organization. The State Bar of California pays exam proctors $13.50 per hour.

TEST SCORER

SERVICE PROVIDED Score standardized tests online.

SKILLS AND EXPERIENCE NEEDED +++ | At least a bachelor's degree and training in how to score the test. To score some tests you may need a teaching license or an advanced degree.

SPECIAL EQUIPMENT ★ | You need a computer and an Internet connection sufficient to access and complete the work.

WHERE TO FIND LEADS Testing companies advertise openings and accept online applications.

PAY RANGE $$ | Test scorers typically earn $12–$15 per hour.

TUTOR

SERVICE PROVIDED Help students keep pace with their schoolwork.

SKILLS AND EXPERIENCE NEEDED +++ | Expertise in the subject you're tutoring, such as an academic degree in the subject—or, if you're a student, excellent grades—as well as teaching experience. School districts that employ tutors may require you to have a teaching license.

SPECIAL EQUIPMENT ★ | Teaching materials and, if you are tutoring online, video chat software for meeting with your students.

WHERE TO FIND LEADS Networking in person and on social media, as well as joining an online platform, can help you connect with potential clients. You may be able to apply to be a tutor with your local school district.

PAY RANGE $$ | College students tend to charge $10–$20 per hour, while more experienced tutors charge $30 per hour or more.

VOICE COACH

SERVICE PROVIDED Provide training for singers or help people improve their speaking voice for presentations, speeches, or stage performance.

SKILLS AND EXPERIENCE NEEDED +++ | Similar to musicians who teach instrument lessons, voice coaches typically have studied vocal performance themselves and have experience as singers.

SPECIAL EQUIPMENT ★ ★ ★ | If you are working with singers, you may use a piano.

WHERE TO FIND LEADS You may be able to get referrals from local school districts, choral groups, and current or past students. Online platforms may be able to match you with students, and you can promote your services on social media.

PAY RANGE $$ | Voice coaches charge anywhere from $20—$100 per hour or more. Your rate will depend on whether you teach children or adults, and your professional credentials.

YOGA TEACHER

SERVICE PROVIDED Teach yoga to kids or adults.

SKILLS AND EXPERIENCE NEEDED ++++ | Yoga teachers need at least two hundred hours of training to be certified.

SPECIAL EQUIPMENT ★★ | Access to a space suitable for your class. Yoga mats and props unless your students provide their own.

WHERE TO FIND LEADS You may be able to teach classes at a yoga studio, community center, health club, school, or a student's home. Joining an online platform and networking in person and on social media can help you connect with potential students.

PAY RANGE $$ | Pay for yoga instructors at a health club is similar to that of other fitness trainers: $20 per class on average. Experienced teachers and teachers who give private classes usually earn more—especially in large urban areas.

YOUTH LEADER

SERVICE PROVIDED Supervise youth programs for religious organizations.

SKILLS AND EXPERIENCE NEEDED +++ | You will likely need some experience working with young people, in-depth knowledge of your faith, and possibly academic training in education or theology.

SPECIAL EQUIPMENT ★ | No special equipment needed.

WHERE TO FIND LEADS Houses of worship in your area (especially your own). Your friends and colleagues may provide referrals, and you may learn of openings on social media or advertised in the online classifieds.

PAY RANGE $$ | Most youth leaders for religious organizations earn $12–$20 per hour.

ZUMBA INSTRUCTOR

SERVICE PROVIDED Teach Zumba fitness classes.

SKILLS AND EXPERIENCE NEEDED +++ | Training and a Zumba teaching license. To teach at a health club you'll also need to be certified as a group exercise instructor. Knowledge of music and experience with choreography will enable you to develop unique routines for your students.

SPECIAL EQUIPMENT ★ | No special equipment necessary. You'll need a place to teach your class and equipment to play the music you use for your routine.

WHERE TO FIND LEADS Facilities that offer fitness classes may advertise for instructors, or you can pitch your services. If you belong to a health club, you may learn of opportunities there or at other places by word of mouth. You may also be able to find work by signing up for an on-demand platform that matches trainers with clients.

PAY RANGE $$ | Zumba instructors are paid similarly to group exercise instructors: $20 per hour is common, although you may be able to charge more depending on where you live and whether you host your own classes versus teaching at a health club. If you teach at a health club, membership may be part of your compensation.

"I appreciated getting paid for tutoring, because I wasn't being paid for doing all that extra work in my job."
—Steven, substitute teacher, Houston

People Want to Learn
Jobs for self-enrichment teachers are among the fastest growing of all teaching occupations, according to the US Bureau of Labor Statistics.

CHAPTER 5
Advise

If you have expertise in almost any field, you can get paid to give advice. You can even find some side hustles—such as focus groups and product testing—where companies want your opinion only because of who you are: part of a particular demographic group or engaged in a specific hobby. Most of the time, however, you need to be able to demonstrate that your recommendations are trustworthy and valuable.

An established reputation, a convincing resume, or a compelling story about your experience helps give potential clients confidence that you can guide them. For some advisory work, especially if it involves health, safety, financial, or legal advice, you may be required to have an academic degree or training and a license or certification. In other cases, proof of training may help people feel more comfortable that you know what you're talking about.

Being comfortable with yourself as an adviser may take practice if you aren't used to being in the spotlight or if you're tackling a problem you haven't dealt with before. Even experts in their fields may not have experience giving advice to people they don't work with regularly. You can practice by working for a friend or colleague, who will then be able to give you a reference.

PAID FOR ADVICE

If you can establish a reputation for giving good advice and forming good relationships with your clients, you can often be paid handsomely. Side hustles in this category are among the most remunerative because people are willing to pay high rates in order to take advantage of an adviser's advanced education and years of experience.

Vivek Ravishanker used to work at a brand-name consultancy. Now he works independently, earning money from a variety of gigs. He helps startup companies run their operations and manage their finances—a series of full-time engagements—interspersed with one-off projects doing statistical research or helping clients with short-term projects.

"A whole bunch of people want the quality of insight and rigor and presentation that a big firm gets you but they don't have the budget," he explains. He finds the startup work through his network of professional contacts. The short assignments come from one of five online platforms that match clients with freelance experts and take fees from both to perform the service.

Some years ago, he taught a graduate-level class in data analysis for the hospitality industry as a favor to a professor friend who was shorthanded one semester. Though it seemed "like a crazy idea," Vivek had academic and practical experience using the statistical tools the students had to learn. And because his parents are college professors, he had some knowledge about how to develop and teach a course.

"Short of performing surgery or trial law, if you are willing to give it a try and go above and beyond, anything is doable," he suggests. "In some cases, I get paid less than the market rate to get up the learning curve."

He has decided to revisit the material to develop an online course for sale—another side hustle (see Chapter 4). "This is one model for the gig economy, where you get paid per hour or you need to be there and engaged, versus the side hustle that keeps generating money even when you're not there."

ADVICE-FOCUSED SIDE HUSTLES

BUSINESS CONSULTANT

SERVICE PROVIDED Advise companies on business strategy, management, and finance.

SKILLS AND EXPERIENCE NEEDED +++ | An academic degree and business expertise. Clients may prefer that you have an advanced degree, whether an MBA or in a relevant field, as well as experience working in their industry.

SPECIAL EQUIPMENT ★ | No special equipment needed.

WHERE TO FIND LEADS Network with colleagues in your industry, including by attending conferences and events, to learn about problems they need to solve within their organizations. Use a professionally focused social media platform (for example, *LinkedIn*) to promote your expertise and help potential clients find you. Ask clients to post recommendations online.

PAY RANGE $$$$ | Many business consultants charge $80 per hour and up, depending on their experience, location, and client base.

COLLEGE CONSULTANT

SERVICE PROVIDED Guide high school students in identifying schools to apply to, help with their college essays and applications, and give advice about the admissions process. Some people who do this work specialize in advising certain types of students, such as athletes. Also called educational consultants.

SKILLS AND EXPERIENCE NEEDED +++ | College consultants often complete formal training programs to become certified, or they may have advanced degrees and experience in counseling or related fields. To maintain an in-depth knowledge about individual colleges, admissions, and financial aid, they regularly visit a variety of college campuses.

SPECIAL EQUIPMENT ★ | No special equipment needed.

WHERE TO FIND LEADS Consultants who qualify for membership in one of the leading professional associations can list their services in a directory. You may be able to find part-time work with an educational consulting firm or find clients by networking with your professional and personal contacts. Clients may provide referrals.

PAY RANGE $$$$ | College consultants may charge $85 per hour and up, depending on where they practice.

CORPORATE DIRECTOR

SERVICE PROVIDED As a member of a board of directors, oversee and make decisions about a company's strategy, finances, and performance on behalf of shareholders. Although board positions at some companies, such as the chairman of the board of a fast-growing startup, can be demanding, corporate directorships are generally designed to be part time.

SKILLS AND EXPERIENCE NEEDED ++++ | Have experience as a senior leader or director of another company or a government agency, and have relevant business area or industry expertise.

SPECIAL EQUIPMENT ★ | No special equipment needed.

WHERE TO FIND LEADS Network with other corporate officers and work with recruiters whose companies hire to search for board members.

PAY RANGE $$$$ | Corporate directors' compensation depends on the revenues of the company, with typical pay at the largest US companies exceeding $250,000.

FOCUS GROUP PARTICIPANT

SERVICE PROVIDED Give opinions about consumer products, entertainment, marketing, or political messages.

SKILLS AND EXPERIENCE NEEDED + | You need to qualify for the group based on demographics, lifestyle, product use, or other criteria.

SPECIAL EQUIPMENT ★ | No special equipment needed.

WHERE TO FIND LEADS Sign up and qualify with firms that run the studies.

PAY RANGE $$$$ | Some studies pay participants $75 or more, but you may get gift cards instead of cash.

HEALTH AND WELLNESS COACH

SERVICE PROVIDED Advise people about healthy lifestyle and nutrition practices.

SKILLS AND EXPERIENCE NEEDED +++ | Many coaches have training and experience in a health- or fitness-related field and a health coach certification, but professional standards are relatively new. States differ in how they regulate health and wellness services; for example, in some states coaches have to be licensed to provide nutrition counseling.

SPECIAL EQUIPMENT ★ | You will need video chat software (for example, Skype or FaceTime) if you meet with clients virtually.

WHERE TO FIND LEADS Network with friends and colleagues. Promote your services on social media by posting in local groups and groups focused on wellness.

PAY RANGE $$$$ | Private health and wellness coaches may charge an average of $100 per hour or more.

HOME INSPECTOR

SERVICE PROVIDED Determine the condition of a house for real estate agents, banks, or buyers.

SKILLS AND EXPERIENCE NEEDED +++ | Depending on the state where you work, you may need to obtain a license and certification. Many home inspectors have worked in construction trades.

SPECIAL EQUIPMENT ★★ | Inspectors may need ladders, flashlights, respirators, gloves, safety glasses, cameras, measurement tools, and other equipment to ensure they can access all parts of a building, collect data, and avoid injury.

WHERE TO FIND LEADS Realtors can provide a list of home inspectors to their clients, who may refer you to their friends. Use social media to promote your services, and ask clients to post reviews online.

PAY RANGE $$ | Home inspectors typically earn around $20 per hour, but pay varies depending on the part of the country where the work is performed.

INTERVIEW COACH

SERVICE PROVIDED Help job applicants prepare for their interviews.

SKILLS AND EXPERIENCE NEEDED +++ | Expertise at developing narratives and messages and giving public presentations. Industry knowledge and experience recruiting or hiring is helpful.

SPECIAL EQUIPMENT ★ | No special equipment needed.

WHERE TO FIND LEADS Network with friends and colleagues, promote your business online, and get referrals. Search firms may recommend you to their clients.

PAY RANGE $$$$ | Interview coaches often charge $100 per hour and up.

IT CONSULTANT

SERVICE PROVIDED Advise companies about how to use information technology.

SKILLS AND EXPERIENCE NEEDED ++++ | At least a four-year degree, IT development, management, or consulting experience, and familiarity with current technologies and business management issues. Many consultants have a specialty, such as IT security.

SPECIAL EQUIPMENT ★ | No special equipment needed.

WHERE TO FIND LEADS Independent IT consultants can find work through their professional networks, attending and presenting at events where they can meet potential clients, participating in professional social media groups, and by joining freelance platforms.

PAY RANGE $$$$ | Depending on their level of experience and specialty, IT consultants may charge $100 per hour or more.

LAWYER

SERVICE PROVIDED If you have a law degree and you are licensed, you can earn extra money providing limited on-demand legal advice to businesses or individuals and help them prepare documents.

SKILLS AND EXPERIENCE NEEDED ++++ | Law degree. You have to apply to join an on-demand platform, which may specialize in specific practice areas.

SPECIAL EQUIPMENT ★ | No special equipment needed.

WHERE TO FIND LEADS Online platforms offering legal services help match lawyers with clients based on their needs.

PAY RANGE $$$ | Though there may be exceptions, on-demand platforms tend to pay lower rates than lawyers—especially experienced ones—earn from their firms.

LEADERSHIP COACH

SERVICE PROVIDED Help people—usually executives—improve their leadership skills and techniques.

SKILLS AND EXPERIENCE NEEDED ++++ | Ability and experience understanding personal and organizational dynamics. Expertise getting people to acknowledge their strengths and weaknesses and identify steps to change their behavior.

SPECIAL EQUIPMENT ★ | No special equipment needed.

WHERE TO FIND LEADS Network with colleagues, write about leadership topics, speak at events that potential clients attend. Companies may hire coaches for their executives.

PAY RANGE $$$$ | Executive coaches may charge $300 or more per hour.

LIBRARIAN

SERVICE PROVIDED Help patrons with research, maintain library collections, and develop acquisitions, among other responsibilities.

SKILLS AND EXPERIENCE NEEDED +++ | A library science degree is generally preferred or required.

SPECIAL EQUIPMENT ★ | Know how to use equipment in the library as needed.

WHERE TO FIND LEADS Libraries may advertise part-time openings, or you may hear about them from friends and colleagues.

PAY RANGE $$$ | Librarians make an average of $29 per hour.

LIFE COACH

SERVICE PROVIDED Help clients set personal and professional goals and develop plans to achieve them.

SKILLS AND EXPERIENCE NEEDED +++ | Life experience, especially in an area where clients need advice, is important, as is an ability to listen and draw out potential future paths. Clients may prefer that you have experience with counseling. Many life coaches become certified.

SPECIAL EQUIPMENT ★ | No special equipment needed.

WHERE TO FIND LEADS Choose an area to specialize, then network with friends and colleagues, use social media, and speak at events where potential clients attend. Companies may hire life coaches to work with their employees.

PAY RANGE $$$$ | Life coaches may charge $100 and up.

MYSTERY SHOPPER

SERVICE PROVIDED Visit stores, restaurants, and other businesses, make purchases, and report on how products are displayed, the condition of the store, and other details.

SKILLS AND EXPERIENCE NEEDED + | You do not need any special skills or experience to be a mystery shopper. The Federal Trade Commission warns that companies asking for a fee to register or become "certified" are scams.

SPECIAL EQUIPMENT ★ | A smartphone for taking pictures if the task requires it.

WHERE TO FIND LEADS Register with a legitimate mystery shopper service and apply for assignments.

PAY RANGE $ | Assignments typically pay $5–$20. Sometimes companies may reimburse shoppers for something they buy instead of paying for the job.

PERSONAL FINANCIAL ADVISOR

SERVICE PROVIDED Help individuals set financial goals and create a plan to achieve them.

SKILLS AND EXPERIENCE NEEDED ++++ | If you are going to sell stocks, bonds, or insurance, you need the appropriate licenses. A Certified Financial Planner certification can help attract clients.

SPECIAL EQUIPMENT ★ | No special equipment needed.

WHERE TO FIND LEADS Network with friends and colleagues, and use social media to promote your services. Giving presentations or webinars may help potential clients learn about you.

PAY RANGE $$$$ | Financial planners have different ways of charging for their services, including hourly, flat fee, and commission (if they sell financial products). Common fees for a comprehensive financial plan range from $2,000 to $5,000.

PERSONAL STYLIST

SERVICE PROVIDED Recommend clothing items and outfits to clients.

SKILLS AND EXPERIENCE NEEDED +++ | Knowledge of fashion trends and lifestyles, an eye for what looks good on people whatever their shape, size, or skin tone. Experience working in fashion retail is helpful to learn about the business and meet potential clients.

SPECIAL EQUIPMENT ★ | No special equipment needed.

WHERE TO FIND LEADS Style people you know, and use social media promote your work. Some retailers and fashion companies may hire stylists.

PAY RANGE $$$ | Depending where you live, you may be able to charge $25 to $100 or more per hour.

PRODUCT TESTER

SERVICE PROVIDED Use and review new products.

SKILLS AND EXPERIENCE NEEDED + | Your demographics, interests, and lifestyle are among the criteria companies use to determine whether they want you to test their products.

SPECIAL EQUIPMENT ★ | Products are provided by the company sponsoring the tests.

WHERE TO FIND LEADS You have to apply to product testing companies.

PAY RANGE $ | You may get only a few dollars for a test, or as much as $45 per hour. You may get to keep the product in lieu of payment.

PROPERTY APPRAISER

SERVICE PROVIDED Evaluate property and advise about its value.

SKILLS AND EXPERIENCE NEEDED ++++ | The Appraisal Standards Board sets criteria for education, training, and experience to become a qualified appraiser. To appraise real estate you also need to obtain a license in the state where you work. Several professional associations offer certifications. Property appraisal is one area where industry watchers anticipate automation will eliminate many traditional jobs in the coming years, so as a side hustle this work may be best for people who already have the qualifications, or who are interested in exploring new business ideas.

SPECIAL EQUIPMENT ★ | A computer and appraisal software.

WHERE TO FIND LEADS Banks, insurance companies, and government agencies hire appraisers.

PAY RANGE $$$$ | A property appraiser is likely to charge $250–$450 for a job.

RESUME COACH

SERVICE PROVIDED Help people craft resumes and other communications related to job seeking.

SKILLS AND EXPERIENCE NEEDED +++ | Strong writing and editing skills, knowledge of editing practices, and knowledge of resume practices and hiring trends. You may want to focus on a specific industry.

SPECIAL EQUIPMENT ★ | No special equipment needed.

WHERE TO FIND LEADS You can network with friends or colleagues to find potential clients who need your advice and promote your services on social media. Recruiters may recommend you to their clients.

PAY RANGE $$$ | Resume writers charge per project and charge the most for executive-level resumes. Rates may start at $80 and run more than $300.

SEARCH ENGINE EVALUATOR

SERVICE PROVIDED Review web search results for completeness and accuracy.

SKILLS AND EXPERIENCE NEEDED ++ | Have experience using search engines and pass a qualifying exam. Foreign language knowledge may be required for some projects.

SPECIAL EQUIPMENT ★ | You need a computer.

WHERE TO FIND LEADS A few companies provide search engine evaluation services, and you can apply online to be a reviewer.

PAY RANGE $$ | Around $13 per hour.

SEARCH ENGINE OPTIMIZATION CONSULTANT

SERVICE PROVIDED Advise companies how to improve their rankings in web searches.

SKILLS AND EXPERIENCE NEEDED +++ | Experience using SEO strategies.

SPECIAL EQUIPMENT ★ | You need a computer and a high-speed Internet connection.

WHERE TO FIND LEADS Join a freelance platform to learn about and bid on consulting projects. Network online and with colleagues to meet potential clients.

PAY RANGE $$$ | Depending on the project, SEO consultants may charge $35–$185 per hour.

SURVEY TAKER

SERVICE PROVIDED Take online market research surveys.

SKILLS AND EXPERIENCE NEEDED + | You will be screened to determine whether you are part of the target demographic for the survey.

SPECIAL EQUIPMENT ★ | You need a computer and a reliable Internet connection.

WHERE TO FIND LEADS You need to register with companies that run the surveys and then qualify for each one. Legitimate research companies do not ask for payment to participate.

PAY RANGE $ | Some surveys pay only a few cents, up to a few dollars each. You may be paid in gift cards rather than cash.

TAX PREPARER

SERVICE PROVIDED Help individuals with their tax returns.

SKILLS AND EXPERIENCE NEEDED ++++ | Tax preparers must be certified, and state requirements vary. However, IRS enrolled agents, who pass an exam and commit to continuing education, can practice in any state. Tax attorneys are also registered tax preparers by virtue of their legal expertise. Certified public accountants (see Chapter 11) can qualify as tax preparers under their state's laws.

SPECIAL EQUIPMENT ★ ★ | Tax preparation software.

WHERE TO FIND LEADS You can get gigs during tax season working for tax preparation services and accounting firms. Find private clients by networking with your friends and promoting your services on social media.

PAY RANGE $$$$ | Tax preparers charge an average of about $175 for a return without any itemized deductions.

TRAVEL ADVISER

SERVICE PROVIDED Create itineraries and make travel arrangements.

SKILLS AND EXPERIENCE NEEDED +++ | Travel extensively and have excellent research skills. Specialization in a destination can help you stand out. If you want to have insider access to bookings, you need training to use professional reservation systems.

A few states require travel agents—who book tours, flights, and other reservations for clients—to be licensed.

SPECIAL EQUIPMENT ★ | No special equipment needed.

WHERE TO FIND LEADS A few websites buy itinerary-based travel articles. You can promote your expertise on social media and sell your travel services online. Some travel services hire freelance or part-time employees to research itineraries and travel deals for customers. Travel agencies may advertise openings for part-time jobs.

PAY RANGE $$ | How much you earn will vary based on the types of services you offer. In a 2017 survey, travel agents working 20 or fewer hours per week reported earning an average $7,000 per year, though income rises with experience.

UNDERWRITER

SERVICE PROVIDED Assess the risk of providing a loan or insurance policy and recommend policies and premiums.

SKILLS AND EXPERIENCE NEEDED ++++ | Bachelor's degree, training as an underwriter, and appropriate certifications. Underwriting is one area that industry watchers anticipate will be impacted by automation in the coming years, so as a side hustle this work may be best for people who already have the qualifications, or who are interested in exploring new business ideas.

SPECIAL EQUIPMENT ★★ | You need underwriting software.

WHERE TO FIND LEADS Although most underwriters work full time, part-time jobs are sometimes available.

PAY RANGE $$$$ | Insurance underwriters make an average of $37 per hour.

USABILITY TESTER

SERVICE PROVIDED Test websites and provide feedback about how easy it is to navigate the site and complete tasks.

SKILLS AND EXPERIENCE NEEDED + | No experience needed. You may have to qualify as a tester.

SPECIAL EQUIPMENT ★ | No special equipment needed. Testing services provide software for recording test results and feedback.

WHERE TO FIND LEADS Sign up with usability testing services.

PAY RANGE $ | The major testing sites pay $10 per test.

VIDEO GAME COACH

SERVICE PROVIDED Play video games with clients to help them improve their performance.

SKILLS AND EXPERIENCE NEEDED ++++ | Extensive experience playing one or more video games. Teaching or coaching experience can help you stand out.

SPECIAL EQUIPMENT ★ ★ ★ | Gaming setup and games.

WHERE TO FIND LEADS If players within your gaming community know you to be an expert player and adviser, they may hire or recommend you. You may also apply to join an online platform that matches expert coaches with clients.

PAY RANGE $$ | Coaches may earn $20 per hour or more.

VIDEO GAME TESTER

SERVICE PROVIDED Play video games before they are released to find bugs and other problems.

SKILLS AND EXPERIENCE NEEDED +++ | Have experience playing video games, troubleshooting skills, and an eye for details. You may need specialized knowledge, such as a language or a gaming platform, depending on what aspect of the game you are testing.

SPECIAL EQUIPMENT ★ ★ ★ | Gaming setup.

WHERE TO FIND LEADS Game developers may post job openings, or you may learn about them from other gamers you know and through social media or professional networks.

PAY RANGE $ | Game tester wages start around $8 per hour, but some companies pay $15 or more.

WRITING COACH

SERVICE PROVIDED Help people improve their writing.

SKILLS AND EXPERIENCE NEEDED +++ | Experience as a writer and ideally as an editor. Ability to listen to clients, help them to identify the problems with their writing, and offer solutions.

SPECIAL EQUIPMENT ★ | No special equipment needed.

WHERE TO FIND LEADS It depends on who you want to work with. If your clients are book authors or journalists, attend writer conferences, join writer communities, or network with magazine and newspaper or website editors. To get business clients, join local business organizations. Tap your professional and personal contacts and promote yourself on social media.

PAY RANGE $$$$ | Rates vary, but some writing coaches charge $70–$150 per hour.

> *"Short of performing surgery or trial law, if you are willing to give it a try and go above and beyond, anything is doable."*
> —Vivek Ravishanker, business consultant

Investment Opportunity

Jobs for personal financial advisors are projected to grow 15 percent by 2026, making it one of the fastest-growing professions.

Source: US Bureau of Labor Statistics

CHAPTER 6

Care for People and Pets

Side hustles that involve taking care of other humans and animals require empathy, compassion, patience, commitment, and in many cases a specific type of training, certification, or degree.

As side hustles, many of these jobs are best for people who are already working professionals who pick up private clients to earn some extra money, or work part time while taking care of family responsibilities. Even when credentials aren't legally required, having related work experience or training is often important to reassure clients that you have the knowledge and skills to ensure their safety and well-being, or that of their relatives or pets. With the credibility you get from professional credentials and experience, you can also get paid more (true for many types of work that people hire for based on a person's knowledge).

SPECIAL RISKS

There are, of course, ways to help without investing in more education, or spending years learning the ropes. For example, you can walk dogs or provide companionship to elderly people in your community.

Although legal, regulatory, and liability concerns can arise with any type of work, caring for people or animals carries special risks. If you are working for relatives, friends, or even friends of friends, they might not blame you if something goes wrong under your care. Strangers are more likely to sue you if they or a loved one is injured when you are present or after following your advice. It can be wise to protect yourself by setting up a formal business and having liability insurance.

After exploring a second career as a dog trainer after she retired, Ilene decided on a low-key side hustle.

She had taken an online course and got a part-time job in a pet store where she learned the company's training method. But teaching dogs to sit and stay is easy. Calling herself a dog trainer would have meant she had to be able to work with dogs that need serious behavior modification. "You need to practice with a lot of dogs," she said, and it takes years.

Meanwhile, hanging out a shingle even to provide basic training would require devoting time to advertising and social media, finding a place to hold classes, becoming bonded, and having clients sign contracts to protect her from liability if one of her trainees bit someone.

"I just wanted to spend more time with dogs," she concluded. Rather than invest the time and money that would be necessary to open a business, she decided give private lessons occasionally, if clients come to her—teaching dogs basic skills and addressing low-level behavior problems.

CARING SIDE HUSTLES

ACUPUNCTURIST

SERVICE PROVIDED Perform acupuncture treatment for human or animal patients.

SKILLS AND EXPERIENCE NEEDED ++++ | Most states regulate acupuncturists, and you need to have proper training, licensing, or certification to practice.

SPECIAL EQUIPMENT ★★★ | Equipment necessary to perform treatments, such as needles.

WHERE TO FIND LEADS Network and use social media to promote your practice and connect with potential patients.

PAY RANGE $$$$ | Acupuncturists may get $50 or more for a routine session, but rates may also be determined by the patient's insurance.

ANIMAL BREEDER

SERVICE PROVIDED Breed animals for show, sports, pets, or food.

SKILLS AND EXPERIENCE NEEDED +++ | Know animal biology, genetics, and reproduction, as well as how to care for and groom animals and keep them healthy. In addition, you should know about the standards for different breeds. Your state may require you to have a license.

SPECIAL EQUIPMENT ★ ★ ★ | Supplies and equipment needed to house and care for your animals.

WHERE TO FIND LEADS Clients will provide word-of-mouth referrals. You can promote your business at animal shows, on social media, and in professional communities.

PAY RANGE $$$ | Animal breeders make an average of $21 per hour.

BABY CONCIERGE

SERVICE PROVIDED Help expectant families plan for their baby's arrival.

SKILLS AND EXPERIENCE NEEDED ++ | Depending on the services you are providing, you will need experience shopping for nursery items, decorating, baby shower planning, or finding childcare.

SPECIAL EQUIPMENT ★ | No special equipment needed.

WHERE TO FIND LEADS Parents you work with will provide word-of-mouth referrals. You can also promote your services on social media and by networking with businesses and groups that assist expectant mothers or new parents.

PAY RANGE $$$$ | Rates vary widely by location, clientele, and service offered, with some providers charging around $35 per hour, $75 per hour, or monthly fees of $2,500 or more.

BABYSITTER

SERVICE PROVIDED Supervise children for a few hours at a time.

SKILLS AND EXPERIENCE NEEDED ✦✦ | Knowledge of basic first aid and safety. If you are not a teenager, parents are likely to want you to have experience as a nanny or babysitter and possibly formal training in childcare, child development, or education.

SPECIAL EQUIPMENT ✦ | No special equipment needed.

WHERE TO FIND LEADS Connect with clients by word-of-mouth referrals, networking in your neighborhood and on social media, and joining an online platform that matches babysitters with parents seeking help.

PAY RANGE $$ | Although pay varies by location (less in rural areas, more in cities) the average rate for a babysitter is around $16 per hour. You can charge more to watch multiple children.

BEEKEEPER

SERVICE PROVIDED Maintain beehives and sell honey.

SKILLS AND EXPERIENCE NEEDED ✦ | Read up on beekeeping before you start. Learn how to respond if you are stung, including what to do if you have an allergic reaction. Be aware of regulations concerning keeping hives and selling honey.

SPECIAL EQUIPMENT ✦✦✦ | You need a hive, protection for you from bee stings, and equipment for extracting honey.

WHERE TO FIND LEADS Find customers for your honey by word of mouth. Depending on how much you produce, you may be able to sell at farmers' markets or in shops. Make sure you comply with regulations for manufacturing and selling food products.

PAY RANGE $ | Honey typically retails for around $7 per pound, but beekeepers can often sell local honey for significantly more.

BLOOD PLASMA DONOR

SERVICE PROVIDED Donate your blood plasma to blood banks.

SKILLS AND EXPERIENCE NEEDED + | You need to pass a medical screening and donate twice before your plasma can be used for treatments. Be aware of potential health risks and consequences.

SPECIAL EQUIPMENT ★ | No special equipment needed.

WHERE TO FIND LEADS You can find a plasma donation center online.

PAY RANGE $$$ | Pay ranges from $30 to $50 depending on how much you donate, which is regulated according to your weight.

CHAPLAIN

SERVICE PROVIDED Conduct religious services and counsel people in hospitals, hospices, nursing homes, and other institutional settings.

SKILLS AND EXPERIENCE NEEDED ++++ | Training and certification as a chaplain. You may need to be ordained in a religious faith.

SPECIAL EQUIPMENT ★ | Depending on the organization where they work, some chaplains may wear uniforms.

WHERE TO FIND LEADS Tap your professional network. Look for work with hospitals, hospices, nursing homes, prisons, and other facilities where patients or residents and their family members need comfort and spiritual guidance.

PAY RANGE $$$ | Chaplains typically earn $24–$30 per hour.

DOG TRAINER

SERVICE PROVIDED Train dogs to behave.

SKILLS AND EXPERIENCE NEEDED +++ | Experience with your own dogs and some dedicated research or a class may prepare you to offer basic training. Learning how to train dogs that have behavior problems such as aggression can require years of study and working with many dogs. You also need to be able to develop rapport with dog owners, who need to implement your lessons at home.

SPECIAL EQUIPMENT ★★ | You need a space to work, unless you train dogs in their owners' homes.

WHERE TO FIND LEADS Word of mouth and social media. Some pet stores will teach employees to provide basic training classes.

PAY RANGE $$ | Dog trainers charge about $20 per hour for basic training.

DOG WALKER

SERVICE PROVIDED Take dogs for walks.

SKILLS AND EXPERIENCE NEEDED + | Enjoy being around dogs, and know how to handle them.

SPECIAL EQUIPMENT ★ | Clients usually provide any gear you need, but dog walkers recommend having extra leashes, a portable water dish, treats, and supplies for cleaning up waste.

WHERE TO FIND LEADS Joining local community groups on social media, creating a profile on an online platform (there are some especially for pet care), and networking with friends and colleagues are good ways to learn about opportunities and get referrals or job offers.

PAY RANGE $$ | Many dog walkers charge around $15 for a 30-minute walk, though rates vary according to location and the number of dogs.

DOULA

SERVICE PROVIDED Assist expectant (antepartum) mothers with high-risk pregnancies, or help postpartum. Some doulas also assist during births, but this is a difficult commitment for anyone who isn't able to be on call twenty-four hours a day. Antepartum or postpartum doulas can make their own hours.

SKILLS AND EXPERIENCE NEEDED ++++ | Although doulas are not regulated, training and certification are necessary to establish credibility in order to get work.

SPECIAL EQUIPMENT ★ | No special equipment needed.

WHERE TO FIND LEADS Join professional networking groups and promote your services on social media. Clients will provide word-of-mouth referrals.

PAY RANGE $$$ | Doulas charge anywhere from $25 and up per hour, depending on their location. Birth doulas may charge as much as $1,000–$1,500 a birth.

EGG DONOR

SERVICE PROVIDED Donate human eggs to help families conceive children.

SKILLS AND EXPERIENCE NEEDED ✦ | You need to pass medical and psychological screenings and comply with the donation process, which includes hormone injections. Be aware of potential health risks and consequences.

SPECIAL EQUIPMENT ★ | No special equipment needed.

WHERE TO FIND LEADS Egg donation centers.

PAY RANGE $$$$ | Donors receive an average of $8,000 for a donation.

ELDER COMPANION

SERVICE PROVIDED Assist elderly people with housework, errands, projects, and getting to appointments, and provide companionship.

SKILLS AND EXPERIENCE NEEDED + | No special experience is needed for work that does not involve healthcare.

SPECIAL EQUIPMENT ★ | You may need a car.

WHERE TO FIND LEADS Clients will provide word-of-mouth referrals. You can promote your availability on social media as well as join an online platform that matches providers with individuals or families that need help.

PAY RANGE $$ | Homemaker services for elderly people cost about $130 per day on average.

EMERGENCY MEDICAL TECHNICIAN (EMT)

SERVICE PROVIDED Deliver frontline medical care to patients who are injured or have a life-threatening medical emergency.

SKILLS AND EXPERIENCE NEEDED ++++ | EMTs must complete a training course and meet physical fitness and other requirements mandated by state law. Employers may want you to have experience working in a hospital, clinic, or other facility that encounters emergency patients.

SPECIAL EQUIPMENT ★★★ | The service you work for typically provides the gear you need.

WHERE TO FIND LEADS Hospitals, ambulance services, and other agencies post openings on websites run by EMT professional organizations as well as on general help wanted sites. If you already work in the healthcare field, you may learn of jobs from colleagues.

PAY RANGE $$ | EMTs earn an average of $17 per hour.

HAIR STYLIST

SERVICE PROVIDED Cut and style hair.

SKILLS AND EXPERIENCE NEEDED +++ | Have experience cutting and styling hair. Most states require you to have a license if you are charging money to cut hair, but you may not need one for styling, including African braiding. Some states have regulations concerning home salons as well as the type of services you are allowed to provide in them.

SPECIAL EQUIPMENT ★★★ | Cutting and styling tools, salon equipment, and supplies appropriate to the services you offer.

WHERE TO FIND LEADS Referrals from friends and, if you work in a salon, existing clients. If you do bridal hair, other wedding professionals, including planners, caterers, and photographers, can help you find clients. Registering as a service provider on a wedding planning website may also help you find work.

PAY RANGE $$$$ | Earnings depend on several factors, including the hairstyle and your location. For wedding hair, stylists may charge $50 an up, plus extra for travel to the wedding location.

HEAD LICE REMOVAL TECHNICIAN

SERVICE PROVIDED Remove head lice for clients in their homes. You may be treating entire families.

SKILLS AND EXPERIENCE NEEDED +++ | Know how to remove lice and advise people how to eliminate them from their homes. People who hire lice removal technicians often prefer a chemical-free process. Training as a nurse is helpful to know how to work with clients, especially children.

SPECIAL EQUIPMENT ★★★ | Lice combs and supplies appropriate to your method.

WHERE TO FIND LEADS Network with pediatricians, school nurses, and childcare providers and promote your services on social media. You will also get referrals from clients.

PAY RANGE $$$$ | Head lice technicians typically charge according to the amount of hair a client has—$50–$150 or more per treatment or per hour. You may be able to charge more for house calls. A part-time job with a lice removal salon may pay $10–25 per hour.

HENNA ARTIST

SERVICE PROVIDED Paint henna body tattoos.

SKILLS AND EXPERIENCE NEEDED +++ | Have experience mixing and applying natural henna. Be familiar with product safety: some products marketed as henna, such as "black henna," or henna with color additives, can cause severe injury. In addition, the US Food and Drug Administration has approved henna only as a hair dye. You need to comply with state health and safety regulations concerning tattoo practices, and you may need a cosmetology license to charge money to work on people's skin.

SPECIAL EQUIPMENT ★★★ | Henna and supplies for mixing and applying it.

WHERE TO FIND LEADS Paint your friends and get referrals, teach classes, get jobs at festivals. You may be able to work out of a salon.

PAY RANGE $$$$ | Henna artists often charge per design: $5 for a small tattoo, $50 and up for larger sizes. For parties, you may be able to charge $40–$100 per hour and get several hundred dollars for bridal designs.

HOME HEALTH AIDE

SERVICE PROVIDED Help people who are ill, or who have disabilities or cognitive or emotional impairments with personal care, meals, and routine housekeeping; check vital signs; and assist with exercise and medications.

SKILLS AND EXPERIENCE NEEDED ++ | Typically you will need experience with bathing someone, giving medications, moving a person safely, and related tasks. If you work through an agency, they may want you to have formal training and certification.

SPECIAL EQUIPMENT ★ | Depending on the client, you may need to use basic tools for checking vital signs or helping with artificial limbs, walkers, or medical equipment.

WHERE TO FIND LEADS You can get a job with an agency or offer your services privately. Joining an online matching service can help you to connect with potential clients.

PAY RANGE $ | Pay starts at around minimum wage, but home health aides in urban areas may charge $35 per hour or more depending on the work involved.

Similar Jobs

Hospice aide: care for people who are bedridden or terminally ill to ensure their comfort. You may need training as a certified nursing assistant.

LACTATION CONSULTANT

SERVICE PROVIDED Educate women in breastfeeding mechanisms and techniques and troubleshoot problems.

SKILLS AND EXPERIENCE NEEDED ✦✦✦ | Many states require lactation consultants to be licensed or certified, especially if they charge for their services. In addition, clients' insurance may only cover licensed services. It can be easier to meet licensing or certification requirements if you are trained as a healthcare provider or you work in a setting where you help care for breastfeeding mothers and their babies.

SPECIAL EQUIPMENT ★ | No special equipment needed.

WHERE TO FIND LEADS Healthcare providers who care for pregnant women and newborns, professional organizations, referrals, word of mouth from mother to mother, social media.

PAY RANGE $$$ | Lactation consultants typically make more than $30 per hour, and a certified lactation consultant may charge $100 or more, depending on her location.

LIFE SKILLS COUNSELOR

SERVICE PROVIDED Help people who may have suffered trauma, are in recovery from addiction, or have difficulty functioning for other reasons by coaching them in a variety of skills, including communication, stress management, goal setting, and problem solving. Life skills counselors may also teach practical skills, such as keeping a budget.

SKILLS AND EXPERIENCE NEEDED ++ | Some jobs may prefer or require an academic degree in counseling, psychology, or a related field. A license or certification is typically required for mental health counseling.

SPECIAL EQUIPMENT ★ | No special equipment needed.

WHERE TO FIND LEADS Social services and education programs.

PAY RANGE $ | Pay varies with the type of work and level of education and experience required. An entry-level position pays around $11 per hour.

LIFEGUARD

SERVICE PROVIDED Maintain safety at pools and beaches, and rescue swimmers who are injured or drowning.

SKILLS AND EXPERIENCE NEEDED ++++ | Training and certification as a lifeguard, which must be renewed every two years.

SPECIAL EQUIPMENT ★ | A whistle, water rescue, and first aid equipment.

WHERE TO FIND LEADS Beaches, health clubs, and public or private pools. You may find advertised openings or hear of jobs by word of mouth.

PAY RANGE $ | Pay varies widely, but averages $9.25 per hour, which is at or near the minimum wage in some states.

MAKEUP ARTIST

SERVICE PROVIDED Do makeup for clients.

SKILLS AND EXPERIENCE NEEDED ++ | Expertise applying makeup for people with different types of skin and skin tones. You may need a cosmetology license to charge money to work on people's skin.

SPECIAL EQUIPMENT ★★ | Makeup and tools for applying it.

WHERE TO FIND LEADS Referrals from friends and, if you work in a salon, existing clients. If you do bridal makeup, networking with other wedding professionals, including planners, caterers, and photographers, can help you find clients. Registering as a service provider on a wedding planning website may also help you find work.

PAY RANGE $$$$ | Rates vary according to your location and the service you provide. Some makeup artists earn around $20 per hour. Others may charge $65 or more per session, and rates of more than $100 per session for weddings.

MANICURIST OR NAIL TECHNICIAN

SERVICE PROVIDED Cut, trim, and polish clients' nails, and apply fake nails.

SKILLS AND EXPERIENCE NEEDED +++ | You will need a license from the state where you work in order to charge people.

SPECIAL EQUIPMENT ★★ | Tools and supplies appropriate to the services you provide.

WHERE TO FIND LEADS You can work at a salon, network with colleagues in other cosmetology fields, do nails for your friends, and promote your work on social media.

PAY RANGE $ | Depending on location and the services provided, manicurists typically charge as little as $10 to more than $100.

MASSAGE THERAPIST

SERVICE PROVIDED Give massages.

SKILLS AND EXPERIENCE NEEDED +++ | Training in massage techniques. Most states require massage therapists be licensed in order to charge people.

SPECIAL EQUIPMENT ★★ | Table, chair, hot stones, and aromatherapy oils depending on the services you provide.

WHERE TO FIND LEADS Spas, health clubs, and medical practices. You may also be able to offer massages at events, as a service for a corporate wellness program, or privately. Referrals from friends and colleagues, promoting your services on social media, and listings on professional websites may help you find clients.

PAY RANGE $$$$ | Massage therapists typically charge $60 per hour or more.

OCCUPATIONAL THERAPIST

SERVICE PROVIDED Help patients who have been sick, disabled, or injured recover or improve their ability to perform daily activities. Some occupational therapists use their training and experience to provide home safety assessments.

SKILLS AND EXPERIENCE NEEDED ++++ | A master's degree in occupational therapy and a license from the state where you work. Occupational therapy aides or assistants need only a high school diploma or two-year degree, respectively.

SPECIAL EQUIPMENT ★★★ | Equipment for evaluating patients.

WHERE TO FIND LEADS Network with colleagues at hospitals, private practices, skilled nursing facilities, and home healthcare agencies.

PAY RANGE $$$$ | Licensed occupational therapists earn an average of $40 per hour.

PARENTING COACH

SERVICE PROVIDED Help parents solve problems in their relationships with their young children and adolescents.

SKILLS AND EXPERIENCE NEEDED +++ | Parenting coaches typically have academic and professional backgrounds in education and counseling. Although parenting coaches aren't regulated, a certification can help attract clients.

SPECIAL EQUIPMENT ★ | No special equipment needed.

WHERE TO FIND LEADS You can list your services in professional directories, promote your business on social media, and get word-of-mouth referrals from your clients. You can also blog, give presentations, and offer group workshops to spread the word about your work.

PAY RANGE $$$$ | Though charges vary, some parenting coaches advertise rates of $75 per hour or more.

PET GROOMER

SERVICE PROVIDED Groom dogs and other pets.

SKILLS AND EXPERIENCE NEEDED +++ | Training in how to give baths, trim hair, clip nails, brush teeth, and other grooming practices.

SPECIAL EQUIPMENT ★ ★ ★ | You need grooming tools.

WHERE TO FIND LEADS Work in a pet salon, get referrals from veterinarians and others involved with animal care, promote your services among friends and colleagues and on social media.

PAY RANGE $$$$ | Dog groomers charge anywhere from $30 to $100 or more per appointment or may charge separately for specific services.

> ### *Similar Jobs*
> Dog washing: if you have experience with dogs of different sizes, you may be able to help dog owners by giving their pets baths.

PET MASSAGE THERAPIST

SERVICE PROVIDED Give dogs and cats massages to relax muscles and improve health.

SKILLS AND EXPERIENCE NEEDED +++ | Know animal anatomy and physiology, and be trained in animal massage. Some states require professional certification.

SPECIAL EQUIPMENT ★★ | You need a massage table.

WHERE TO FIND LEADS Get word-of-mouth referrals from pet owners, promote your services on social media, and connect with veterinarians.

PAY RANGE $$$$ | Animal massage therapist rates range from around $45 to $100 per treatment.

PET SITTER

SERVICE PROVIDED Take care of pets when their owners are away, sometimes staying overnight.

SKILLS AND EXPERIENCE NEEDED ++ | Experience taking care of cats, dogs, and other small animals.

SPECIAL EQUIPMENT ★ | Clients usually provide the equipment you need.

WHERE TO FIND LEADS Join local community groups on social media, create a profile on an online platform (there are some especially for pet care), and get referrals from clients, friends, and colleagues.

PAY RANGE $$ | Your rates will depend on your location, how much time you spend with the pet, and your responsibilities. About $16 per hour is average.

Similar Jobs

Work in a kennel or a shelter: check with local kennels or pet day-care providers for part-time openings. Though many shelter jobs are for volunteers, you may find a paid position.

PHLEBOTOMIST

SERVICE PROVIDED Draw blood for medical assessments.

SKILLS AND EXPERIENCE NEEDED +++ | Training and experience drawing blood. In some states you need a license or certification to practice, and many jobs require it.

SPECIAL EQUIPMENT ★★ | Equipment for drawing, collecting—and if you are mobile phlebotomist, storing and transporting blood. The facility where you work may provide supplies.

WHERE TO FIND LEADS Insurance companies employ phlebotomists for life- and health-insurance exams. Healthcare staffing agencies supply phlebotomists to hospitals and other medical facilities. If you have your own practice, you may be able to contract directly with clinics, labs, and other healthcare providers, or work during blood drives.

PAY RANGE $$ | Phlebotomists make nearly $17 per hour on average.

PHYSICAL THERAPIST

SERVICE PROVIDED Help patients improve movement, and manage pain after illness or injury.

SKILLS AND EXPERIENCE NEEDED ++++ | You need a Doctor of Physical Therapy degree and a license.

SPECIAL EQUIPMENT ★★★ | Equipment appropriate to the treatment you are providing.

WHERE TO FIND LEADS Physical therapy practices, hospitals, home healthcare agencies, and other organizations that provide healthcare services. Job openings may be advertised.

PAY RANGE $$$$ | Most physical therapists earn more than $40 per hour.

PSYCHOLOGIST

SERVICE PROVIDED Provide therapy for patients with mental or behavioral disorders.

SKILLS AND EXPERIENCE NEEDED ++++ | Depending on the state where you work and the focus of your practice, you need either a master's degree or a doctorate to obtain a license.

SPECIAL EQUIPMENT ★ | No special equipment needed.

WHERE TO FIND LEADS Get referrals from other healthcare professionals, or by word of mouth. List your services in professional directories. Some psychologists are joining online therapy services.

PAY RANGE $$$$ | Many psychologists charge $100 and up per session. In private practice, your client's insurance will impact how much you earn.

SOCIAL WORKER

SERVICE PROVIDED Help people manage personal and family problems and crises, and advocate for them if they need assistance with food, healthcare, childcare, and other services.

SKILLS AND EXPERIENCE NEEDED +++ | A degree in social work. You need a master's degree and a license for clinical work.

SPECIAL EQUIPMENT ★ | No special equipment needed.

WHERE TO FIND LEADS Healthcare and mental health providers, social services agencies, and schools. Crisis hotlines and online counseling services may hire social workers to counsel callers.

PAY RANGE $$ | Most social workers earn $25–$30 per hour. In private practice, your clients' insurance will impact how much you earn.

SPEECH-LANGUAGE PATHOLOGIST

SERVICE PROVIDED Treat patients with speech, language, and related disorders.

SKILLS AND EXPERIENCE NEEDED ++++ | A master's degree or doctorate and meet state licensing and certification requirements.

SPECIAL EQUIPMENT ★ | Tools for diagnosis and therapy.

WHERE TO FIND LEADS Schools and hospitals hire speech-language pathologists. You may also find work in a private practice or find your own clients by networking with health and education professionals and promoting your services to parenting or patient communities.

PAY RANGE $$$$ | Most speech-language pathologists earn more than $35 per hour.

SPERM DONOR

SERVICE PROVIDED Donate human sperm to help families conceive children.

SKILLS AND EXPERIENCE NEEDED + | Sperm banks have age, education, and lifestyle criteria for donors, and you need to pass a medical screening.

SPECIAL EQUIPMENT ★ | No special equipment needed.

WHERE TO FIND LEADS Sperm banks.

PAY RANGE $$$ | $35–$50 per donation. You need to take a blood test six months after donating before receiving payment.

STABLE HAND

SERVICE PROVIDED Care for horses, including feeding and cleaning stalls.

SKILLS AND EXPERIENCE NEEDED ✦✦ | Experience with horses is usually required.

SPECIAL EQUIPMENT ★ | Necessary equipment provided by the stable.

WHERE TO FIND LEADS You may hear of openings by word of mouth and by contacting stables in your area. Stables may advertise openings.

PAY RANGE $ | Around $10 per hour.

SURROGATE MOTHER

SERVICE PROVIDED Bear a child for another woman.

SKILLS AND EXPERIENCE NEEDED ✦ | No experience needed. Learn about the state laws and regulations concerning surrogate pregnancy where you live. Paid surrogacy is illegal in some states.

SPECIAL EQUIPMENT ★ | No special equipment needed. You will need to pass a medical screening that includes some invasive tests to assess your reproductive health.

WHERE TO FIND LEADS You may decide to be a surrogate for a friend or relative. Surrogacy agencies help match surrogates with couples that need one.

PAY RANGE $$$$ | Rates start at $25,000 plus expenses. Having a lawyer can help ensure you are adequately compensated.

TELEMEDICINE DOCTOR

SERVICE PROVIDED Provide remote exams for patients on demand.

SKILLS AND EXPERIENCE NEEDED ✦✦✦✦ | You need to be a board-certified physician.

SPECIAL EQUIPMENT ★★★ | Have high-speed Internet access, and a computer with a camera and microphone for videoconferencing.

WHERE TO FIND LEADS Join a network that offers telemedicine services.

PAY RANGE $$$ | Many doctors who work for telemedicine services earn $100–$120 per hour, though wages depend somewhat on their location.

"I just wanted to spend more time with dogs."
—Ilene, pet store employee

CHAPTER 7
Create

If you make crafts, clothing, or art, or you engage in other creative work as a hobby, you can turn it into a side hustle that covers your expenses and may even turn a profit. You can also earn money making food and drinks and, if you have the space, growing niche crops like mushrooms.

To succeed with any type of creative side hustle, however, you have to price your products right and choose a profitable way to sell them. Start by tracking how much you spend on your materials and pay attention to how much time you work. Some hobbyists—who are, after all, creating because they enjoy it—will need to get comfortable with the idea of paying themselves (see Chapter 2).

Earning back what you spend on materials may be sufficient if your goal is to pay for your yarn habit. If you want to make extra money, your prices should take into account not only the effort you put in, but also what customers are willing to pay for a handmade item. It may require trial and error to learn what you can charge and which venues—an online store, a gallery, or an outdoor market—are profitable. But artisans who undervalue their creations don't earn as much as they could.

WATCH OUT FOR LEGAL ISSUES

Creative side hustles can face legal hurdles. For example, products that are derived from copyrighted or trademarked designs—such as a knitted hat featuring a video game character—require a license from the owner of the character in order to be sold. That's too expensive for most side hustlers, and so is litigation. It's smarter not to risk a lawsuit.

On the flip side, if you create images—including illustrations and photographs—or original clothing designs, you will want to take steps to protect your own copyright.

Food products also need to steer clear of trademark infringement. "Most things in food are not very unique; what sets your product apart is your branding," says Lauren Handel, a food lawyer and principal with Handel Food Law LLC in Hackettstown, New Jersey. It's wise to be sure a brand name isn't infringing on someone else's trademark, and to register it. "If selling food is just a hobby, maybe you don't need to register your trademark. If you are trying to build a business that has some value, the biggest asset for a food business often is its brand," Handel adds.

Furthermore, to grow, prepare, and sell food, producers may have to comply with a host of federal, state, and local regulations concerning food safety, kitchen sanitation, or labeling. Government regulations may also apply to personal care products, from cosmetics to soap.

Carol, who works as a marketing writer for a software company, started her clothing upcycling business by making Christmas ornaments. "I started messing around with felted sweaters, making these little wool ornaments, and that turned into other Christmas-y things. Then I think I started adding shirttails to the sweaters."

Next came flannel shirts, deconstructed, reassembled, and embellished. "As I got more comfortable with sewing, it became more of a designing and sewing thing than a craft thing."

She sells the upcycled clothing at two or three craft fairs every year. Her earnings cover the cost of renting the booth and her materials—which come from thrift stores, flea markets, and the swap bin at the local recycling center. Instead of paying herself, she donates the proceeds—usually a few hundred dollars from each event—to local charities.

To have enough items in her inventory for each sale, Carol sews during her vacations and on the weekends, ramping up her work in September for the holiday season and again in January for a fair in May. "I do it because I enjoy it. And people like the things that I make."

She'd like to expand her sales if she can find a way to make product distribution "painless." Many artisans get tripped up on business management and logistics; they open an online store without thinking through how orders will be assembled, packaged, and shipped, for example.

"The making process has to bring you enough joy to make you enthusiastic about paying attention to the administrative process too," Carol advises. "You have to find a way to streamline and make a very efficient process so you spend as little time as possible on the business stuff." In her case, it's a system for setting up her table.

Many—if not most—artisans dream of turning their creative side hustle into full-time work. Carol envisions a company that she would run for profit but with charitable giving built into the business model. "It's something I will probably do when I retire."

Meanwhile, she has more charitable side hustles in mind: a class that would help people in need start their own creative businesses, and a co-op where they could sell their creations. "I'm not sure how it would work, but it would be cool."

CREATIVE SIDE HUSTLES

3-D PRINTMAKER

SERVICE PROVIDED Use a 3-D printer to make items you design or as a service printing objects for others.

SKILLS AND EXPERIENCE NEEDED +++ | Know how to use a 3-D printer, software, and materials, including how to troubleshoot. Educate yourself about copyright and trademark laws to avoid being held liable for infringement. For example, you need permission from the copyright or trademark owner to sell products that are derived from their designs, and some items, such as a statue of a cartoon character, need to be licensed in order to be sold.

SPECIAL EQUIPMENT ★★★ | A 3-D printer, filament, and software.

WHERE TO FIND LEADS Sell your original creations online. Find potential customers who have designs they need printed in online 3-D printing communities.

PAY RANGE $ | Some 3-D printed objects sell for under $1 (for a plastic tree ornament) while others sell for hundreds of dollars (complex artwork or gold jewelry).

ANIMATOR

SERVICE PROVIDED Create computer animations.

SKILLS AND EXPERIENCE NEEDED +++ | You need artistic ability, and skill in your chosen medium.

SPECIAL EQUIPMENT ★★★ | A computer and tools, including software, necessary for creating your work.

WHERE TO FIND LEADS You can sell animations as messaging app stickers, enter contests, or offer your services on freelancing platforms. If you post animated shorts to *YouTube* and create enough traffic, you can qualify for paid advertising.

PAY RANGE $ | Sticker packs sell in the Apple App Store for about $1, and it's a crowded field. *YouTube* pays qualified channels a few dollars per 1,000 views. Freelancers charge anywhere from $20 per hour to more than $100 per hour to create animations for clients.

BAKER

SERVICE PROVIDED Sell baked goods, such as cookies.

SKILLS AND EXPERIENCE NEEDED ++ | In addition to being able to bake tasty treats, you need to comply with state and local cottage food laws.

SPECIAL EQUIPMENT ★ | As long as selling food from your home is legal in your state, you probably will not need additional special equipment, though your kitchen may need to pass an inspection.

WHERE TO FIND LEADS Depending on state and local laws, you may be able to sell your products from your home—in which case referrals from customers and social media will generate orders. You may also be able to set up a booth at local farmers' markets or events, or sell through local stores.

PAY RANGE $ | Price your products to cover your costs and your time to earn an acceptable rate. Your state may have limits to how much you can earn as a home-based food business.

BARISTA

SERVICE PROVIDED Make coffee drinks.

SKILLS AND EXPERIENCE NEEDED ++ | You can learn on the job, but some coffee shops may prefer to hire someone who is trained.

SPECIAL EQUIPMENT ★ ★ ★ | You need to know how to use coffee grinding and brewing equipment.

WHERE TO FIND LEADS Learn about jobs by word of mouth, including people who work in the coffee shops you frequent. The shops may advertise openings.

PAY RANGE $ | Baristas earn around $8.50 per hour with tips, on average.

BARTENDER

SERVICE PROVIDED Make cocktails and pour beer and wine.

SKILLS AND EXPERIENCE NEEDED ++ | Taking a bartending class can improve your chances of getting a job, and some states require it.

SPECIAL EQUIPMENT ★ | Know your bar tools and accessories.

WHERE TO FIND LEADS Get work by word of mouth through connections with bars, restaurants, and other venues that serve alcohol, as well as caterers and event planners. You may also find work through help wanted sites.

PAY RANGE $$ | Tips may account for more than half of bartenders' earnings. In big cities, at private parties, or on busy nights, bartenders can earn $23 per hour or more.

BREWER

SERVICE PROVIDED Make beer.

SKILLS AND EXPERIENCE NEEDED +++ | Practice brewing your own beer and developing recipes.

SPECIAL EQUIPMENT ★ ★ ★ | Brewing equipment for your personal use.

WHERE TO FIND LEADS It's illegal in the United States to sell beer you have brewed at home. Home brewers who want to sell their beer need to obtain the necessary licenses and a facility to produce their beer. Hiring a contract brewer to make the beer and distribute it is one option. Starting a small brewery is another.

PAY RANGE $ | It can take several years to become profitable and may be worthwhile only if you eventually plan to make your beer business your full-time job.

CAKE DECORATOR

SERVICE PROVIDED Decorate cakes.

SKILLS AND EXPERIENCE NEEDED ++ | Artistic ability, as well as experience making and piping frosting and royal icing, crafting decorations with fondant, and creating other embellishments. Make sure you comply with state and local cottage food laws.

SPECIAL EQUIPMENT ★ ★ | In addition to your cake decorating tools, if the law requires it, your kitchen may need to pass an inspection.

WHERE TO FIND LEADS Decorate cakes for your friends and get them to refer you. Do your own networking on social media to promote yourself and learn about potential customers.

PAY RANGE $$ | Charge enough to cover your costs and earn an acceptable rate for your time. State laws may limit the amount of money you can make as a home-based food business.

CALLIGRAPHER

SERVICE PROVIDED Create hand-lettered documents or artwork.

SKILLS AND EXPERIENCE NEEDED +++ | Excellent calligraphy skills.

SPECIAL EQUIPMENT ★★★ | Pens, ink, paper, and other supplies you need to complete your projects.

WHERE TO FIND LEADS Do work for friends and get them to refer you, and network on social media. Sell your work or list your services on platforms for artists or wedding planning.

PAY RANGE $$ | Calligraphers price their work by the piece. According to a 2016 survey by calligraphy studio Carla Hagan Designs, "hobbyist calligraphers" charge an average of $150 to design a menu for a wedding. Custom documents may sell for as little as $15 for a quote on a poster to more than $1,000 for artwork.

CANDLE MAKER

SERVICE PROVIDED Make candles for sale.

SKILLS AND EXPERIENCE NEEDED ++ | Practice making candles of different sizes, shapes, and color combinations.

SPECIAL EQUIPMENT ★★ | Candle-making supplies and equipment, such as wax and molds.

WHERE TO FIND LEADS Sell your products online, at farmers' markets and craft markets, and at stores that specialize in handmade items. Use social media to promote your work.

PAY RANGE $ | When pricing your work, you should cover your costs and pay yourself for your time, as well as take into account the value customers place on having a handmade item. Some tea lights sell online at six for $3.00.

CARICATURE ARTIST

SERVICE PROVIDED Draw caricatures.

SKILLS AND EXPERIENCE NEEDED ++ | Ability to draw quickly and accurately while expressing humor about your subject.

SPECIAL EQUIPMENT ★★ | Paper, pens, pencils, or markers as you prefer, a portable easel.

WHERE TO FIND LEADS Theme parks hire caricaturists. You may be able to sell your work in public parks (check whether you need a permit) or work at an outdoor event like a street fair. You can also join an online platform to help connect you with potential clients who want a caricaturist for a private event.

PAY RANGE $$$$ | Working at an event can net you $80 per hour or more.

CARTOONIST

SERVICE PROVIDED Draw cartoons as art, to illustrate products, magazines, and blogs, or as graphic novels.

SKILLS AND EXPERIENCE NEEDED ++ | Have the ability to tell a story and convey a point of view through simple drawings.

SPECIAL EQUIPMENT ★ | Drawing supplies or software.

WHERE TO FIND LEADS It's a competitive field, and people make a lot of cold submissions to magazines and web publishers. Promoting your work on social media and listing on freelance platforms may get you commissions. Sell stickers or T-shirts, draw at art shows and trade shows, or self-publish your graphic novel.

PAY RANGE $ | You can earn anywhere from pennies to hundreds of dollars per drawing depending on where you sell it.

CATERER

SERVICE PROVIDED Cook food for customers' events.

SKILLS AND EXPERIENCE NEEDED ✦✦ | Be an experienced cook and specialize in a type of food or event. Have excellent organizational skills and be comfortable handling surprises. Obtain any necessary licenses and training you need to operate a food service business.

SPECIAL EQUIPMENT ★ ★ ★ | A commercial kitchen for preparing clients' food.

WHERE TO FIND LEADS Get your friends and customers to recommend you. Connect with wedding planners, event managers, and others who hire or recommend caterers for events, and network on social media.

PAY RANGE $$$ | Caterers usually charge per person, and rates can vary by location and the type of event or food served. As the head of your catering side hustle, you can expect to earn an average of $23 per hour.

CHOCOLATIER

SERVICE PROVIDED Make chocolate candies for sale.

SKILLS AND EXPERIENCE NEEDED ✦✦ | Learn how to make a variety of chocolate candies. You may want to develop a specialty or signature creation to differentiate your products from others. Become familiar with cottage food laws in your state.

SPECIAL EQUIPMENT ★ | As with baked goods, as long as selling food from your home is legal in your state, you probably will not need additional special equipment beyond candy-making tools, though your kitchen may need to pass an inspection.

WHERE TO FIND LEADS Depending on state and local laws, you may be able to sell your products from your home—in which case referrals from customers and social media will generate orders. You may also be able to set up a booth at local farmers' markets or events, or sell through local stores.

PAY RANGE $ | Price your products to cover your costs and your time to earn an acceptable rate. Your state may have limits to how much you can earn as a home-based food business.

CHRISTMAS TREE FARMER

SERVICE PROVIDED Grow and sell Christmas trees.

SKILLS AND EXPERIENCE NEEDED +++ | Have experience growing plants, and know how to grow evergreen trees. You can learn about growing trees from agriculture extension programs and professional associations. Research and comply with applicable laws for a farming business.

SPECIAL EQUIPMENT ★ ★ ★ | Suitable land and soil, equipment, and supplies for preparing the land and soil, fertilizing, controlling pests, and pruning. It takes an average of seven years to grow a tree.

WHERE TO FIND LEADS Decide how you are selling your trees: from a retail lot or as U-cut on the farm. Market them using advertising, paper flyers, social media, and word of mouth.

PAY RANGE $$$$ | How much you can charge depends on your location. Christmas tree farmers typically earn $15,000–$20,000 per season, though the amount depends on the price of the trees and how many they sell. Some Christmas tree farmers earn additional revenue by selling wreaths and other decorations.

CLOTHING UPCYCLER

SERVICE PROVIDED Repurpose secondhand clothing to create new designs.

SKILLS AND EXPERIENCE NEEDED ++ | Have sewing and craft skills, and the ability to deconstruct and reimagine existing items in new ways. Be aware of the potential for trademark infringement if your products involve repurposing items with logos or other trademarks.

SPECIAL EQUIPMENT ★★ | A sewing machine and related tools are necessary for sewing, ripping out seams, cutting fabric, and embellishing.

WHERE TO FIND LEADS You can sell your products online, at farmers' and craft markets, and at stores that specialize in handmade items. Social media will help you promote your work and meet potential customers.

PAY RANGE $$ | When pricing your work, you should cover your costs and pay yourself for your time, as well as take into account the value customers place on having a handmade item. People who sew for a living make an average of $15 per hour.

COFFEE ROASTER

SERVICE PROVIDED Roast coffee beans for sale to consumers.

SKILLS AND EXPERIENCE NEEDED +++ | Knowledge of different coffee beans and roasts, and experience roasting. Make sure you comply with state and local food handling and food production laws.

SPECIAL EQUIPMENT ★★★ | A coffee roaster that can handle the volume of beans you're roasting, or a contract roasting arrangement.

WHERE TO FIND LEADS Sell your coffee online, at farmers' markets, and in specialty food shops. Promote your business on social media and through advertising.

PAY RANGE $$ | Depending on your location, you may be able to sell your coffee for $16 or more per pound.

FIBER ARTIST

SERVICE PROVIDED Make knitted, crocheted, or woven clothing, accessories, or home goods.

SKILLS AND EXPERIENCE NEEDED ++| Be able to knit, crochet, or weave good-quality items. Because there may be copyright or trademark restrictions on published patterns, designing your own ensures you won't infringe on someone else's work.

SPECIAL EQUIPMENT ★★ | Yarns and other materials to execute your designs, along with knitting needles, crochet hooks, or a loom.

WHERE TO FIND LEADS You can sell your creations online, at farmers' or craft markets, and in stores that specialize in hand-made goods. Use social media to market your work and meet potential customers.

PAY RANGE $$ | When pricing your work, you should cover your costs and pay yourself for your time, as well as take into account the value customers place on having a unique piece of art. If you sell through a store, it will take a cut. Craft artists make an average of $19 per hour.

FINE ARTIST

SERVICE PROVIDED Create original works of art for sale.

SKILLS AND EXPERIENCE NEEDED ♦♦ | Artistic ability and expertise in your chosen medium.

SPECIAL EQUIPMENT ★★ | Supplies as needed for your work. These will depend on the type of art you create; painters, for example, usually need paints, paintbrushes, and canvasses.

WHERE TO FIND LEADS Artists exhibit and sell their work at art fairs and in galleries, as well as from their own studios. Some artists also offer their work for sale online or in shops that specialize in handmade goods. People who like your work may commission a piece from you.

PAY RANGE $$$$ | Prices for original art vary depending on the size of the work and the medium. If you are selling through a gallery, it will take a cut. A drawing may sell for less than $50 and a large painting may sell for several hundred. When pricing your work, you should cover your costs and pay yourself for your time, as well as take into account the value customers place on having a handmade item.

FLORAL DESIGNER

SERVICE PROVIDED Arrange flowers for customers.

SKILLS AND EXPERIENCE NEEDED ✦✦ | Familiarity with a variety of flowers and techniques for arranging them in vases or containers.

SPECIAL EQUIPMENT ★★★ | A source for flowers and other plants—whether live, artificial, or dried—to use in your arrangements, along with containers and materials to create and stabilize your designs.

WHERE TO FIND LEADS Make arrangements for your friends and get them to refer you. Use social media and network with friends and colleagues to connect with people who are planning events or who need an arrangement for a special occasion. Online platforms that help people plan events may help you find potential customers.

PAY RANGE $$ | Cover your costs and pay yourself an acceptable rate for your time. Floral designers earn $13 per hour on average.

FURNITURE MAKER

SERVICE PROVIDED Make furniture for sale.

SKILLS AND EXPERIENCE NEEDED ✦✦✦ | Woodworking skills (see "Woodworker" in this chapter). The originality of your designs and skill at executing them will contribute to the quality of your work, its appeal, and how much you can charge for it.

SPECIAL EQUIPMENT ★★★ | Tools, equipment, and supplies needed to complete your projects.

WHERE TO FIND LEADS Sell your furniture online using *craigslist* or through an online store. Get a booth at craft fairs.

PAY RANGE $$$$ | When pricing your work, you should cover your costs and pay yourself for your time, as well as take into account the value customers place on having a handmade item. A small wooden bench might sell for less than $100, while a headboard for a bed might sell for several hundred.

FURNITURE RESTORER

SERVICE PROVIDED Restore old furniture for resale.

SKILLS AND EXPERIENCE NEEDED +++ | Expertise in various techniques for restoring furniture to usable or like-new condition. Vintage items may be valuable as antiques, and that value can be reduced when restored. Knowledge about the period and the value of similar pieces can help you determine the type of restoration you do (see Chapter 8).

SPECIAL EQUIPMENT ★ ★ ★ | Tools, equipment, and supplies for completing restoration projects.

WHERE TO FIND LEADS Sell your furniture online using *craigslist* or through an online store. Get a booth at a craft fair or antique fair.

PAY RANGE $$$$ | When pricing your work, you should cover your costs and pay yourself for your time, as well as take into account the value customers place on having a hand-restored item. A repainted wood dresser might sell for more than $500.

GLASS ARTIST

SERVICE PROVIDED Create decorative objects and glassware.

SKILLS AND EXPERIENCE NEEDED ++ | Artistic ability and experience with glass-making techniques.

SPECIAL EQUIPMENT ★ ★ ★ | Tools and supplies needed to make your creations.

WHERE TO FIND LEADS Sell your work online, at craft shows, and in stores that specialize in handmade goods. People who like your work may commission pieces.

PAY RANGE $ | When pricing your work, you should cover your costs and pay yourself for your time, as well as take into account the value customers place on having a handmade item. Handcrafted glass beads may sell for less than $1, while unique art pieces may sell for hundreds.

HOPS FARMER

SERVICE PROVIDED Grow hops for use in brewing beer.

SKILLS AND EXPERIENCE NEEDED +++ | Know how to grow hops and become familiar with the market for different varieties.

SPECIAL EQUIPMENT ★★★ | Suitable garden or farmland and appropriate equipment for planting, tending, and harvesting.

WHERE TO FIND LEADS Breweries and suppliers, brewing magazines, brewing message boards and other communities of professional or amateur brewers.

PAY RANGE $ | A pound of hops sold for an average of just under $6 in December 2017.

ILLUSTRATOR

SERVICE PROVIDED Create images to illustrate books, magazine articles, cards, brochures, advertisements, and other published print and electronic material.

SKILLS AND EXPERIENCE NEEDED +++ | Have artistic ability, expertise telling stories with pictures, and experience drawing or painting. Be able to take direction from clients.

SPECIAL EQUIPMENT ★★ | Supplies for making illustrations in your chosen medium. If you create your illustrations traditionally (for example, using paint or pencil), you will need a scanner to create a digital file for publication.

WHERE TO FIND LEADS Promote your work in professional directories, on social media, and with postcards and business cards that feature your illustrations. Find agencies and publishers who commission freelancers (bookstores are good places to research book, magazine, greeting card, and music publishers who use work in styles like yours). You can also tap your personal and professional contacts for jobs or referrals.

PAY RANGE $$$$ | Illustrators' earnings vary from $50 for a greeting card illustration to more than $1,000 to illustrate a book.

JEWELRY DESIGNER

SERVICE PROVIDED Make original earrings, necklaces, rings, or bracelets.

SKILLS AND EXPERIENCE NEEDED ✦✦ | Artistic ability and experience designing and making jewelry.

SPECIAL EQUIPMENT ★★ | Equipment and supplies you need to produce your designs.

WHERE TO FIND LEADS Sell your jewelry online, at farmers' markets, craft fairs, and in stores that specialize in handmade goods. Use social media to promote your work.

PAY RANGE $ | Handmade jewelry prices vary widely depending on the materials and the complexity of design. When pricing your work, you should cover your costs and pay yourself for your time, as well as take into account the value customers place on having a handmade item.

LOGO DESIGNER

SERVICE PROVIDED Create logos for businesses.

SKILLS AND EXPERIENCE NEEDED ✦✦ | Artistic ability and graphic design training. You also need to be able to understand your client's audience, needs, and goals.

SPECIAL EQUIPMENT ★ | Design software (many designers use Adobe Illustrator) and drawing supplies.

WHERE TO FIND LEADS Join an online freelance platform to learn about and bid on projects. Network with friends and colleagues and promote your services on social media. Professional associations for graphic designers sponsor directories where members can list their profiles and search for jobs, while online portfolio sites provide another venue to display your work.

PAY RANGE $$ | Pay for logo projects varies widely depending on factors such as where you live, the amount of competition you face, and your reputation. You could earn a few bucks creating logos using prepackaged templates and clip art for clients who don't want to pay much, up to a few thousand dollars for complex projects for which you produce completely original work.

MUSHROOM FARMER

SERVICE PROVIDED Grow gourmet mushrooms for sale.

SKILLS AND EXPERIENCE NEEDED ✦✦ | Learn to grow mushrooms by starting with a kit, and then determine ways to cultivate enough to sell. You'll need to make sure selling home-grown mushrooms is legal where you live and that you comply with regulations concerning home-based farming, food safety, and sales.

SPECIAL EQUIPMENT ★★ | Mushrooms require relatively less space than other crops, and you can grow them indoors. But you'll need to have enough space and the proper equipment to grow the quantity you want.

WHERE TO FIND LEADS You may be able to sell at farmers' markets or to restaurants. As with selling any food product, make sure you comply with the relevant laws and regulations.

PAY RANGE $$ | Farming any crop is labor intensive. Growing shiitake or oyster mushrooms, which are said to be easiest, takes an estimated 10–12 hours a week, but they command relatively high prices. Shiitakes retail for as much as $15 per pound.

Similar Jobs

Grow flowers, herbs, fruits, or vegetables: if you have enough land, you may be able grow more than you need for your personal use, but in most cases the work amounts to more than a side hustle. You may, however, save money with a large garden that yields enough for canning and preserving.

PATTERN DESIGNER

SERVICE PROVIDED Create patterns for sewing, knitting, crocheting, or weaving.

SKILLS AND EXPERIENCE NEEDED +++ | Know how to construct garments, accessories, or home décor; create patterns; and write instructions.

SPECIAL EQUIPMENT ★★ | Materials for making samples, a computer, and software for generating your patterns.

WHERE TO FIND LEADS Sell your patterns online, including through online crafting communities.

PAY RANGE $ | Figure your costs, including an hourly rate for your time and the unique value of your work. Choose a price that will enable you to sell enough copies to recoup your costs and earn a profit. Knitting and crochet patterns typically sell for under $10 each.

PERSONAL CARE PRODUCTS

SERVICE PROVIDED Make soaps, lotions, and other personal care products for sale.

SKILLS AND EXPERIENCE NEEDED ++ | Have experience making your products and be aware of FDA regulations that cover cosmetics, drugs, soap, and labeling.

SPECIAL EQUIPMENT ★★ | Supplies and equipment needed to make your products.

WHERE TO FIND LEADS Give products as gifts to your friends and have them help spread the word. Sell at farmers' markets, craft fairs, and online.

PAY RANGE $$ | Homemade bars of soap and bottles of lotion typically sell for $5–$15 each, though prices vary. Consider your costs and an acceptable rate for your time. Craft artists make an average of $19 per hour.

PERSONAL CHEF

SERVICE PROVIDED Cook meals for clients in their homes.

SKILLS AND EXPERIENCE NEEDED ++ | Know how to cook nutritious everyday meals. Professional training or restaurant kitchen experience can help you get work.

SPECIAL EQUIPMENT * | Standard home equipment in the client's kitchen.

WHERE TO FIND LEADS Get friends and customers who have had your cooking to spread the word. Network with friends and on social media to promote your services and meet potential customers.

PAY RANGE $$$ | Private chefs can earn $30 per hour or more.

PHOTOGRAPHER, DRONE

SERVICE PROVIDED Operate a drone to take aerial photos for clients.

SKILLS AND EXPERIENCE NEEDED +++ | Know how to operate a drone and shoot photos and videos with it. Have a pilot license and make sure you comply with any federal, state, or local regulations for flying drones.

SPECIAL EQUIPMENT * * * | Drone with a camera, computer and software.

WHERE TO FIND LEADS If you work for a company in the real estate, construction, or insurance industry—or any industry that needs to inspect buildings, land, or equipment—you may be able to offer your services and get paid extra. Social media and online platforms for freelancers help to connect you with potential clients and get referrals, including for work at parties or weddings.

PAY RANGE $$$$ | Drone photographers may charge $100–$500 per hour or more.

PHOTOGRAPHER, EVENTS

SERVICE PROVIDED Photograph events such as weddings and parties.

SKILLS AND EXPERIENCE NEEDED +++ | Artistic ability, expertise shooting live events indoors and outdoors, and familiarity with "must get" shots. Flexibility, attentiveness to clients' needs, and communications skills will help you set expectations, respond to unexpected snags and opportunities, and deliver a final product that clients like. Having a portfolio enables you to showcase your abilities.

SPECIAL EQUIPMENT ★★★ | Camera, lenses, and related equipment.

WHERE TO FIND LEADS Shoot a friend's wedding or party, and get the word out. You can also ask event managers at hotels and other venues to put you on their list of service providers they recommend, and use social media and online platforms that help people plan events to promote your services.

PAY RANGE $$$$ | Experienced event photographers may charge $100 or more per hour. Wedding photographers get an average of $2,000 per event.

PHOTOGRAPHER, PORTRAITS

SERVICE PROVIDED Photograph individuals, families, children, or pets.

SKILLS AND EXPERIENCE NEEDED +++ | Artistic ability, expertise capturing individual personalities and group relationships, and ability to create rapport with reluctant subjects.

SPECIAL EQUIPMENT ★★★ | Camera, lenses, and related equipment.

WHERE TO FIND LEADS List your services on platforms such as *Thumbtack* or *GigSalad* that connect individuals with service providers. Network with friends and colleagues and use social media to promote your work, meet potential customers, and get referrals. For a traditional part-time job, you could work at a department store photo studio.

PAY RANGE $$ | Price your work based on your costs, your time, and the value you bring for your clients. Photographers make an average of $20 per hour.

PHOTOGRAPHER, PRINTS

<u>**SERVICE PROVIDED**</u> Shoot images to sell as artwork.

<u>**SKILLS AND EXPERIENCE NEEDED**</u> ++++ | Artistic ability. Know how to compose, shoot, and edit artistic photos.

<u>**SPECIAL EQUIPMENT**</u> ★★★ | Camera, lenses, and related equipment.

<u>**WHERE TO FIND LEADS**</u> Sell your photos online. Institutions in your community such as hospitals, libraries, and places of worship may offer space to display work for sale by local artists. Network with galleries and shops that sell handmade goods, or get a booth at an art fair.

<u>**PAY RANGE**</u> $$ | When pricing your work, you should cover your costs and pay yourself for your time, as well as take into account the value customers place on having a handmade item. If you are selling through a gallery or shop, they will take a cut. Photographers make an average of $20 per hour.

PHOTOGRAPHER, STOCK PHOTOS

<u>**SERVICE PROVIDED**</u> Shoot images that can be licensed or sold for repeated use.

<u>**SKILLS AND EXPERIENCE NEEDED**</u> ++ | Artistic ability. Know how to compose, shoot, and edit photos of people, animals, scenery, and cityscapes.

<u>**SPECIAL EQUIPMENT**</u> ★★ | Camera, lenses, and related equipment.

WHERE TO FIND LEADS Stock photography agencies want professional-quality photos (they will vet your work before you can sell it). Online marketplaces that enable you to sell products customized with your images will give you more control.

PAY RANGE $ | You get royalties—at the beginning, maybe only a few cents at a time—when your photos are licensed from a stock agency. On *Zazzle*, you can determine your royalty percentage on the sale of products that use your images.

PORTRAIT ARTIST

SERVICE PROVIDED Draw or paint portraits of people or pets.

SKILLS AND EXPERIENCE NEEDED ++ | Artistic ability and experience in your chosen medium.

SPECIAL EQUIPMENT ★★ | Art supplies needed for the work.

WHERE TO FIND LEADS Use social media and network with friends and colleagues to meet potential customers and get referrals.

PAY RANGE $$$ | Some portrait artists charge based on size and complexity of the work, including the medium (for example, a pencil drawing or an oil painting). Take into account your costs, your time, and the value of the work to your customer. Fine artists typically earn less than $30 per hour for their time. With experience, you may be able to charge several hundred dollars or more for a single portrait.

POTTERY ARTIST OR CERAMIST

SERVICE PROVIDED Create clay pots, vases, and other vessels.

SKILLS AND EXPERIENCE NEEDED +++ | Know how to work with clay, a wheel, glazes, and a kiln.

SPECIAL EQUIPMENT ★★★ | Supplies and access to a kiln for firing.

WHERE TO FIND LEADS Sell your products online and in galleries or shops specializing in art or handmade goods. Use social media to promote your work and meet potential customers.

PAY RANGE $$$ | When pricing your work, you should cover your costs and pay yourself for your time, as well as take into account the value customers place on having a handmade item. Fine artists typically earn less than $30 per hour for their time. Artisans sell their work for a wide range of prices, including coffee mugs for $35 and serving bowls for more than $100.

QUILTER

SERVICE PROVIDED Make original quilts.

SKILLS AND EXPERIENCE NEEDED ++ | Artistic ability, sewing skills, and quilting expertise.

SPECIAL EQUIPMENT ★ ★ ★ | A sewing machine, fabric, and quilting tools appropriate for your projects.

WHERE TO FIND LEADS You may be able to sell your work online, at local farmers' markets, craft fairs, flea markets, and shops that specialize in handmade products.

PAY RANGE $$ | Large handmade quilts may sell for hundreds of dollars, while small items, such as table runners, may sell for less than $100. When pricing your work, you should cover your costs and pay yourself for your time, as well as take into account the value customers place on having a handmade item. People who sew for a living make an average of $15 per hour.

SCRAPBOOKER

SERVICE PROVIDED Assemble scrapbooks for clients.

SKILLS AND EXPERIENCE NEEDED +++ | Design sense, storytelling ability, expertise using scrapbooking materials and tools, and a portfolio of your work.

SPECIAL EQUIPMENT ★ ★ | Scrapbooking materials and tools.

WHERE TO FIND LEADS Make some scrapbooks for friends and get the word out. Networking with friends and colleagues in person and on social media can help you meet potential customers and get referrals.

PAY RANGE $$ | One way scrapbookers determine pricing is by the page, taking into account any materials they use and an hourly charge. Rates may range from $5 to $30 per page.

Similar Jobs

Photo book designer: you can use the same design skills that animate your scrapbook pages to design photo books for people from their digital photos.

SEWER OR TAILOR

SERVICE PROVIDED Mend, alter, or make clothing or accessories to order.

SKILLS AND EXPERIENCE NEEDED +++ | Good sewing skills, including an understanding of garment construction and facility with using patterns.

SPECIAL EQUIPMENT ★★★ | A sewing machine suited to the kinds of projects you do.

WHERE TO FIND LEADS Join local social media groups to meet potential customers and get referrals. Youth and community theater companies sometimes need volunteers to help make, alter, or repair costumes, providing an opportunity for you to show off your talents to actors and audiences alike.

PAY RANGE $$ | People who sew for a living—tailors, dressmakers, and custom sewers—make around $15 per hour.

SPINNER

SERVICE PROVIDED Spin and dye wool to make yarn.

SKILLS AND EXPERIENCE NEEDED +++ | Know how to spin yarn and work with dyes to create the colors you want.

SPECIAL EQUIPMENT ★★★ | If you raise sheep or goats or have access to wool roving from farmers near you, you can dye and spin yarn. You need a spinning wheel and related supplies, as well as supplies for dyeing.

WHERE TO FIND LEADS Sell your yarn online, at farmers' markets and festivals, and in yarn shops.

PAY RANGE $$$ | Handspun yarn sells at a premium—sometimes $30 or more per skein depending on the amount of yarn, the type of fiber, and how much you decide to charge for your time.

TATTOO ARTIST

SERVICE PROVIDED Ink tattoos for people.

SKILLS AND EXPERIENCE NEEDED +++ | Know how to make tattoos and comply with state and local health codes. You may need a license or certification.

SPECIAL EQUIPMENT ★★★ | Access to tattooing equipment and supplies, as well as medical and sterilization supplies.

WHERE TO FIND LEADS Tattoo parlors.

PAY RANGE $$$$ | Depending on your experience, you can make between $80 and $200 or more per hour.

T-SHIRT DESIGNER

SERVICE PROVIDED Create T-shirt designs and produce T-shirts for customers.

SKILLS AND EXPERIENCE NEEDED + | Artistic ability.

SPECIAL EQUIPMENT ★ | Supplies for creating your designs. If you produce your T-shirts through an online service for creating custom products, you don't need to invest in equipment or shirts.

WHERE TO FIND LEADS Sell your T-shirts online. Promote your designs using social media. Rent booths at conventions, craft fairs, farmers' markets, and festivals.

PAY RANGE $$ | Custom designs retail for $15 and up.

VIDEOGRAPHER, EVENTS

SERVICE PROVIDED Film events such as weddings.

SKILLS AND EXPERIENCE NEEDED +++ | Have expertise shooting live video (and editing, unless you have a partner who can do that), as well as familiarity with the conventions of the genre (including "must have" shots). Flexibility, friendliness, attentiveness to clients' needs, and communications skills will help you set expectations for your projects, respond to unexpected snags and opportunities, and deliver a final product that clients like.

SPECIAL EQUIPMENT ★ ★ ★ | If you are an amateur, or you do not have experience shooting events, look into whether you have the right equipment, and buy or rent what you need.

WHERE TO FIND LEADS Shoot a friend's wedding or event, and get the word out. Event managers at hotels and other venues often keep lists of service providers whom they recommend to clients. Use social media and network with friends and colleagues to promote your work.

PAY RANGE $$$$ | Wedding videographers charge anywhere from a few hundred dollars to several thousand, depending on location, experience, and the hours and the complexity of the job.

WOODWORKER

SERVICE PROVIDED Create decorative and practical objects from wood.

SKILLS AND EXPERIENCE NEEDED ++ | Your skills at woodworking and the originality of your designs will contribute to the quality of your work, its appeal, and how much you can charge for it.

SPECIAL EQUIPMENT ★ ★ ★ | Tools and a workshop. If you have access to a maker space in your community—a facility where you can pay a membership fee to use shared tools—you may be able to complete projects that you don't have the equipment or space for in your basement or garage.

WHERE TO FIND LEADS You may be able to sell your work online, at local farmers' markets, craft fairs, flea markets, and shops that specialize in handmade products.

PAY RANGE $ | Small items such as Christmas ornaments may sell for a few dollars, while large, unique items may sell for hundreds or even thousands. When pricing your work, you should cover your costs and pay yourself for your time, as well as take into account the value customers place on having a handmade item.

Similar Jobs

Metalworker: like woodworkers, artists who work with metal can sell both decorative and practical creations.

"The making process has to bring you enough joy to make you enthusiastic about paying attention to the administrative process too."
Carol, clothing upcycler

CHAPTER 8

Rent or Sell

Side hustles that involve selling or renting are among the easiest to start. You don't need any experience to open a store on *eBay*. Peer-to-peer platforms such as *Airbnb* have made it simple to offer unused assets for rent—not only spare rooms, but also parking spaces, backyards, and infrequently used tools.

Digital technologies have also created opportunities to earn money by writing social media copy, and investing through online trading platforms. You don't have to be a celebrity to be paid as an *Instagram* influencer, promoting brands to your followers. If you have a knack for catchy names, you can enter brand-naming contests.

UNDERSTAND YOUR MARKET

That doesn't mean easy money, as anyone who sells for a living will tell you. You can fail to make any money, or lose it, if you don't understand your market, don't do enough work to cultivate your customers, or take risky bets. Income is not predictable.

Running a used book business from your basement, for example, costs less and is more flexible than having a storefront, making it amenable to a side hustle. But your profit margins may still be narrow due to the cost of your inventory and the competition. If you prefer a predictable side income, a part-time sales job working for an employer, such as in a store, could be better for you.

Renting is appealing in part because the main investment people have to make is their time. Interacting with renters isn't trivial; they have questions, problems, and maybe complaints.

They may damage your house or your things (make sure you have insurance or otherwise have a way to recover repair and replacement costs). But renting doesn't require additional financial investment beyond what you've already paid for your asset. Hosting a paying guest in your spare room a few dozen nights a year could cover a chunk of your mortgage. Leasing an empty driveway in a busy neighborhood is about as close as you can get to free money.

Robin is an independent personal stylist who sells clothing from a direct-to-customer women's fashion brand. She develops relationships with her customers by bringing samples to show at people's houses and helping guests assemble outfits. And she earns commissions on the pieces they buy.

She began her job eleven years ago, when her two children were in middle school and high school and a friend needed an assistant. "I was mom, wife, and daughter, and I had really lost my identity," she said, and she wanted her own business. Robin accompanied her friend to shows, took orders, and handled returns and exchanges. She had been a math teacher and helped companies set up IT support groups. Her customer service skills, and "being honest and caring," carried over.

Four years after Robin began working with her friend, she went into business on her own. "My daughter was graduating from high school, and I wanted to take her on a train trip across the United States. I needed to make that plus what I had spent on my initial investment." (She has buy her samples, which she sells for a discount when the season is over.)

With her children grown, the business has become a bigger focus. "I probably spend thirty hours a week sometimes." But it's still flexible. She has taken a season off to focus on family responsibilities.

"At this point, it makes me feel good to make financial decisions on my own. It's not that my husband tells me I can't do something, but I like to have the independence."

SELLING AND RENTING SIDE HUSTLES

AFFILIATE MARKETER

SERVICE PROVIDED Write about companies or support advertising in content you publish in exchange for a commission when your efforts produce a sale.

SKILLS AND EXPERIENCE NEEDED ++ | Writing ability, social media savvy, and an interest in the category you are promoting. You need to be able to write credibly about the products you are promoting and drive traffic to your blog.

SPECIAL EQUIPMENT * | You need a computer and a reliable Internet connection, as well as familiarity with a website platform that will host your content.

WHERE TO FIND LEADS Join an affiliate network.

PAY RANGE $$$$ | How much you make depends on your niche, your experience, and the amount of time you put in. Some affiliate marketers are able to turn profits of a few hundred to a few thousand dollars in a day, but earnings can be volatile.

ANTIQUES AND COLLECTIBLES DEALER

SERVICE PROVIDED Resell furniture and objects from the past.

SKILLS AND EXPERIENCE NEEDED +++ | Sales skills, along with an ability to spot pieces that you resell for a markup (typically 50 percent) or restore if in need of repair (sometimes that reduces its value). Specializing in a category that interests you, such as mid-century modern, or lamps, will help your credibility with customers.

SPECIAL EQUIPMENT * | Vehicle for transporting your finds. If you sell your products in a physical space, you may need tables, cabinets, or signage to display them.

WHERE TO FIND LEADS You can sell to other dealers, open a store online, get a booth at an antiques mall or flea market, or sell in a cooperative store or on consignment.

PAY RANGE $$ | As a side hustle, selling antiques and collectibles earns from a few hundred to a few thousand dollars per year.

ART RENTAL

SERVICE PROVIDED Rent out your original artwork or prints.

SKILLS AND EXPERIENCE NEEDED +++ | Artistic ability and an inventory of work to rent. Art rental companies won't rent just anyone's artwork; you have to meet criteria that may include experience, reputation, and location.

SPECIAL EQUIPMENT ★ | No special equipment needed.

WHERE TO FIND LEADS A variety of art rental companies serve local, regional, or national markets.

PAY RANGE $$ | Art rental companies pay commissions on rented work and artists may be able to sell it to customers. Rates depend on factors including the artist, the artwork, and how the company structures payments.

ARTIST MODEL

SERVICE PROVIDED Pose for drawings, paintings, or sculptures.

SKILLS AND EXPERIENCE NEEDED + | Be able to hold a pose. Some poses may last for thirty minutes. Many life-modeling jobs require models to pose nude.

SPECIAL EQUIPMENT ★ | No special equipment needed.

WHERE TO FIND LEADS Anywhere that offers art classes, and artists' studios. You may find help wanted ads for models; do research to find out if these are legitimate jobs.

PAY RANGE $$ | Artist models earn about $20 per hour.

AUCTIONEER

SERVICE PROVIDED Run auctions.

SKILLS AND EXPERIENCE NEEDED +++ | Attend auctioneer training and obtain licenses or permits as required by state or local laws. Many auctioneers have a background working in auction houses or gain experience working as apprentices.

SPECIAL EQUIPMENT ★ | You'll need a gavel.

WHERE TO FIND LEADS Auction houses, estate liquidation companies, county sheriffs (they usually run foreclosure auctions), storage companies, and social media. List your profile on platforms that provide referrals for auction services.

PAY RANGE $$$$ | Auctioneers may take a percentage commission on sales in a for-profit auction. For charity events, auctioneers may earn $2,500 or more.

BOAT RENTAL

SERVICE PROVIDED Rent out your boat.

SKILLS AND EXPERIENCE NEEDED + | Be willing and able to interact with renters.

SPECIAL EQUIPMENT ★ ★ ★ | You need a boat.

WHERE TO FIND LEADS Several online platforms offer peer-to-peer boat rentals.

PAY RANGE $$$$ | Boat owners typically set their own rates per day or half day and give the platform a cut.

BOOKSELLER

SERVICE PROVIDED Buy and sell used books.

SKILLS AND EXPERIENCE NEEDED + | Unless you are dealing in antique books, you don't need experience.

SPECIAL EQUIPMENT ★ ★ | Storage space and, if you're selling online, shipping materials.

WHERE TO FIND LEADS Sell books online or at flea markets. If you are selling your own collection (rather than books you have purchased to resell), local used bookstores or online booksellers may purchase your books, usually for a few cents each.

PAY RANGE $ | The amount of money you make depends on how many books you sell and how much profit you can make on each book. On *eBay*, prices for hardcover fiction published since 2000 start at $1.

BOOTH ASSISTANT

SERVICE PROVIDED Staff vendor booths at trade shows to help companies greet visitors, hand out information, demonstrate products, and run presentations.

SKILLS AND EXPERIENCE NEEDED ++ | Enthusiasm, ability to initiate conversations, good presentation and performance skills. Customer service and sales experience is helpful.

SPECIAL EQUIPMENT * | No special equipment needed, although vendors usually have a dress code for the event.

WHERE TO FIND LEADS Staffing agencies. Some vendors will advertise openings.

PAY RANGE $ | Rates start at around minimum wage, which varies by state.

BRAND AMBASSADOR

SERVICE PROVIDED Promote brands or products at an event or to a specific audience.

SKILLS AND EXPERIENCE NEEDED ++ | Enthusiasm, social media savvy. Sales or marketing experience can be helpful. For some jobs, companies may want you to have experience using the product you are representing.

SPECIAL EQUIPMENT * | No special equipment needed.

WHERE TO FIND LEADS Event staffing agencies, marketing agencies. Event companies and product companies may advertise openings.

PAY RANGE $ | Pay for brand ambassadors starts at about $10 per hour, which is minimum wage in some states.

BUSINESS NAME CREATOR

SERVICE PROVIDED Suggest business names for new companies.

SKILLS AND EXPERIENCE NEEDED + | Anyone can sign up to participate in name-generating contests. If the names you submit are chosen, you can gain points that enable you to submit more names. Some knowledge of branding may be useful.

SPECIAL EQUIPMENT ★ | No special equipment needed.

WHERE TO FIND LEADS Register on sites that run the contests.

PAY RANGE $$$$ | Winners get $50–$500.

CANVASSER

SERVICE PROVIDED Go door to door or engage people on the street to generate sales leads, conduct a survey, or collect signatures.

SKILLS AND EXPERIENCE NEEDED + | No experience needed, but customer service or sales experience is helpful. You need to be comfortable knocking on doors or starting a conversation with random people in the street.

SPECIAL EQUIPMENT ★ | No special equipment needed.

WHERE TO FIND LEADS Companies and nonprofit organizations may advertise openings.

PAY RANGE $ | Most canvassing jobs pay $9–$21 per hour.

CAR PARTS RESELLER

SERVICE PROVIDED Sell parts from used cars (called "parting out").

SKILLS AND EXPERIENCE NEEDED +++ | Experience working on cars is useful to be able to know whether the parts are usable and how to price them.

SPECIAL EQUIPMENT ★★★ | Tools for disassembling cars.

WHERE TO FIND LEADS Sell parts online or through classified listings.

PAY RANGE $$$$ | Individually, parts may sell for less than $10 up to $100.

CAR RENTAL

SERVICE PROVIDED Rent your car out to people who need one.

SKILLS AND EXPERIENCE NEEDED + | No experience needed.

SPECIAL EQUIPMENT ★ | A car that is available for people to rent. Peer-to-peer rental platforms may provide insurance, but check the policy and discuss with your insurer to confirm you're covered.

WHERE TO FIND LEADS Join a peer-to-peer car-sharing platform. Some carmakers offer them in addition to independent companies.

PAY RANGE $ | Car-sharing platforms offer tools to help you set prices based on factors such as the type of car you have, its mileage, its age, and your location. How much you charge will depend on the type of car you have and how old it is, but rates start around $10 per day, and the platform takes a cut.

Similar Jobs
Reselling cars: you will need a dealer license to buy cars and resell them. Otherwise, flipping—or "curbstoning"—cars is illegal, although your state may allow you to sell a very small number of cars per year (in South Dakota, it's four).

CASHIER

SERVICE PROVIDED Work at the register in a retail store.

SKILLS AND EXPERIENCE NEEDED + | No experience usually needed.

SPECIAL EQUIPMENT ★ | No special equipment needed.

WHERE TO FIND LEADS Companies advertise openings, and you may find work by word of mouth.

PAY RANGE $ | Cashier jobs typically pay minimum wage.

CATALOG MODEL

SERVICE PROVIDED Pose for pictures that will be used in a catalog.

SKILLS AND EXPERIENCE NEEDED ++ | Aside from your appearance, you will need a portfolio, or "book," to market yourself.

SPECIAL EQUIPMENT ★ | No special equipment needed.

WHERE TO FIND LEADS Most modeling jobs come through agencies, so you will likely need to sign with one to get work. Agencies may have open casting calls; otherwise, you need to submit your book. Promoting yourself on social media may help you be discovered. Legitimate agencies do not ask for money up front or require you to pay for photographs in order to be signed.

PAY RANGE $$$$ | You can earn a few hundred dollars per shoot, and your agency will take a cut.

CHICKEN EGG SALES

SERVICE PROVIDED Sell eggs from your backyard chickens.

SKILLS AND EXPERIENCE NEEDED ++ | Know how to raise and care for chickens in order to produce good quality eggs. You will need to comply with laws and regulations for keeping chickens and selling the eggs.

SPECIAL EQUIPMENT ★★★★ | Equipment and supplies for raising chickens and preparing eggs for sale. You'll need cartons and a table if you sell at a market or farm stand.

WHERE TO FIND LEADS You can sell at farmers' markets or set up your own farm stand if local laws allow it.

PAY RANGE $ | It's difficult to make a profit on a small scale. In Vermont, a dozen eggs sold for $4–$6 per dozen at farmers' markets early in 2018.

CLOTHING RENTAL

SERVICE PROVIDED Rent your designer clothing to people.

SKILLS AND EXPERIENCE NEEDED + | No experience needed. Sales and marketing experience or good instincts can be helpful for taking appealing photographs and writing descriptions of your clothes.

SPECIAL EQUIPMENT ★★ | Clothing offered on peer-to-peer rental sites tends to be from popular or designer brands and leans toward special occasion and eveningwear.

WHERE TO FIND LEADS Peer-to-peer clothing rental platforms. Some platforms may serve limited locations.

PAY RANGE $$$$ | Owners can price their items and earn a few hundred dollars for every rental. You may have to cover your own cleaning costs.

Similar Jobs

Clothing sales: you can sell your clothes directly to customers online, through classified listings, or on consignment. Unless you have a regular supply of clothes—whether your own or finds from yard sales or estate sales—you won't be able to make regular money this way any more than by renting.

DIGITAL MARKETING CONSULTANT

SERVICE PROVIDED Help companies decide where to promote their brands and their products online and assist them with developing content for websites, blogs, and social media.

SKILLS AND EXPERIENCE NEEDED +++ | Knowledge of how to use marketing techniques to promote brands, products, and services using content, social media, search engines, email, and video on different technology platforms. A portfolio of work that showcases the results you are able to get can help you get work.

SPECIAL EQUIPMENT ★ | You will need a computer and a reliable Internet connection, as well as familiarity with software used to track the results of digital campaigns.

WHERE TO FIND LEADS Join a freelancing platform to get access to project listings. Pitch companies you would like to work for with ideas.

PAY RANGE $$$$ | How much you can charge depends in part on how much experience you have and your location; $50–$150 per hour is typical.

DIRECT SALES REPRESENTATIVE

SERVICE PROVIDED Sell a company's products directly to friends, colleagues, and people in your local area.

SKILLS AND EXPERIENCE NEEDED + | Believe in the products you're selling. You may need to spend time learning about them and the company's sales approach.

SPECIAL EQUIPMENT ★ | You may have to purchase a starter sales kit or inventory.

WHERE TO FIND LEADS Research direct sales companies to find one with a business model that suits your time and your goals. Before you sign on, investigate to ensure the sales quotas are realistic for you and that you're not joining an illegal pyramid scheme.

PAY RANGE $$ | How much money you make depends on how much time you put in, your sales prowess, the value of the products you sell, and the business model of the company you work for. Commission rates vary, but successful sellers report earning anywhere from a few hundred to several thousand dollars per month.

DROP SHIPPER

SERVICE PROVIDED Act as a middleman for manufacturers by selling products online that ship to customers directly from the factory or wholesaler, who may be overseas.

SKILLS AND EXPERIENCE NEEDED ++ | You don't need a lot of experience to start a drop shipping business, but if you have never worked in sales and you don't know anything about e-commerce or importing, you will need time to learn the ropes before you make any money.

SPECIAL EQUIPMENT * | You need a computer and a reliable Internet connection.

WHERE TO FIND LEADS Once you have chosen the type of products you want to sell, you need to find a supplier and set up an online store. Then you need to promote your products using some combination of social media, advertising, a blog, and emailing your customers.

PAY RANGE $$$$ | Some drop shippers claim to earn thousands of dollars (or tens of thousands) a month. Assume that takes a ton of work. The margins are low and the industry is competitive.

ELECTRONICS RECYCLER

SERVICE PROVIDED Resell your used electronic devices.

SKILLS AND EXPERIENCE NEEDED + | Know how to wipe your personal data from your devices.

SPECIAL EQUIPMENT * | You need used devices.

WHERE TO FIND LEADS Many device manufacturers, recyclers, and some retailers pay cash for old devices. You may get more money by selling directly to a buyer online or by advertising in the classifieds (but beware of scammers who will claim your device arrived damaged to get out of paying).

PAY RANGE $ | Depending on the device, how old it is, and whether or not it works, you can get a few dollars or a few hundred.

FIT MODEL

SERVICE PROVIDED Help clothing designers test samples.

SKILLS AND EXPERIENCE NEEDED ++ | Your body needs to be well-proportioned and your measurements have to match those of the clothing brand's sizing. Have photos to submit to agencies.

SPECIAL EQUIPMENT * | No special equipment needed.

WHERE TO FIND LEADS Sign with a modeling agency. Legitimate agencies do not ask for money up front or require you to pay for photographs in order to be signed. If you have contacts in the fashion industry, you may be able to get hired directly by a designer or manufacturer.

PAY RANGE $$$$ | Fit models earn more than $100 per hour, depending on their experience.

FLYER DISTRIBUTOR

SERVICE PROVIDED Hand out advertisements to people on the street.

SKILLS AND EXPERIENCE NEEDED * | Experience usually isn't necessary. You need to be able to walk for several hours at a time.

SPECIAL EQUIPMENT * | No special equipment needed.

WHERE TO FIND LEADS Marketing firms that manage flyer distribution for clients advertise openings, and some companies hire people directly for this work. You may hear about jobs by word of mouth.

PAY RANGE $ | Flyer distribution jobs pay minimum wage or slightly above.

FORAGER

SERVICE PROVIDED Collect wild edible or medicinal plants and sell them.

SKILLS AND EXPERIENCE NEEDED ++++ | Ability to identify wild edible or medicinal plants and find places to harvest them. To keep your "patch" producing, know how to harvest from a plant without killing it. Be aware of local regulations and have permits or permission from property owners to harvest what you find.

SPECIAL EQUIPMENT ★★★ | Foraging tools, including a knife, scissors, and basket or other storage containers.

WHERE TO FIND LEADS Local restaurants may want to buy your edible bounty, while companies that use botanicals in drugs, personal care products, and cosmetics may purchase other plants. Online retailers and wholesalers may want your finds. You can also make jam from foraged berries and sell it (keeping in mind regulations for selling homemade food items—see Chapter 7).

PAY RANGE $$$ | Mushrooms earn the most; short-season varieties such as morels can bring in $35 or more per pound.

FUNDRAISER

SERVICE PROVIDED Help an organization raise money for a campaign or a cause.

SKILLS AND EXPERIENCE NEEDED ++ | Sales experience and knowledge about the cause may be preferred or required.

SPECIAL EQUIPMENT ★ | No special equipment needed.

WHERE TO FIND LEADS Telemarketing companies advertise openings for jobs making calls.

PAY RANGE $ | Telemarketing jobs pay around $10 per hour, which is minimum wage in some states.

HAIR SALES

SERVICE PROVIDED Sell your hair.

SKILLS AND EXPERIENCE NEEDED + | No experience needed.

SPECIAL EQUIPMENT ★ | The long, healthy, untreated hair from your head.

WHERE TO FIND LEADS Look for buyers among wigmakers and salons, as well as on social media and in the classifieds. Some websites provide a platform for sellers to list their hair, for a fee.

PAY RANGE $$$$ | Earnings depend on the amount of hair and the color. At the low end, you might make $100. Since hair takes a long time to grow, you can't sell it often.

HOME OR ROOM RENTAL

SERVICE PROVIDED Rent your house or a room to visitors.

SKILLS AND EXPERIENCE NEEDED + | No experience needed. You need to be comfortable having people in your house, using your things. Check your insurance coverage and be aware of local regulations on rentals as well as homeowners' association rules.

SPECIAL EQUIPMENT ★ | A key box is useful.

WHERE TO FIND LEADS List your house or spare room on a home-sharing site.

PAY RANGE $$$$ | What you earn will depend on your location, the size of your house, the number of people you rent to, and the number of days you offer it. A room may rent for as little as $20 per night, and a house or apartment may rent for more than $100.

HUMAN BILLBOARD OR SIGN WALKER

SERVICE PROVIDED Wear a sandwich board or hold a sign to advertise a business.

SKILLS AND EXPERIENCE NEEDED + | Be able to remain enthusiastic and cheerful while walking around wearing or carrying a sign.

SPECIAL EQUIPMENT ★ | Your sign will be provided.

WHERE TO FIND LEADS Some advertising agencies supply sign walkers. You may hear of a business that needs one by word of mouth, and some businesses may independently advertise an opening.

PAY RANGE $ | Sign walkers earn around $10 per hour, which is minimum wage in some states.

INSURANCE SALES

SERVICE PROVIDED Sell insurance policies.

SKILLS AND EXPERIENCE NEEDED +++ | You need to have a license to sell insurance.

SPECIAL EQUIPMENT ★ | No special equipment needed.

WHERE TO FIND LEADS Insurance companies advertise part-time openings, including some jobs that can be done from home. Insurance agencies where you live may need help.

PAY RANGE $$ | Most insurance agents are paid between $17 and $37 per hour but may be able to earn more through commissions and bonuses.

JUNK REMOVER

SERVICE PROVIDED Clean out basements and resell the materials and items you collect.

SKILLS AND EXPERIENCE NEEDED ++ | An eye for items and materials that are saleable is helpful. You need to be able to lift heavy objects.

SPECIAL EQUIPMENT ★ | A truck for hauling, hand trucks or dollies for moving items, and storage space.

WHERE TO FIND LEADS Promote your services on social media, advertise in the classifieds, and tell your friends and colleagues. Sell items at flea markets, antique stores, online, or to recyclers.

PAY RANGE $$$$ | Junk removal companies may charge less than $100 or more than $300, depending on the location and the size of the job.

LANDLORD

SERVICE PROVIDED Rent property that you own to tenants.

SKILLS AND EXPERIENCE NEEDED ++ | Be comfortable negotiating. Know how to make basic home repairs. You also need to be responsive, empathetic, and flexible.

SPECIAL EQUIPMENT ★ | A well-equipped toolbox.

WHERE TO FIND LEADS Advertise your property locally.

PAY RANGE $$$$ | Landlords need to be able to charge in rent in order to turn a profit after covering all of their expenses, including the mortgage on the property, taxes, and maintenance.

MALL SANTA

SERVICE PROVIDED Perform as Santa at shopping malls during the holiday season.

SKILLS AND EXPERIENCE NEEDED + | No experience needed, but you should be able to look the part and have a good rapport with children. Event companies run Santa training programs.

SPECIAL EQUIPMENT ★ ★ | Santa costume and props.

WHERE TO FIND LEADS Malls often book Santas through event companies.

PAY RANGE $$ | Santa gets $10–$40 per hour. Santas who visit kids in hospitals or perform at other events earn more.

MERCHANDISER

SERVICE PROVIDED Organize products for display in a store, and provide sales materials.

SKILLS AND EXPERIENCE NEEDED ✦ | Usually experience isn't required for an entry-level job, although retail sales and marketing experience can be helpful.

SPECIAL EQUIPMENT ★ | No special equipment needed.

WHERE TO FIND LEADS Companies advertise job openings, or you may hear about them by word of mouth.

PAY RANGE $ | About $11 per hour, which is minimum wage in some states.

PARKING SPOT RENTAL

SERVICE PROVIDED Get paid to let someone keep their car in a parking spot you own or rent and don't use.

SKILLS AND EXPERIENCE NEEDED ✦ | No experience needed. If you don't own your space, check whether your rental agreement allows re-renting your spot.

SPECIAL EQUIPMENT ★ | No special equipment needed.

WHERE TO FIND LEADS Peer-to-peer parking apps serve some cities and enable you to rent your parking space on demand. You can also advertise in your local newspaper classifieds or on *craigslist*.

PAY RANGE $$$ | The amount you can charge will vary based on where your space is located. In a crowded city where parking is scarce, you may get $200 and up per month.

PEER-TO-PEER LENDING

SERVICE PROVIDED Lend money to people as an investment.

SKILLS AND EXPERIENCE NEEDED ✦✦ | Some knowledge of investing and finance is useful for evaluating the terms of your investment and its risks.

SPECIAL EQUIPMENT ★ | No special equipment needed.

WHERE TO FIND LEADS Join a peer-to-peer lending platform. On these platforms, investors choose which loans to support, and how much to invest. Funds from multiple investors are bundled together for the borrower.

PAY RANGE $ | The peer-to-peer lending platforms estimate returns starting at around 4 percent, with the highest estimated returns assigned to the riskiest loans. You will lose your money if the borrower defaults.

PERSONAL INVESTING

SERVICE PROVIDED Buy and sell stocks, bonds, and other financial investments.

SKILLS AND EXPERIENCE NEEDED ✦✦ | Understand the market for the type of investments you are buying and selling, and know the risks involved.

SPECIAL EQUIPMENT ★ | No special equipment needed. You should have a way to stay informed about how your investments are performing (usually a computer).

WHERE TO FIND LEADS Do research to identify investments that align with your goals and tolerance for risk.

PAY RANGE $$$$ | Returns depend on how much and where you invest. Investments that estimate high returns also carry higher risks, and you can potentially lose money from any investment.

PERSONAL SHOPPER

SERVICE PROVIDED Shop for people who can't shop for themselves.

SKILLS AND EXPERIENCE NEEDED + | It depends on what you are shopping for and how much discretion you have. For example, if you are buying personal items such as clothes or gifts, your clients may want to you to be able to understand their tastes.

SPECIAL EQUIPMENT ★ | You may need your own transportation.

WHERE TO FIND LEADS On-demand platforms for task-based work include shopping and errand-running jobs, among them grocery shopping. In addition, individuals who are homebound or busy may hire someone to shop for them on a regular basis: you could find this type of work by offering your services on social media or by word of mouth.

PAY RANGE $$$ | Errand runners typically earn $25 per hour, but you can charge more if you have to drive (see Chapter 3).

POLL INTERVIEWER

SERVICE PROVIDED Call people on the phone and survey them about their opinions.

SKILLS AND EXPERIENCE NEEDED + | Experience isn't necessary, but you should be able to handle rejection when people are rude or hang up on you.

SPECIAL EQUIPMENT ★ | No special equipment needed.

WHERE TO FIND LEADS Organizations looking for interviewers advertise openings.

PAY RANGE $ | The average pay for interviewers is around minimum wage or slightly above, depending on the organization conducting the research and the state where the job is located.

PRODUCT DEMONSTRATOR

SERVICE PROVIDED Show people in a store how to use a product (or if the product is food, give them tastes).

SKILLS AND EXPERIENCE NEEDED + | Usually no experience is needed.

SPECIAL EQUIPMENT ★ | Employers will provide the products you demonstrate.

WHERE TO FIND LEADS Companies that need product demonstrators advertise openings. Product demonstrators often work for a marketing company, which assigns them to clients' projects.

PAY RANGE $ | About $11 per hour on average, though experienced product demonstrators can make more.

PROPERTY MANAGER

SERVICE PROVIDED Handle the day-to-day business of running rental property for a landlord.

SKILLS AND EXPERIENCE NEEDED +++ | Some states require property managers to have a real estate license.

SPECIAL EQUIPMENT ★ | No special equipment needed.

WHERE TO FIND LEADS Real estate companies advertise openings for property managers. You can also network with friends and professional colleagues on social media, and you may hear of jobs by word of mouth.

PAY RANGE $$$ | Property managers earn an average of $35 per hour.

REAL ESTATE AGENT

SERVICE PROVIDED Market and show homes for sale to prospective buyers.

SKILLS AND EXPERIENCE NEEDED +++ | You need to take a course and obtain a real estate license in the state where you work. Most states require that you have experience working for a brokerage before you can work on your own.

SPECIAL EQUIPMENT ★ | You will need transportation to visit the properties you are showing and a computer along with a reliable Internet connection and software to communicate with clients, manage listings, and sign documents.

WHERE TO FIND LEADS If you are working with a brokerage, you will have an arrangement with them for receiving leads.

PAY RANGE $$$$ | You get a commission that is a percentage of every sale; your earnings depend on how much you work and the selling prices of the properties you sell.

REAL ESTATE FLIPPER

SERVICE PROVIDED Invest in property that can be upgraded and sold quickly for a profit.

SKILLS AND EXPERIENCE NEEDED +++ | Knowledge of local housing markets, real estate financing, and tolerance for risk. Familiarity with housing construction and materials will help you estimate how much you will need to invest in order to update the property and ensure you can make a profit.

SPECIAL EQUIPMENT ★ | If you are remodeling the property yourself, you'll need the tools and equipment for it (see Chapter 10). Research what type of software you might need to manage your investments and associated remodeling projects.

WHERE TO FIND LEADS Real estate websites and listings of distressed properties, such as foreclosures.

PAY RANGE $$$$ | How much profit you can make flipping real estate depends on housing prices where you live and your ability to manage expenses. It's possible to make thousands of dollars in profit from flipping a property, but as with any investment, you can lose money if you spend too much or the market drops.

REAL ESTATE STAGER

SERVICE PROVIDED Redecorate homes that are for sale to make them more appealing to prospective buyers.

SKILLS AND EXPERIENCE NEEDED ++ | Interior design experience, whether formal or informal.

SPECIAL EQUIPMENT ★★ | You need access to furniture for decorating. You can use furniture you own or lease it.

WHERE TO FIND LEADS Team up with real estate agents.

PAY RANGE $$$$ | Most real estate stagers charge between $300 and $1,300 per project, though rates vary a lot by location. Some stagers base their rates on the listing price for the property.

RESELLER

SERVICE PROVIDED Buy used goods from sources such as yard sales or collect free cast-offs, refurbish if needed, and resell them.

SKILLS AND EXPERIENCE NEEDED ++ | Knowing the value of the products you buy and sell will help you spot deals and price items to make a profit.

SPECIAL EQUIPMENT ★ | No special equipment needed. If you ship your products, you will need shipping materials.

WHERE TO FIND LEADS Sell your products at flea markets, consignment shops, or online. You can promote your business on social media.

PAY RANGE $$ | How much you earn depends on the value of the goods you sell, how much you are able to mark them up, and whether the site or store that hosts your listings or items takes a cut.

RETAIL SALES

SERVICE PROVIDED Work as a sales associate or cashier in a retail store.

SKILLS AND EXPERIENCE NEEDED + | Experience may be preferred or required for some retail jobs.

SPECIAL EQUIPMENT ★ | No special equipment needed.

WHERE TO FIND LEADS Stores will advertise openings or you may hear of them by word of mouth.

PAY RANGE $ | Pay rates start at minimum wage.

RV RENTAL

SERVICE PROVIDED Rent out an RV you own when you aren't using it.

SKILLS AND EXPERIENCE NEEDED ✦ | Be willing and able to interact with renters.

SPECIAL EQUIPMENT ★ ★ ★ | Your RV.

WHERE TO FIND LEADS List your RV on an RV-sharing site or advertise in the classifieds.

PAY RANGE $$$$ | Rental rates on RV-sharing sites range from less than $100 to more than $900 per day. Check your insurance policy and the policy offered by the sharing site to make sure your RV is covered for loss or damage.

SALES REPRESENTATIVE

SERVICE PROVIDED Make sales calls, assist with prospecting, manage customer relationships, help to close sales.

SKILLS AND EXPERIENCE NEEDED ✦✦✦ | Sales experience, knowledge of the product and the target buyer.

SPECIAL EQUIPMENT ★ | No special equipment needed.

WHERE TO FIND LEADS Companies may hire salespeople for part-time jobs, and you may hear of work through your professional or social network. You may also find opportunities by joining an online freelance platform.

PAY RANGE $$ | Sales representatives' earnings vary widely based in part on the products they sell. The average pay for sales work is around $20 per hour, encompassing cashiers and retail sales workers earning minimum wage as well as more highly paid securities brokers.

SCRAP METAL COLLECTOR

SERVICE PROVIDED Collect discarded metal from households and industrial sites and resell it to a recycler.

SKILLS AND EXPERIENCE NEEDED ++ | Be knowledgeable about different types of scrap metal and the market for selling them. Know the scrap metal collection laws or regulations in your state.

SPECIAL EQUIPMENT ★★★ | A truck, appropriate tools for collecting and identifying metals, and safety equipment.

WHERE TO FIND LEADS You can find scrap metal advertised as free and make connections with housing developments and other businesses that discard appliances and metal equipment. To sell, develop relationships with scrap yards. Some apps offer directories of scrap yards and pricing.

PAY RANGE $$$ | Scrap yards buy by the pound or by the ton, and prices depend on the metal.

SOCIAL MEDIA INFLUENCER

SERVICE PROVIDED Get paid to promote brands and products on social media.

SKILLS AND EXPERIENCE NEEDED +++ | Expertise using your social media platform of choice, an account focused on a specific topic, and a large, engaged following.

SPECIAL EQUIPMENT ★ | You'll need a smartphone.

WHERE TO FIND LEADS Interact on social media with brands you want to represent.

PAY RANGE $$$$ | Earnings depend on the platform and how many followers you have, among other factors. For example,

Instagram influencers with fewer than one thousand followers charge less than $100 per post on average.

SOCIAL MEDIA MARKETER

SERVICE PROVIDED Write social media posts for companies, interact with followers, and manage social media accounts.

SKILLS AND EXPERIENCE NEEDED +++ | You need writing ability, digital marketing experience, a social media presence, and knowledge of social media metrics. You may need a degree in marketing or a related field.

SPECIAL EQUIPMENT ✶ | A computer, a smartphone, and reliable Internet service.

WHERE TO FIND LEADS Join an online freelance platform, network with your colleagues, and promote your services on social media.

PAY RANGE $ | Freelance social media marketers charge wide-ranging rates, starting at $10 per hour up to $50 per hour or more.

STADIUM CONCESSIONAIRE

SERVICE PROVIDED Sell concessions and souvenirs at sports events.

SKILLS AND EXPERIENCE NEEDED + | Usually no experience is needed. Employers generally train workers as needed.

SPECIAL EQUIPMENT ✶ | Employers usually provide any necessary equipment.

WHERE TO FIND LEADS Local sports arenas, word of mouth. Openings may be advertised.

PAY RANGE $$ | Concession vendors earn an average of $13 per hour.

STREET VENDOR

SERVICE PROVIDED Sell products on the street, such as from a cart or food truck.

SKILLS AND EXPERIENCE NEEDED ++ | Knowledge of your products and good sales and customer service skills. You need to obtain proper licenses and permits, and if you are selling food, comply with local health, safety, and insurance regulations.

SPECIAL EQUIPMENT ★ ★ ★ | Any equipment you need to set up and sell your products.

WHERE TO FIND LEADS Do research to determine the optimal location to set up your wares and to understand the competition.

PAY RANGE $$ | How much you earn depends on many factors, including what you sell, where you're set up, and how often you work.

TELEMARKETING SALESPERSON

SERVICE PROVIDED Make calls to prospective customers to sell products or schedule appointments.

SKILLS AND EXPERIENCE NEEDED ++ | You need to be able to take rejection if prospects are rude or hang up on you. Companies frequently want people with some sales experience.

SPECIAL EQUIPMENT ★ | No special equipment needed.

WHERE TO FIND LEADS Companies hiring telemarketers advertise openings, or you may hear of work by word of mouth.

PAY RANGE $ | Telemarketers make an average of $10 per hour.

TIRE RECLAIMER

SERVICE PROVIDED Collect used tires and sell them to recyclers.

SKILLS AND EXPERIENCE NEEDED ++ | Comply with laws and regulations in your state concerning tire storage and disposal.

Be able to assess the condition of the tires you collect so that you can negotiate a fair price for them.

SPECIAL EQUIPMENT ★★ | A truck and somewhere to store tires until you can sell them.

WHERE TO FIND LEADS Contact businesses such as tire retailers and car rental companies to find sources of used tires, which you can collect for a fee or take for free. Develop relationships with retreading companies, which will purchase repairable tires, or recycling companies, which will take them for a fee—you profit from the margin.

PAY RANGE $$$ | Retreading shops may purchase tires for $25 to $75 each.

TOOL RENTAL

SERVICE PROVIDED Rent out tools you aren't using.

SKILLS AND EXPERIENCE NEEDED ✦ | Be willing and able to interact with renters.

SPECIAL EQUIPMENT ★★ | Your tools.

WHERE TO FIND LEADS Join a peer-to-peer platform that lists tools for rent, or advertise locally.

PAY RANGE $$$$ | How much money you make will depend on how much demand there is for your tools. You set the rental prices; for example, a tiller might be available for $40 per day.

VIDEO ACTOR

SERVICE PROVIDED Perform in demo and instructional videos.

SKILLS AND EXPERIENCE NEEDED ✦✦ | You have to fit the part and be available to work on shooting days. Audition applications require a headshot or photo.

SPECIAL EQUIPMENT ★ | No special equipment needed.

WHERE TO FIND LEADS Websites that cater to actors post casting calls. You may have to pay a membership or subscription fee.

PAY RANGE $$ | Pay varies depending on the project and the role, but a flat fee that works out to around $20 per hour is typical.

WEB DOMAIN FLIPPER

SERVICE PROVIDED Purchase abandoned or unused web domains and resell them to someone who wants the domain name.

SKILLS AND EXPERIENCE NEEDED ✦✦ | Research skills and market knowledge to identify web domains that may be valuable.

SPECIAL EQUIPMENT ★ | You'll need a computer and a reliable Internet connection.

WHERE TO FIND LEADS Domain auction sites, domain hosting companies.

PAY RANGE $$$$ | Web domains can sell for thousands of dollars, but your return depends on how much you paid for it initially.

YARD RENTAL

SERVICE PROVIDED Rent out your yard for people to host their events.

SKILLS AND EXPERIENCE NEEDED ✦ | Be able and willing to interact with renters. Check local regulations for restrictions. Make sure your neighbors are okay with what you're doing.

SPECIAL EQUIPMENT ★ | Check your insurance policy to make sure you're covered if a renter damages your property.

WHERE TO FIND LEADS Join a peer-to-peer platform and list your yard or land, or advertise locally.

PAY RANGE $$$$ | Depending on the land and location, you might be able to get a few hundred dollars a month or a few thousand for a weekend.

*"At this point, it makes me feel good to make
financial decisions on my own."*
Robin, direct sales representative and
independent personal stylist

Social Selling

Forty-four percent of online sellers say social media is at least somewhat important for promoting their items.

Source: Pew Research Center, November 2016

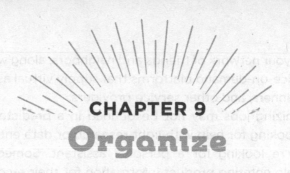

CHAPTER 9
Organize

Side hustles that involve organizing people, things, and information cover a range of part-time jobs, short-term projects, and work with the potential to develop into full-time businesses. These jobs pay you to save people time and help them become more productive or enable a business to run more efficiently.

You can find organizing jobs for a wide range of experience, education, and work environments. Some jobs, like data entry, are rote work. Others, like wrapping gifts, require creativity. You might spend your time by yourself delving into documents and data, using the research skills you learned as a librarian or journalist or exploring your family history. If your closets and your kitchen are meticulous, you could help clients get rid of clutter in their homes. As a party planner, you find yourself in the center of the action; as a personal assistant, you're behind the scenes.

DECIDE ON A STRATEGY

Finding an organizing side hustle requires various strategies, depending on the type of work you want to do. If you want to work for a company, whether as a professional in your field or an entry-level helper, tapping business contacts and joining an agency or freelance platform that specializes in the type of work you do will be your best source of leads. Part-time jobs may be advertised on both general and industry-focused help wanted sites, or you might find an opening by cold calling. If your clients are individuals, and your work is to help them at home or with personal projects, you're most likely to find work through your network of friends and neighbors, along with task- and service-on-demand platforms that supply virtual assistants, event planners, and other service providers.

Organizing jobs may not be defined in a predictable way. People looking for help with light research or data entry might say they're looking for a personal assistant. Someone who wants help entering product information for their e-commerce site may also need someone to edit the item descriptions. When you're creating online profiles on freelancing and on-demand platforms, think broadly about the job categories and skills you can tag to ensure the system refers you to potential clients who want to hire someone like you.

Olivia Quintanilla, a PhD candidate, planned her first event during high school, when she organized a walk to raise money for breast cancer research. "I noticed planning events and programming was something I enjoyed," she says, and she took on jobs planning campus events to pay her way through school.

She has started an event business with her sister, who is studying to be a dietician. WEmpower San Diego will offer workshops, retreats, and special events about health, wellness, and personal and professional growth. She's motivated to educate people; planning events is a means to that end. "With all the jobs I've had, I've seen the budgets I'm given and I see ways that money was wasted. I can take my skills and plan better events."

ORGANIZING SIDE HUSTLES

ART STUDIO ASSISTANT

SERVICE PROVIDED Help artists run their studios or with their work.

SKILLS AND EXPERIENCE NEEDED ++ | It depends on what the artist needs. You may need art-making skills to help produce the artist's work, or you may need administrative skills to pay bills, keep records, or buy supplies.

SPECIAL EQUIPMENT ★ | No special equipment needed.

WHERE TO FIND LEADS You are most likely to find this work in places where there are a lot of working artists, or if you are in art school. Networking with artists and art dealers can help you learn about openings, and some artists may advertise for help.

PAY RANGE $ | Wages start at around $10 per hour.

BANK TELLER

SERVICE PROVIDED Assist customers with bank transactions and information.

SKILLS AND EXPERIENCE NEEDED ✦ | Banks train entry-level tellers. The bank will probably run a credit check on you, so be prepared.

SPECIAL EQUIPMENT ★ | No special equipment needed.

WHERE TO FIND LEADS Inquiring at banks, word of mouth, advertised openings.

PAY RANGE $ | Bank tellers' pay rates start at minimum wage.

BELLHOP

SERVICE PROVIDED Carry bags, set up patron's hotel rooms, and answer questions for hotel guests.

SKILLS AND EXPERIENCE NEEDED ✦ | Be able to be on your feet and lift heavy objects for hours at a time. Enjoy interacting with people.

SPECIAL EQUIPMENT ★ | No special equipment needed.

WHERE TO FIND LEADS Inquire at hotels and look for openings on help wanted sites. You may hear about jobs by word of mouth.

PAY RANGE $ | Pay for bellhops starts at minimum wage. Usually bellhops also get tips.

DATA CLEANSER

SERVICE PROVIDED Identify erroneous or corrupt data in databases or spreadsheets and delete or correct it.

SKILLS AND EXPERIENCE NEEDED +++ | Experience working with a variety of data formats, spreadsheets, or databases. Jobs may require knowing how to use specific software, programming languages, or database platforms.

SPECIAL EQUIPMENT ★ | You need a computer and a reliable Internet connection.

WHERE TO FIND LEADS Join freelance platforms and network with your professional contacts.

PAY RANGE $$$ | Data cleansing work pays around $25–$30 per hour.

DATA COLLECTOR

SERVICE PROVIDED Gather and report data for businesses to use for varied purposes, including publishing, research, contact lists, and product development.

SKILLS AND EXPERIENCE NEEDED ++ | Varies depending on the data you're collecting and how you obtain it. Some jobs may involve Internet research; others may require taking notes and photos on location, or taking precision measurements from mechanical equipment.

SPECIAL EQUIPMENT ★ | If you are taking measurements or readings from mechanical equipment, you may need to use specialized tools.

WHERE TO FIND LEADS Advertised openings, freelance platforms, professional contacts.

PAY RANGE $$ | Data collectors earn an average of $15 per hour.

DATA ENTRY

SERVICE PROVIDED Enter data into a database.

SKILLS AND EXPERIENCE NEEDED + | Computer skills. Some employers look for data entry experience.

SPECIAL EQUIPMENT ★ | If you are working remotely, you will need your own computer and a reliable Internet connection.

WHERE TO FIND LEADS Join freelance platforms and network with your professional contacts. Companies who need data entry help may advertise openings.

PAY RANGE $$ | Data entry clerks earn an average of $13 per hour.

EVENT ASSISTANT

SERVICE PROVIDED Help with a variety of tasks at conferences, lectures, or social events, such as registering guests, seating them, giving directions, or serving food and drinks.

SKILLS AND EXPERIENCE NEEDED + | You need good customer service skills.

SPECIAL EQUIPMENT ★ | No special equipment needed.

WHERE TO FIND LEADS Inquire at staffing agencies, hotels, and conference centers. Venues and agencies may advertise openings.

PAY RANGE $$ | Event assistants make $18 per hour on average.

EVENT PLANNER

SERVICE PROVIDED Plan and organize conferences, lectures, or social events.

SKILLS AND EXPERIENCE NEEDED ++ | Ability to bring an event concept to fruition. Be able to develop and work within a budget as well as coordinate vendors such as caterers, florists, and speakers or entertainers. You can start without a lot of experience planning small social, community, or business events for friends, organizations you support, or a local small business. Though not required in order to get work, professional training programs teach relevant business and planning skills.

SPECIAL EQUIPMENT ★ | No special equipment needed.

WHERE TO FIND LEADS Network with people you know, promote your services on social media, and get referrals from people who have attended events you planned.

PAY RANGE $$$ | Most event planners earn at least $25 per hour.

GENEALOGY RESEARCHER

SERVICE PROVIDED Research people's family history.

SKILLS AND EXPERIENCE NEEDED +++ | Expertise developed through researching and documenting your own family history provides a good start. Many professional genealogists are certified or have advanced degrees in library science or history.

SPECIAL EQUIPMENT ★ | You will need a computer and a reliable Internet connection to do some of your research. Learn about available genealogy software for organizing information.

WHERE TO FIND LEADS Blog about your research, teach classes, join professional organizations, and get referrals from your clients.

PAY RANGE $$ | Base your rates on your expertise and experience. You should be able to charge $20–$100 per hour or more.

GIFT WRAPPER

SERVICE PROVIDED Wrap presents for individuals or businesses.

SKILLS AND EXPERIENCE NEEDED ++ | Have design ability and skill at wrapping packages creatively.

SPECIAL EQUIPMENT ★★ | Wrapping paper, ribbons, bags, embellishments, and related supplies.

WHERE TO FIND LEADS Work for friends, neighbors, and colleagues, who will also provide referrals. Promote your services on social media.

PAY RANGE $ | How much you charge depends on your location, the size and complexity of the wrapping job, and whether you travel to the customer's site. In urban areas, you could charge anywhere from a few dollars for a small box, $20 for a large box, and $40 or more per hour to wrap multiple boxes at someone's home or business.

GOLF CADDY

SERVICE PROVIDED Carry golfers' bags, find lost balls, support golfers with advice and insights about the course and their game, and related duties.

SKILLS AND EXPERIENCE NEEDED ++ | Knowledge of golf and experience playing the game. Be able to walk a golf course carrying bags several times a shift. You need to have weekend days, especially mornings, free.

SPECIAL EQUIPMENT ★ | You'll need appropriate attire for the club where you work.

WHERE TO FIND LEADS Find work at golf courses and resorts. Openings may be advertised. A peer-to-peer platform matches players with independent caddies at some country clubs.

PAY RANGE $$$ | Pay varies with location and how much experience you have, but some caddies make $100 or more for an eighteen-hole round, plus tips.

HOME ORGANIZER

SERVICE PROVIDED Help people arrange their space and reduce clutter.

SKILLS AND EXPERIENCE NEEDED ++ | Expertise organizing closets, drawers, and living spaces. You can read books and take classes to improve your skills.

SPECIAL EQUIPMENT ★ | Your organizing tools, such as a label maker.

WHERE TO FIND LEADS Do projects for your friends, get referrals, and use social media. Watch for posts from people in your community seeking help.

PAY RANGE $$$$ | Typical rates range from $40 to $200 per hour, depending on your experience and location.

INFORMATION RESEARCHER

SERVICE PROVIDED Find information for clients.

SKILLS AND EXPERIENCE NEEDED +++ | Good Internet and database research skills. Having a specialty in a particular subject, such as business financial records, or a type of information, such as academic databases, can help you stand out to potential clients and potentially enable you to charge more.

SPECIAL EQUIPMENT ★ | You will need a computer and a reliable Internet connection if the job entails acquiring information online. You may need access to proprietary databases to help clients (public and university libraries are good sources). For some jobs where information is not online, including some public records, you may need transportation to collect physical documents.

WHERE TO FIND LEADS Tap your professional contacts, get word-of-mouth referrals, and look for work on freelance platforms.

PAY RANGE $$$ | Rates vary widely depending on the topic, the complexity of the project, and how much subject matter expertise is required. Researchers are typically paid $15–$40 per hour.

> ### *Similar Jobs*
> Fact checker: confirm factual information in articles, books, and reports before they are published.

ITEM LISTING OR CLASSIFIED AD POSTER

SERVICE PROVIDED Upload product listings to e-commerce sites or post classified ads to help wanted or for sale sites.

SKILLS AND EXPERIENCE NEEDED ++ | Data entry skills, knowledge of e-commerce, and classified listing platforms. If you can help with copywriting and proofreading entries, search engine optimization, and keyword tagging, you may have an edge getting work.

SPECIAL EQUIPMENT ★ | You will need a computer and, if you are working remotely, a reliable Internet connection.

WHERE TO FIND LEADS You may be able to find work on freelance platforms. Promote yourself to professional and personal contacts with e-commerce businesses.

PAY RANGE $$ | These jobs are part data entry, part marketing, and the pay is likely to depend on whether or not you are creating or editing content as well as uploading data. Expect to earn an average of $13 per hour for data entry; marketing copywriters earn $20 and up (see Chapter 13)

LEAD GENERATOR

SERVICE PROVIDED Research sales leads for businesses and compile lists of contact information.

SKILLS AND EXPERIENCE NEEDED ++ | Good Internet, database research skills. Knowledge of your client's market can make your services more marketable.

SPECIAL EQUIPMENT ★ | You'll need a computer and a reliable Internet connection.

WHERE TO FIND LEADS Network with professional contacts, and look for work on freelance platforms. Companies may advertise open positions.

PAY RANGE $$ | Lead generation is a type of sales job. Pay for this type of work averages around $20 per hour and varies by industry as well as experience.

LIBRARY WORKER

SERVICE PROVIDED Help librarians and assist patrons.

SKILLS AND EXPERIENCE NEEDED + | You don't need prior experience to help shelve and retrieve books or assist patrons with checking out and returning materials. More technical work such as cataloging or doing research may require work experience or college study.

SPECIAL EQUIPMENT ★ | No special equipment needed.

WHERE TO FIND LEADS Libraries. Openings may be advertised.

PAY RANGE $$ | About $13 per hour.

LINE WAITER

SERVICE PROVIDED Wait in line to buy food, tickets, electronics, or other products for people who don't want to wait themselves.

SKILLS AND EXPERIENCE NEEDED + | No experience needed, but you have to be able to show up early and tolerate standing or sitting around, potentially in bad weather.

SPECIAL EQUIPMENT ★ | No special equipment needed, but having books to read, homework, or movies to watch on your phone helps to pass the time.

WHERE TO FIND LEADS Join an on-demand platform that matches line waiters with people who want to hire them. You'll find the most line-waiting gigs in big cities.

PAY RANGE $$$ | Around $25 for a typical job, waiting up to an hour.

MOVIE THEATER CREW

SERVICE PROVIDED Sell tickets, take tickets, sell concessions, and clean up in a movie theater.

SKILLS AND EXPERIENCE NEEDED + | No experience needed. Movie theaters train employees for these jobs.

SPECIAL EQUIPMENT ★ | No special equipment needed.

WHERE TO FIND LEADS Apply online to cinema operators.

PAY RANGE $ | These jobs typically pay minimum wage.

MUSEUM EDUCATOR

SERVICE PROVIDED Give tours of a museum or exhibit to educate patrons—often school groups—about its collection and significance.

SKILLS AND EXPERIENCE NEEDED +++ | The exact experience required varies depending on the institution and the job, but academic background in a relevant subject is usually preferred or required. Some programs want people to have teaching experience.

SPECIAL EQUIPMENT ★ | No special equipment needed.

WHERE TO FIND LEADS Museums, historic sites, cultural organizations. Openings may be advertised.

PAY RANGE $ | Pay for museum educators ranges from $8–$20 per hour.

> ### Similar Jobs
> Museum docent: usually these jobs, which also involve giving tours of a museum collection, go to volunteers in exchange for access to the collection and programs, but you can sometimes find a paid, part-time position. Museums provide training.

ONLINE COMMUNITY MANAGER

SERVICE PROVIDED Interact with customers in a social media community, analyze and report metrics.

SKILLS AND EXPERIENCE NEEDED ++ | Writing ability, social media expertise, and customer service skills. Some organizations may want you to have a marketing background, experience with a specific platform, and industry experience.

SPECIAL EQUIPMENT ⋆ | You'll need a computer and a reliable Internet connection.

WHERE TO FIND LEADS Network with your professional contacts, and use social media to search for opportunities.

PAY RANGE $$ | Rates vary, starting at $13 per hour.

PARALEGAL

SERVICE PROVIDED Support lawyers by reviewing documents, doing research, evaluating cases, and preparing for litigation, among other responsibilities. Virtual jobs are increasingly common.

SKILLS AND EXPERIENCE NEEDED +++ | Paralegals usually have at least a two-year degree in paralegal studies and may specialize in a specific area of the law, such as contracts, real estate, or immigration. You may be able to get jobs based on your work experience without having academic credentials.

SPECIAL EQUIPMENT ⋆ | If you work remotely, you will need a computer and a reliable Internet connection.

WHERE TO FIND LEADS Network with your professional contacts, join an on-demand legal platform or staffing agency, and look for advertised openings.

PAY RANGE $$$ | Pay varies according to location, experience, and legal specialty, but many freelance paralegals report rates of $20–$50 per hour.

PARTY PLANNER

SERVICE PROVIDED Plan and organize parties, such as for birthdays and special occasions.

SKILLS AND EXPERIENCE NEEDED ++ | Have experience planning successful parties. You may want to identify a niche or theme that takes advantage of an interest or skill you have, such as children's birthday parties, baby showers, or spa treatments.

SPECIAL EQUIPMENT ★ ★ | Equipment and supplies needed for your parties.

WHERE TO FIND LEADS Your friends, social media, online platforms that match event planners with potential clients.

PAY RANGE $$$$ | Party planners charge anywhere from $250 to $2,000 depending on the type of event and number of guests.

PATENT RESEARCHER

SERVICE PROVIDED Help lawyers prove whether an invention is original.

SKILLS AND EXPERIENCE NEEDED +++ | An academic degree in a scientific or technical field.

SPECIAL EQUIPMENT ★ | You'll need a computer to conduct your research.

WHERE TO FIND LEADS Network with your professional contacts, promote your services on social media, join a patent research service, and look for advertised openings.

PAY RANGE $$ | Experienced researchers can earn $30 per hour or more.

PERSONAL ASSISTANT

SERVICE PROVIDED Make appointments and reservations, manage schedules, pay bills, run errands, help with tasks, and do research for individuals, either virtually or in person.

SKILLS AND EXPERIENCE NEEDED ++ | Have excellent organizational, time management, and research skills. Be able to multitask and meet deadlines, and be creative about suggesting additional work that you can do. Whether handling someone's business or personal affairs, have discretion and respect for privacy.

SPECIAL EQUIPMENT ★ | You may need transportation to run errands. If you work remotely, you will need your own computer and a reliable Internet connection.

WHERE TO FIND LEADS Tap your friends and professional contacts. You could also join a platform specializing in virtual assistant work to get matched with clients, or sign up for an on-demand platform to get access to requests for one-off tasks.

PAY RANGE $$ | Virtual personal assistants make an average of $16 per hour.

> ### *Similar Jobs*
> Administrative assistant: working for a business, you may be able to charge $35 per hour and up if you are filling an executive assistant role.

PHOTO BOOTH ATTENDANT

SERVICE PROVIDED Set up and operate the photo booth at parties.

SKILLS AND EXPERIENCE NEEDED + | You should enjoy interacting with people. Some employers want photography experience.

SPECIAL EQUIPMENT ★ | You'll operate the photo booth supplied by the company you work for.

WHERE TO FIND LEADS Party or event-planning companies.

PAY RANGE $$ | Typical pay rates range from $12 to $20 per hour.

PHOTOGRAPHY ASSISTANT

SERVICE PROVIDED Help photographers in the studio or on photo shoots.

SKILLS AND EXPERIENCE NEEDED ++ | Have experience as a photographer and a portfolio of work, knowledge of photography equipment, computers, and studio equipment.

SPECIAL EQUIPMENT ★ | Your own professional-quality digital camera. You may also need your own computer for editing.

WHERE TO FIND LEADS Photographers and photography studios.

PAY RANGE $$ | Around $17 per hour.

PROJECT ARCHIVIST

SERVICE PROVIDED Help museums, historical societies, universities, and other organizations with projects to organize and preserve their records.

SKILLS AND EXPERIENCE NEEDED ++++ | You need an advanced degree in archives and records management and work experience. Some jobs may require you to know a language other than English to be able to work with the collection.

SPECIAL EQUIPMENT ★ | No special equipment needed.

WHERE TO FIND LEADS Museums, historical societies, universities, professional contacts. Openings may be advertised.

PAY RANGE $$ | Project archivists typically earn $20–$25 per hour.

PROJECT MANAGER

SERVICE PROVIDED Keep projects on track for a business. Responsibilities include managing the project budget, maintaining and updating schedules, and coordinating team members to produce deliverables.

SKILLS AND EXPERIENCE NEEDED +++ | You need experience working in your industry to be able to establish and maintain schedules, and to assign and manage deliverables. You should also have knowledge of budgeting and practice leading, facilitating, and resolving conflicts within teams, as well as advocating for resources.

SPECIAL EQUIPMENT ★ | No special equipment needed, but you should be familiar with the project management tools used in your industry.

WHERE TO FIND LEADS Network with your friends and colleagues to meet people who have projects, including by attending conferences and events.

PAY RANGE $$$$ | Most project managers earn $50 per hour and up, depending on the industry.

RECEPTIONIST

SERVICE PROVIDED Answer phones and greet visitors for a business.

SKILLS AND EXPERIENCE NEEDED + | You need good customer service skills.

SPECIAL EQUIPMENT ★ | No special equipment needed.

WHERE TO FIND LEADS Learn about jobs from friends and colleagues. Openings for part-time positions may be advertised.

PAY RANGE $ | Receptionists make an average of $12 per hour.

RESTAURANT HOST

SERVICE PROVIDED Manage reservations and table assignments at a restaurant, greet and seat guests.

SKILLS AND EXPERIENCE NEEDED + | You don't need experience, but you should be able to remain composed and polite when handling complaints.

SPECIAL EQUIPMENT ★ | No special equipment needed.

WHERE TO FIND LEADS Inquire at restaurants, and learn about jobs from friends and colleagues or find advertised openings.

PAY RANGE $ | Restaurant hosts make $8 per hour on average. Sometimes they share tips with the wait staff.

STAGEHAND

SERVICE PROVIDED Load and strike sets; move equipment and props; set up lights, rigging, and audio for theatrical performances and concerts; and other behind the scenes work as needed.

SKILLS AND EXPERIENCE NEEDED ++ | Physical strength, knowledge of lighting and audio equipment, carpentry skills. Some venues prefer you have experience.

SPECIAL EQUIPMENT ★ | Basic tools and equipment necessary to complete the work.

WHERE TO FIND LEADS Find jobs by word of mouth and advertised openings, especially on websites that specialize in entertainment jobs (you may have to pay a fee to join or subscribe)

PAY RANGE $ | Most stagehands earn $10–$25 per hour.

TABLE BUSSER

SERVICE PROVIDED Clean and set tables in restaurants.

SKILLS AND EXPERIENCE NEEDED + | No experience needed. Restaurants will train you. Be able to spend many hours on your feet and lift heavy objects.

SPECIAL EQUIPMENT ★ | No special equipment needed.

WHERE TO FIND LEADS Inquire at restaurants, and learn about jobs by word of mouth. Openings may be advertised.

PAY RANGE $ | Rates start at minimum wage.

TITLE SEARCHER OR EXAMINER

SERVICE PROVIDED Research the ownership history of real estate for buyers.

SKILLS AND EXPERIENCE NEEDED ✦✦ | Knowledge of real estate records and legal training (for example, as a paralegal) is often preferred or required.

SPECIAL EQUIPMENT ★ | You will need a computer and a reliable Internet connection to search online records. If records are not online, you will need transportation to visit the local courthouse or tax assessors' offices where they're stored.

WHERE TO FIND LEADS Title search companies, law firms, banks, and staffing agencies may hire part-time or freelance workers. You can network with your professional contacts to learn about openings. Jobs may be advertised. You can also offer your services on a freelance platform.

PAY RANGE $$ | Title search companies typically pay researchers $15–$20 per hour.

TRADEMARK RESEARCHER

SERVICE PROVIDED Research and register brand names, logos, and product names for companies or individuals.

SKILLS AND EXPERIENCE NEEDED ✦✦ | You should be familiar with the US Patent and Trademark Office trademark database and filing procedures (for example, as a paralegal). You need a law degree to advise clients about what to do if their application is rejected.

SPECIAL EQUIPMENT ★ | You'll need a computer and a reliable Internet connection.

WHERE TO FIND LEADS Network with your professional contacts, and inquire at law firms. Join an online freelance platform to offer your services and get access to requests for trademark help.

PAY RANGE $$$ | Paralegals specializing in trademark research may earn $20–$30 per hour.

TRANSCRIPTIONIST

SERVICE PROVIDED Create transcripts of audio recordings.

SKILLS AND EXPERIENCE NEEDED +++ | Good listening and fast typing skills. Background in the subject matter of recordings you are transcribing will make you more efficient. The faster you are, the more likely you will be able to get regular work.

SPECIAL EQUIPMENT ★ | You will need a computer and transcription software that enables you to easily pause, rewind, or slow down playback of the recording.

WHERE TO FIND LEADS Network with your professional contacts and inquire at transcription companies. Join a freelance platform to offer your services and find people or companies that need help.

PAY RANGE $$ | Set your rates based on how long it takes you to transcribe an hour of audio (three hours for an experienced transcriber). Average pay for a transcriptionist is $13 per hour, though you may be able to charge more for legal, medical, or other specialty work.

TRANSLATOR

SERVICE PROVIDED Translate written documents.

SKILLS AND EXPERIENCE NEEDED +++ | Fluency in a language other than English.

SPECIAL EQUIPMENT ★ | You will need a computer and access to word processing software.

WHERE TO FIND LEADS Network with professional contacts and friends. Join an agency that supplies translators. Join a freelance platform to offer your services and find out about projects.

PAY RANGE $$ | Translators often charge by the word or by the page, with higher rates for rush work. Typical rates range from 8-11 cents per word, depending on the language, or $25-$45 per hour. Certified translators can usually charge more than people who are not certified.

"With all the jobs I've had, I've seen the budgets I'm given and I see ways that money was wasted. I can take my skills and plan better events."
—Olivia Quintanilla, event planner

Many side hustles that involve helping and fixing capitalize on skills that aren't hard for most people to learn: making repairs, putting up shelves, or doing household chores. When people don't want to do them, don't have time, can't do them well, don't want to learn, or don't have the strength, they hire someone to do the tasks for them.

That means that side hustlers can find jobs they have already learned how to do through practice, without additional training or work experience, as well as those that they can easily be taught. There are some exceptions: to do most electrical or plumbing work, you need training and a license.

Regardless of whether you've had special training or learned by doing, the side hustles in this category requiring expert knowledge or skills—carpentry or computer repair, for example—pay better than jobs that primarily involve unskilled physical labor.

On-demand platforms have targeted this market for small and one-off jobs with tools that take some of the effort out of finding help and getting work. You list the type of work you do and your availability, and the platform matches you with people who want help. For side hustlers, the platforms have a couple of selling points: the jobs come to you when you have the time for them, and you can usually get paid immediately.

LEARN THE SETTING

Before diving into these platforms, though, take time to learn their ways. Some platforms require you to work at rates they set. Others allow you to set your own rates but take a large cut of your earnings. Still others charge service providers a fee for listings or referrals. If you don't do much work through the platform, or you spend a lot of time traveling from gig to gig, it might not be worth it to participate.

You can still find work the old-fashioned way, by word of mouth. But social media mastery works to your advantage here. People who hire household workers or repair people often start by asking their friends and neighbors for recommendations. These days, instead of calling around, they'll post a question on *Facebook*. If you participate, you can respond quickly if someone suggests you—or you can recommend yourself.

When Jessica Lane started her garden design, installation, and maintenance business, she created a *Facebook* page before building a website and posted pictures of her own gardens and others she liked to build a following.

"I jumped right in, so it's not a true side job, but it could have been. I could have started evenings and weekends and gotten the word out to friends."

Providing the full spectrum of gardening services—ranging from one-hour consultations to new garden installations—could be challenging for side hustlers because so much of the work is seasonal, such as from early spring to midsummer. But a more limited set of services or small projects could be managed alongside other, full-time work, she says. "A lot of people have this attitude that there's not work out there, but you can be creative."

HELPING AND FIXING SIDE HUSTLES

BICYCLE MECHANIC

SERVICE PROVIDED Fix bicycles.

SKILLS AND EXPERIENCE NEEDED +++ | Know how to fix bicycles. Formal training or certification may make you more marketable.

SPECIAL EQUIPMENT ★★ | Your tools.

WHERE TO FIND LEADS Bicycle shops and repair services may hire part-time employees. You could also start your own bicycle repair business and promote it among your friends and neighbors, and on social media.

PAY RANGE $$ | Bicycle mechanics typically earn around $14 per hour. You may be able to earn more as a business owner, especially if you also offer classes to teach cyclists how to repair their own bikes.

CAR OR MOTORCYCLE MECHANIC

SERVICE PROVIDED Fix cars or motorcycles.

SKILLS AND EXPERIENCE NEEDED +++ | Know how to repair passenger vehicles, motorcycles, and light trucks. Most professional mechanics have formal training.

SPECIAL EQUIPMENT ★ ★ ★ | You need a garage or driveway, and tools to make repairs.

WHERE TO FIND LEADS Work part time or lease space at a local garage. Promote your services on social media, and get referrals from customers. If you live in an area served by an online platform that matches car owners with mechanics, you may be able to find work by joining.

PAY RANGE $$ | Most automotive mechanics make $14–$31 per hour, depending on experience and location.

CAR WASHER AND DETAILER

SERVICE PROVIDED Wash and detail people's cars.

SKILLS AND EXPERIENCE NEEDED + | No experience needed.

SPECIAL EQUIPMENT ★ ★ | You'll need water, a hose, a bucket, rags, cleaning and detailing products, a vacuum, and other tools as appropriate to the service you're providing.

WHERE TO FIND LEADS Find work through friends and neighbors, get referrals from customers, and promote your services on social media. You may be able to find work by joining a task-on-demand platform.

PAY RANGE $$ | You're competing with car washing shops that charge around $10 for a car wash and up to $150 for detailing. If you can differentiate your services, such as by making house calls, you may be able to charge more.

CARPENTER

SERVICE PROVIDED Remodel homes or make repairs, such as installing cabinets, replacing windows, or building shelves. If you are skilled at remodeling, you can buy houses and fix them up to sell at a profit (see Chapter 8).

SKILLS AND EXPERIENCE NEEDED +++ | Most carpenters learn on the job. Know how to measure and cut wood, use tools, read blueprints, and build or repair structures. Good business skills and project choices are essential to be able to manage costs. Be familiar with local laws and regulations concerning licenses, building permits, waste disposal, and safety.

SPECIAL EQUIPMENT ★★ | Your tools.

WHERE TO FIND LEADS Do work for friends and neighbors, and get referrals from customers. Promote your services on social media. You can also invest in traditional advertising, list your business on platforms that rate home improvement contractors and provide referrals, and join platforms that match workers with tasks.

PAY RANGE $$$ | Self-employed carpenters make $20–$35 per hour. You may be able to make extra money by salvaging waste for reuse and selling it or making furniture or decorative objects.

COMPUTER REPAIR

SERVICE PROVIDED Fix desktop and laptop computers.

SKILLS AND EXPERIENCE NEEDED +++ | Expertise repairing commonly used computer equipment and troubleshooting software problems. You can learn these skills by building and repairing your own equipment and that of your friends. Some professionals obtain certifications.

SPECIAL EQUIPMENT ★ ★ | Your tools.

WHERE TO FIND LEADS Word of mouth, social media. You may find work by joining an online platform where people post tasks with which they need help.

PAY RANGE $$ | You're competing against big box and brand-name stores that typically pay $8–$20 per hour. You may be able to charge more by offering personalized services, such as house calls.

CONSTRUCTION LABORER

SERVICE PROVIDED Prepare and clean up construction sites, move materials, build and dismantle scaffolding and other temporary structures, operate machinery, control traffic.

SKILLS AND EXPERIENCE NEEDED ★★ | A license or certification may be required in your state to perform certain types of work, but many jobs do not require any experience.

SPECIAL EQUIPMENT ★ | No special equipment needed.

WHERE TO FIND LEADS Find work through your professional and personal contacts, and look for advertised openings.

PAY RANGE $$ | Most construction laborers earn $13–$30 per hour, depending on the work and location.

CUSTODIAN OR JANITOR

SERVICE PROVIDED Clean inside and outside buildings.

SKILLS AND EXPERIENCE NEEDED ★ | Usually no experience or training is needed, but knowing how to repair things is useful.

SPECIAL EQUIPMENT ★ | No special equipment needed.

WHERE TO FIND LEADS Find part-time jobs by word of mouth or advertised openings.

PAY RANGE $ | Custodians make an average of $12 per hour.

DOORMAN

SERVICE PROVIDED Monitor the entrance of an apartment, hotel, or office building; sign in guests; accept packages; give directions; hail taxis; keep an eye out for suspicious behavior.

SKILLS AND EXPERIENCE NEEDED + | No special experience needed. Good customer service skills are important. Depending on where you work, you may need to be able to stand for long periods, tolerate being outside in poor weather, or eject disruptive patrons.

SPECIAL EQUIPMENT ★ | You may need to wear a uniform provided by your employer.

WHERE TO FIND LEADS These jobs are most available in large cities and vacation spots. Find them by contacting property managers and hotel managers, and by word of mouth. You may also find advertised openings.

PAY RANGE $$ | Doormen make about $16 per hour on average.

ELECTRICIAN

SERVICE PROVIDED Install electrical wiring and lighting and make repairs.

SKILLS AND EXPERIENCE NEEDED ++++ | You need to be licensed as an electrician.

SPECIAL EQUIPMENT ★ ★ | Your tools.

WHERE TO FIND LEADS Get customer referrals, and promote your services on social media. You can also list your services on platforms that rate home improvement contractors and provide recommendations, as well as join online platforms that match workers with available tasks.

PAY RANGE $$$$ | Licensed electricians typically charge $50–$100 per hour, depending on the job and their level of experience.

FARM HAND

SERVICE PROVIDED Provide labor for a farm, such as harvesting and maintaining crops, operating farm machinery, and irrigating. On livestock farms, help with breeding or animal care.

SKILLS AND EXPERIENCE NEEDED ✦ | Usually employers will train their workers. Farm work is physically demanding; you'll be on your feet, and sometimes on your knees. You need to be able to tolerate physical labor outdoors in hot or inclement weather.

SPECIAL EQUIPMENT ★ | No special equipment needed.

WHERE TO FIND LEADS Inquire at local farms and learn about openings from people you know. Many farms hire workers seasonally, such as vegetable or berry farms for harvesting in the summer. Farms may advertise for workers.

PAY RANGE $ | Farmworkers are typically paid minimum wage.

FURNITURE ASSEMBLY

SERVICE PROVIDED Put furniture together for people in their homes.

SKILLS AND EXPERIENCE NEEDED ✦ | You should have the ability to work quickly and follow directions.

SPECIAL EQUIPMENT ★★ | Your tools.

WHERE TO FIND LEADS Furniture assembly gigs are emblematic of on-demand platforms for task-based labor. IKEA bought *TaskRabbit* in 2017 in part to bolster its customer service. You can also use social media to let people in your community know about your services.

PAY RANGE $$$ | Typical charges for assembling home furniture range from $25 to $75 per hour, depending on location, experience, and the complexity of the project.

GARDENER

SERVICE PROVIDED Design, plant, and maintain home gardens.

SKILLS AND EXPERIENCE NEEDED +++ | Your experience designing and planting your own gardens.

SPECIAL EQUIPMENT ★★ | You'll need gardening tools and a vehicle to transport plants.

WHERE TO FIND LEADS Work for your friends and neighbors, and get customer referrals. Promote your services to community organizations, and on social media.

PAY RANGE $$ | Gardening services range from $10 per hour for labor (cleaning up leaves, spreading mulch) to $150 per hour or more for design. You might charge several hundred dollars and up for a project that includes design, plant purchases, and planting, depending on the size of the property.

HANDYPERSON

SERVICE PROVIDED Do odd jobs such as install shelves, and make small repairs.

SKILLS AND EXPERIENCE NEEDED +++ | Know how to use tools and have basic carpentry skills. Some types of work may require you to have a professional license.

SPECIAL EQUIPMENT ★★ | Your tools.

WHERE TO FIND LEADS Work for friends and neighbors, and get referrals from customers. Members of local community pages on social media often ask for recommendations, and you can find leads directly or get referrals there. You could also join an online platform for task-based work to get referrals when people post jobs.

PAY RANGE $$$$ | Rates vary by location, with an average rate for a handyperson around $60 per hour. If you have professional skills or lots of experience, you can usually charge more. Some states have limits on how much you can charge for a project without having a contractor's license.

HOME MAINTENANCE AND REPAIR

SERVICE PROVIDED Maintain and repair property, home electronics, or large and small appliances.

SKILLS AND EXPERIENCE NEEDED +++ | Carpentry, plumbing, or electrical skills, and where applicable, experience fixing electronics and appliances. You need a license to make plumbing repairs or work on home wiring. If you repair refrigerators, you need to be certified to work with refrigerants.

SPECIAL EQUIPMENT ⋆ | Tools and a vehicle for transporting them along with parts and equipment.

WHERE TO FIND LEADS Your friends, professional contacts, social media, retailers that sell appliances or home improvement products. You can also join an online platform for task-based labor to offer your services.

PAY RANGE $$ | Technicians who repair appliances earn an average of $18 per hour.

HOUSE CLEANER

SERVICE PROVIDED Clean private homes.

SKILLS AND EXPERIENCE NEEDED ++ | Skill at cleaning floors, furniture, bathrooms, appliances, carpets, and other home fixtures, including familiarity with a variety of cleaning products. This work is physically demanding and also requires good customer service skills.

SPECIAL EQUIPMENT ⋆⋆ | Cleaning products, mops, rags, vacuum.

WHERE TO FIND LEADS House cleaners often get work through customer recommendations. You can also promote your services on social media or join an online platform that offers referrals to people looking for household help.

PAY RANGE $$ | You can charge anywhere from $60–$150 or more per visit depending on the size of the house or apartment and its location.

HOUSE PAINTER

SERVICE PROVIDED Paint interiors and exteriors for homeowners.

SKILLS AND EXPERIENCE NEEDED ✦✦ | Gain experience by painting your own home. You can also take classes or work for an experienced painter to improve your skills. Your state may require you to have a license to charge money for house painting.

SPECIAL EQUIPMENT ★★★ | Painting tools and supplies.

WHERE TO FIND LEADS Find work through real estate companies, building contractors, painting companies, and your friends and neighbors. Promote your services on social media.

PAY RANGE $$$ | Painters typically earn $25–$35 per hour.

HOUSE SITTER

SERVICE PROVIDED Take care of people's houses while they're away to maintain the property, take care of plants and pets, and discourage burglars.

SKILLS AND EXPERIENCE NEEDED ✦ | No experience needed. If the job involves taking care of pets, it will help to have experience with animals.

SPECIAL EQUIPMENT ★ | No special equipment needed.

WHERE TO FIND LEADS Find work through your friends and neighbors, and by promoting your services on social media.

PAY RANGE $$$ | Typical rates for housesitting range from around $25 per day to $50 to stay overnight. You may charge more or less depending on your location and your responsibilities.

HOME IT INSTALLER

SERVICE PROVIDED Set up computer equipment, smart devices, and networks in people's homes.

SKILLS AND EXPERIENCE NEEDED ++ | Know how to set up accounts on desktop computers and devices, install software, and connect computers to a home network and the Internet. To install electrical wiring, you need to be a licensed electrician.

SPECIAL EQUIPMENT ⋆ | It depends on the extent of the services you're providing. If you're just running setup scripts and plugging in devices, you won't need any equipment. If you're running cables, hanging monitors, or troubleshooting, you'll need appropriate tools and supplies.

WHERE TO FIND LEADS Friends, neighbors, and colleagues may hire or refer you. Promote your services on social media. You could also join an on-demand platform for task-based work to get referrals when people post jobs.

PAY RANGE $$$ | Research what professionals charge in your area and set competitive rates, or find ways to differentiate your services. Big box stores charge around $100 for in-home computer, Wi-Fi, or software installation.

INTERIOR DECORATOR

SERVICE PROVIDED Help people choose color schemes, furniture, and décor for their homes.

SKILLS AND EXPERIENCE NEEDED ++ | You need design ability, experience decorating your home, knowledge of design trends and sources for furniture, lighting, carpets, curtains, art, and accessories such as throw pillows. Have connections with contractors to paint rooms, install lighting, and perform other work as needed.

SPECIAL EQUIPMENT ⋆ | Have measuring tools, sketching supplies, software for visualizing room layouts, and color palettes. If you're hanging drapes and pictures yourself, have a tool kit.

WHERE TO FIND LEADS Work for friends and neighbors, and get referrals from customers. Promote your work on social media and with real estate agencies, home decorating stores, and home improvement contractors. You can also list your services on platforms that rate home improvement contractors and provide referrals.

PAY RANGE $$$$ | Interior decorators charge by the hour or by the project. Highly regarded, in-demand decorators in wealthy areas may charge $500 per hour or more. If you're new to the business or serve a middle-class clientele, your rates might range from less than $50 to $150 per hour.

IT SUPPORT

SERVICE PROVIDED Troubleshoot software, hardware, and network problems.

SKILLS AND EXPERIENCE NEEDED +++ | You need good problem-solving skills, and experience troubleshooting common IT problems, such as getting rid of malware.

SPECIAL EQUIPMENT ★★ | Tools needed to deliver your services.

WHERE TO FIND LEADS Friends, neighbors, and colleagues may hire or refer you. Promote your services on social media, or join an on-demand platform for task-based work to get referrals when people post jobs.

PAY RANGE $$$ | Research what professionals charge in your area and set competitive rates, or find ways to differentiate your services. Big box stores charge around $100 for in-home diagnostic services.

LABORER

SERVICE PROVIDED Do heavy lifting for homeowners, such as moving furniture, installing a fence, digging and planting, or removing debris. You may need to work with a partner.

SKILLS AND EXPERIENCE NEEDED ✦ | Some work doesn't require any experience. For other work, you will need to know how to use the necessary tools. You need to be able to engage in demanding physical work, possibly for several hours at a time and in hot, cold, or inclement weather. If you are doing gardening work, you should know about plants, such as how to prune them.

SPECIAL EQUIPMENT ★ | If the job requires tools, you may need to provide your own, although customers may let you use theirs.

WHERE TO FIND LEADS Friends, neighbors, and colleagues may hire or refer you. Promote your services on social media, or join an on-demand platform for task-based work to get referrals when people post jobs.

PAY RANGE $ | Typical day-labor rates range from $10 to $25 per hour.

LAUNDERER

SERVICE PROVIDED Wash people's laundry. You could also drop off and pick up dry cleaning.

SKILLS AND EXPERIENCE NEEDED ✦ | Knowledge of fabric care, familiarity with detergents and stain removal methods, ability to read labels—which you know from washing your own clothes.

SPECIAL EQUIPMENT ★ | No special equipment needed, though if you do clients' laundry in your own machines, consider the wear and tear and need to replace your equipment more quickly.

WHERE TO FIND LEADS Friends, neighbors, and colleagues may hire or refer you. Promote your services on social media or register with online sites that provide referrals for housekeeping services. If you provide childcare, elder care, or housecleaning services, you could offer laundering at an additional cost or incorporate it into your rate.

PAY RANGE $$ | Rates vary widely depending on your location. Laundry services may charge per pound—between $1 and $3 is common—or per load ($10 for a typical load, which weighs about 10 pounds).

LAWN CARE

SERVICE PROVIDED Mow and maintain lawns for homeowners.

SKILLS AND EXPERIENCE NEEDED ++ | Know your lawn mowing equipment. If you are also raking, seeding, fertilizing, or providing other lawn services, you need to be familiar with lawn-care products and how and when to use them.

SPECIAL EQUIPMENT ★★ | Have a lawnmower, rakes, spreaders, and other equipment as needed. Some customers may have equipment you can use.

WHERE TO FIND LEADS Friends, neighbors, and colleagues may hire or refer you. Promote your services on social media, or join an online platform that rates home improvement contractors and provides referrals.

PAY RANGE $$$ | You can charge $30 or more per visit for lawn mowing, depending on the rates in your area and the size of the lawn.

LEAF REMOVER

SERVICE PROVIDED Clean up dead leaves for homeowners in the fall or spring.

SKILLS AND EXPERIENCE NEEDED + | If you grew up in a house with a yard and trees, you know how to rake leaves. If you're going to use a leaf blower or vacuum, you have to know how to use the equipment.

SPECIAL EQUIPMENT ★ | Have a rake, leaf blower, or vacuum. You'll need bags if you have to remove the leaves from the property.

WHERE TO FIND LEADS Friends, neighbors, and colleagues may hire or refer you. Promote your services on social media, or join an online platform where people post tasks.

PAY RANGE $$$$ | Many people who do leaf removal charge a flat rate based on the size of the yard and number of trees, with rates starting around $70 for a small lot.

LOCKSMITH

SERVICE PROVIDED Install, repair, and change locks for homeowners.

SKILLS AND EXPERIENCE NEEDED +++ | You need training and experience as a locksmith, and you can become certified, which may help you get work. Some states require locksmiths to have a license.

SPECIAL EQUIPMENT ★★ | You'll need your tools.

WHERE TO FIND LEADS Friends, neighbors, and colleagues may hire or refer you. Promote your services on social media, and advertise locally. You can also list your services on platforms that rate contractors and provide referrals.

PAY RANGE $$ | Locksmiths charge anywhere from a few dollars to copy a key to more than $100 for changing locks.

MOVER

SERVICE PROVIDED Pack and transport boxes for people who are moving houses.

SKILLS AND EXPERIENCE NEEDED ++ | Know how to pack items efficiently and so they don't break. Be able to lift heavy boxes and furniture repeatedly.

SPECIAL EQUIPMENT ★★ | If you work independently, you'll need supplies for packing, equipment for loading and unloading, and your own truck.

WHERE TO FIND LEADS If you're working for yourself, network with friends, neighbors, colleagues, and on social media. You can also list your business on a platform that rates service providers and offers referrals. Moving companies hire part-time workers, and in some locations, you can join an on-demand platform to get gigs.

PAY RANGE $$ | Movers working as employees make an average of $13 per hour and may get tips.

PICTURE FRAMER

SERVICE PROVIDED Mat and frame photographs, artwork, or documents, or mount and frame objects.

SKILLS AND EXPERIENCE NEEDED +++ | Have artistic ability and woodworking skills. You can teach yourself framing or attend a training course.

SPECIAL EQUIPMENT ★★★ | Framing tools and supplies and workshop space.

WHERE TO FIND LEADS Market your services to photographers, artists, and galleries directly, and use social media to promote your work to individuals. Do work for friends and colleagues to generate referrals.

PAY RANGE $$ | Framing designers employed by frame shops earn around $15 per hour on average. As a business owner, you may be able to earn more.

PICTURE HANGER

SERVICE PROVIDED Hang art and design wall displays for homeowners.

SKILLS AND EXPERIENCE NEEDED ++ | Be able to hang a picture cleanly on a variety of wall surfaces. If you are making a display, have good design skills.

SPECIAL EQUIPMENT ★★ | Tools and supplies for hanging.

WHERE TO FIND LEADS Friends, neighbors, and colleagues may hire or refer you. Promote your services on social media. People also post this job on on-demand platforms.

PAY RANGE $ | You might charge $10 to hang a single picture on drywall, and $100 or more for large items, a complex display, or a project that requires climbing a ladder.

PLUMBER

SERVICE PROVIDED Install plumbing fixtures and make repairs.

SKILLS AND EXPERIENCE NEEDED +++ | You need to be licensed as a plumber.

SPECIAL EQUIPMENT ★★ | You'll need your tools.

WHERE TO FIND LEADS Friends, neighbors, and professional contacts may hire or refer you. You can also promote your services on social media or list them on platforms that rate home improvement contractors and provide referrals.

PAY RANGE $$$$ | Plumbers typically charge $45–$150 per hour, depending on location.

POOL CLEANER

SERVICE PROVIDED Clean and service swimming pools for homeowners.

SKILLS AND EXPERIENCE NEEDED +++ | You can take training courses to learn how to clean pools, and some business owners are certified.

SPECIAL EQUIPMENT ★★★ | Pool-cleaning equipment and supplies.

WHERE TO FIND LEADS Promote your business to pool owners with advertising and through social media. You may be able to get work or referrals from friends and neighbors.

PAY RANGE $$$$ | You can charge anywhere from $50 to $200 per hour depending on whether you are only cleaning pools or doing maintenance and equipment repairs.

SNOW REMOVAL

SERVICE PROVIDED Clear driveways and walkways or plow streets after a snowstorm.

SKILLS AND EXPERIENCE NEEDED + | Know how to use a snow shovel or a snow blower, or drive a snowplow.

SPECIAL EQUIPMENT ★ ★ | Have a snow shovel, snow blower, or truck with a plow.

WHERE TO FIND LEADS Friends, neighbors, and colleagues may hire or refer you. Promote your services on social media and to local businesses and public works departments.

PAY RANGE $$$ | Individuals typically charge $25–$75 per hour for clearing driveways and walkways.

WAITER

SERVICE PROVIDED Work in restaurants, for caterers, or for private customers to serve food.

SKILLS AND EXPERIENCE NEEDED + | You can get trained on the job. Some restaurants, caterers, or private customers may prefer to hire people with experience. You need to be able to deal with rude or complaining customers, work on your feet for hours at a time, and carry heavy trays.

SPECIAL EQUIPMENT ★ | Wear comfortable, supportive shoes.

WHERE TO FIND LEADS If you let friends and neighbors know you're available to help at private parties, you may get work by word of mouth. You can also find work with restaurants, catering companies, and hotels, which often advertise openings.

PAY RANGE $ | Depending on the state where you work, restaurants may pay only $2.13 per hour, the federal minimum wage for tipped employees. Most states set higher rates, though only a few require paying servers the same minimum wage as workers in other jobs. The rest of your earnings come from tips. Caterers pay an average of $11 per hour, which is more than the minimum wage in most states.

WAREHOUSE WORKER

SERVICE PROVIDED Pick and pack products, load and unload trucks, and other tasks relative to stocking goods and order fulfillment.

SKILLS AND EXPERIENCE NEEDED + | Entry-level jobs don't require experience. You need to be able to work on your feet for hours and lift heavy items.

SPECIAL EQUIPMENT ★ | Employers will train you to use scanners and other equipment.

WHERE TO FIND LEADS Logistics companies, manufacturers, and retailers all need warehouse workers. Some jobs are available through on-demand platforms.

PAY RANGE $ | Wages for warehouse workers start at around $10 per hour.

"A lot of people have this attitude that there's not work out there, but you can be creative."
—Jessica Lane, gardener

Personal Connections Matter

Fifty-two percent of consumers believe that getting connected directly with a service provider rather than a company is an advantage of on-demand platforms.

Source: National Technology Readiness Survey, Rockbridge Associates & Robert H. Smith School of Business, 2018

CHAPTER 11
Solve a Problem

Problem-solving side hustles usually use math, science, computer, design, foreign language, or communications skills to help others answer questions, reach conclusions, untangle dilemmas, or invent solutions. They are similar to the helping and fixing side hustles in Chapter 10, but here we're focused more on business-related services than on doing tasks for individuals in their homes.

These jobs include maintaining and analyzing financial records, developing software, producing music, editing video, and participating in research studies. A few jobs, such as actuary, private investigator, and some language interpreters, require professional training and licensing—making them suitable side hustles only for people who have the credentials. However, you can master the skills needed for many other side hustles in this category on your own, whether in the course of other work you do or by learning online and then practicing with personal projects or unpaid work. If your skills are new, you'll have to prove yourself before you can get hired for complex projects or charge the highest rates.

HOURS MAY VARY

Some problem-solving side hustles offer potentially predictable work. Customer service representatives, for example, may have regular shifts. When a business hires a freelance bookkeeper, the job is likely to have ongoing, well-defined tasks. Most side hustles in this category, however, are time-limited or intermittent. As a software developer or audio engineer, you may have to work intensively to meet a deadline for a project. As a foreign language interpreter, you may go long stretches without an assignment. If you are developing your own mobile app or inventing a new product, you will probably put in long hours before you know whether you'll get a payoff and how big it will be.

Freelance platforms can be a source of work for projects. As discussed in earlier chapters, you need to research these platforms to understand how they operate and how you get paid, as well as to decide how much effort you want to put into your profile or portfolio to ensure you get noticed. For any type of work that can be performed virtually, you're competing on these platforms with a global talent pool of thousands of professionals. For many problem-solving side jobs, and for many of the side hustles covered in the next two chapters, engaging your personal and professional contacts may be more fruitful, especially if you are flexible about the type of work you do.

Linda trained as an actuary but quit her job in the annuities group of a large insurance company after she had her second child. She spent the next six years mainly "being a mom and volunteering." She found her side hustle when a friend who runs a small consultancy hired her to support a health insurance client: twenty hours a week setting up spreadsheets and formulas.

"It was grunt work, probably what I did when I first started out," she says. "But I got to earn some money, and use my brain." And the earnings enabled her family to afford a home renovation and cover their vacations.

Many jobs in this category require a computer. If you're developing software or producing video, the lowest cost machine, or your five-year-old laptop, may not be powerful enough. For Linda to do her job properly, she had to buy new equipment. "The first year my laptop was old and it would crash. That was something I didn't realize would be an issue until I was in it. You don't want to buy a lot of stuff before you know what you need."

PROBLEM-SOLVING SIDE HUSTLES

ACCOUNTANT

SERVICE PROVIDED Maintain financial records for businesses, ensure their accuracy, and prepare financial reports and statements. Accountants may also advise their customers about managing financial risks.

SKILLS AND EXPERIENCE NEEDED ++++ | You need a four-year degree to practice accounting professionally. To be able to create a legally accepted, audited balance sheet or income statement for a company, you need to be licensed by your state as a Certified Public Accountant.

SPECIAL EQUIPMENT ★ | You need a computer and accounting software, as well as a reliable Internet connection to communicate and exchange documents with your clients.

WHERE TO FIND LEADS Get work through your professional and personal contacts, and by advertising. You may also find opportunities by joining an online freelance platform.

PAY RANGE $$$$ | Freelance rates range from $20 to $150 per hour and up, depending on the project, the accountant's experience, and location.

ACTUARY

SERVICE PROVIDED Evaluate financial risk for businesses.

SKILLS AND EXPERIENCE NEEDED ++++ | A college degree and additional coursework necessary to pass multiple certification exams. You also need to know how to work with spreadsheets, databases, and statistical modeling tools.

SPECIAL EQUIPMENT ★ | You need a computer and appropriate software for your projects.

WHERE TO FIND LEADS Find work through your professional contacts, agencies, and freelance platforms. Although insurance and financial companies have traditionally been the most common source of jobs for actuaries, businesses in other industries may hire actuaries to help them understand their financial risks.

PAY RANGE $$$$ | Depending on certifications and years of experience, actuaries may charge anywhere from $30 to $500 per hour.

AI TRAINER

SERVICE PROVIDED Teach artificial intelligence systems to understand human actions, language, and gestures by speaking, translating or transcribing text, or tagging images and videos.

SKILLS AND EXPERIENCE NEEDED + | No experience needed.

SPECIAL EQUIPMENT ★ | You need a computer and a reliable Internet connection.

WHERE TO FIND LEADS Platforms that crowdsource small tasks such as *Amazon Mechanical Turk*. These tasks are not available predictably.

PAY RANGE $ | Tasks typically pay only a few cents each.

AMERICAN SIGN LANGUAGE INTERPRETER

SERVICE PROVIDED Sign spoken language for deaf and hard of hearing people and convey the signed parts of a conversation to people who do not know ASL.

SKILLS AND EXPERIENCE NEEDED +++ | To be hired by an agency or company, you may need a license or certification.

SPECIAL EQUIPMENT ★ | No special equipment needed.

WHERE TO FIND LEADS Network with professional and personal contacts, or sign up with an agency. You may find openings advertised on help wanted sites or posted on freelance platforms.

PAY RANGE $$ | Most interpreters earn $20–$40 per hour.

AUDIO ENGINEER

SERVICE PROVIDED Compile audio tracks and optimize the sound of a recording.

SKILLS AND EXPERIENCE NEEDED +++ | Some professionals have academic training. You can teach yourself how to mix and master audio by practicing or through online tutorials.

SPECIAL EQUIPMENT ★ ★ ★ | Digital audio workstation software and a computer configured to run it efficiently. You will also need a high-speed Internet connection to send and receive audio files.

WHERE TO FIND LEADS Musicians and other contacts in the music business may hire or refer you. Attend shows at local clubs to meet new bands, and use social media to promote your work. You may be able to find jobs on freelance platforms. Have a demo to show potential clients.

PAY RANGE $$ | Many audio mixing and mastering engineers charge rates of $15–$60 per hour.

BANNER ADVERTISING DESIGNER

SERVICE PROVIDED Create ads for display on websites and mobile devices.

SKILLS AND EXPERIENCE NEEDED +++ | Graphic design training and web design experience. Clients will want to see samples or a portfolio of your work.

SPECIAL EQUIPMENT ★ | You need a computer, design software, and a reliable Internet connection.

WHERE TO FIND LEADS Network with your professional contacts, list your services in professional directories, and join freelance platforms. Many advertising agencies work with freelancers and accept pitches.

PAY RANGE $$ | Rates vary widely. Some designers working directly for a business client will charge a flat rate per ad, for example, $20–$80, while others offer packages that include concept development and revision time. Advertising agencies may pay per project, or by the hour.

BANQUET SERVER

SERVICE PROVIDED Serve food and drinks at large social events and conferences.

SKILLS AND EXPERIENCE NEEDED + | Have good customer service skills and the ability to lift and carry heavy trays, staying on your feet for hours.

SPECIAL EQUIPMENT ★ | Sturdy, comfortable shoes.

WHERE TO FIND LEADS Inquire at hotels, banquet halls, caterers. Openings may be advertised, or you may hear of them from friends or colleagues.

PAY RANGE $ | Banquet servers make an average of $11 per hour.

BOOKKEEPER

SERVICE PROVIDED Keep track of financial transactions for a business.

SKILLS AND EXPERIENCE NEEDED ++ | You don't need formal training, but accounting courses, familiarity with accounting software, and work experience will make you more marketable.

SPECIAL EQUIPMENT ★ | No special equipment needed.

WHERE TO FIND LEADS Tap your professional and personal contacts, especially people you know who run small businesses. You may find work on freelance platforms, or through help wanted sites.

PAY RANGE $$ | Depending on experience, bookkeepers typically charge $20–$50 per hour.

CALL CENTER CUSTOMER SERVICE REPRESENTATIVE

SERVICE PROVIDED Field calls from customers to take orders, address complaints, or give information. Some of these jobs enable employees to work from home.

SKILLS AND EXPERIENCE NEEDED + | Experience usually isn't needed, and employers provide training. Minimal industry knowledge or experience may be required or preferred for some positions.

SPECIAL EQUIPMENT ★★ | If you work from home, you will need a home office setup that meets employers' requirements, including a computer and a reliable Internet connection.

WHERE TO FIND LEADS You may learn of jobs through your friends and professional contacts, or on help wanted websites.

PAY RANGE $$ | Customer service representatives make about $16 per hour on average.

CHATBOT DEVELOPER

SERVICE PROVIDED Write software that can carry on a conversation, usually text-based, with a person within a software application or a website.

SKILLS AND EXPERIENCE NEEDED +++ | Have experience with databases, artificial intelligence, machine learning, or natural language processing technologies. You can learn relevant skills through online tutorials. Jobs may require that you have experience using a specific development platform; as with most software development work, the broader your knowledge, the more marketable you are.

SPECIAL EQUIPMENT ★ | You'll need a computer and a reliable Internet connection, as well as software development tools appropriate for your project.

WHERE TO FIND LEADS Attend meetups and conferences, and network with friends and colleagues to meet people who have projects. Contribute to open source projects. You may also find work by joining a freelance platform.

PAY RANGE $$$$ | Depending on experience, chatbot developers charge $40 per hour and up.

CLINICAL TRIAL PARTICIPANT

SERVICE PROVIDED Try new medical treatments as a member of a research study to evaluate whether the treatment is effective.

SKILLS AND EXPERIENCE NEEDED + | You need to qualify for the study by meeting health and demographic criteria. Some studies recruit healthy participants. Research the trial to understand its purpose, process, risks, safety measures, and other factors that might impact your health or lifestyle.

SPECIAL EQUIPMENT ★ | Depending on the trial, you may be given equipment to use. In addition, researchers instruct trial participants about how to record information they need to collect.

WHERE TO FIND LEADS Learn about studies from medical research institutions, including hospitals, pharmaceutical and medical device companies, clinical trial management companies, and organizations that support medical research. Some websites provide a clearinghouse for listings of current trials.

PAY RANGE $$$$ | Although many clinical trials rely on volunteers, compensation for trials that pay can range from a few hundred to a few thousand dollars.

COMPUTER-AIDED DESIGN DRAFTER

SERVICE PROVIDED Draft architectural and engineering blueprints.

SKILLS AND EXPERIENCE NEEDED +++ | Professional drafters usually have at least a two-year degree. Training includes learning how to use AutoCAD or other digital drafting tools.

SPECIAL EQUIPMENT ★★ | You'll need a computer, and, if you are working remotely, a high-speed Internet connection and appropriate software.

WHERE TO FIND LEADS Network with your professional contacts, join freelance platforms, and look for advertised openings.

PAY RANGE $$ | Most CAD drafters earn $18–$25 per hour.

Similar Jobs

3-D modeler: use 3-D modeling software to create product designs or digital objects to use in games or virtual reality.

DATA ARCHITECT OR ENGINEER

SERVICE PROVIDED Design database systems to enable access by end-user applications, enforce Information security, and maintain business continuity in case of disaster.

SKILLS AND EXPERIENCE NEEDED +++ | Have a background In computer science or a related field or work experience, and knowledge of database languages. As with many information technology jobs, the broader your knowledge, the more market able you are.

SPECIAL EQUIPMENT ★ | You'll need a computer, a reliable Internet connection, and your choice of tools.

WHERE TO FIND LEADS Attend meetups and conferences, and network with friends and colleagues to meet people who need help with projects. Contribute to open source projects. You may find work on freelance platforms.

PAY RANGE $$$$ | You may be paid by the hour or by the project. Data architects may earn $40 per hour or more.

DATA ANALYST

SERVICE PROVIDED Analyze data to develop information and insights clients use to make decisions.

SKILLS AND EXPERIENCE NEEDED +++ | Know how to retrieve, transform and analyze data using statistical analysis, data modeling, and data reporting tools. A background in computer science, math, or a related field may be helpful.

SPECIAL EQUIPMENT ★ | You'll need a computer, a reliable Internet connection, and access to the software you will need to complete clients' projects.

WHERE TO FIND LEADS Attend meetups and conferences, and network with friends and colleagues to meet people who have projects. You may find work on a freelance platform.

PAY RANGE $$$ | Earnings vary with experience, location, and the industry. You may be paid by the hour or by the project. Experienced data analysts can make $30 per hour or more.

DATA VISUALIZATION DEVELOPER

SERVICE PROVIDED Create charts, graphs, and renderings that illustrate data.

SKILLS AND EXPERIENCE NEEDED +++ | Knowledge of statistics and data analysis, as well as visual grammar and conventions (such as when to use a bar chart versus a scatter plot). Have experience using data visualization tools. Good storytelling skills are essential; design experience helps.

SPECIAL EQUIPMENT ★ | You'll need a computer and access to the software you need for your projects.

WHERE TO FIND LEADS Attend meetups and conferences, and network with your friends and colleagues to meet people who have projects. Contribute to open source projects. You may find work on freelance platforms.

PAY RANGE $$$$ | Rates for developers and analysts with data visualization experience range widely, depending on skills and experience and the scope of the work. You may be paid by the hour or by the project. Data visualization experts can earn $30 per hour or more.

DIGITAL GAME CONTESTANT

SERVICE PROVIDED Compete in mobile or online games to win prizes.

SKILLS AND EXPERIENCE NEEDED ✦✦ | You need to be skilled at the games you're playing (or in the case of trivia games, have the right kind of knowledge) to win. Research games to make sure they are legitimate. If you have to pay to play, it's gambling.

SPECIAL EQUIPMENT ✦ | Many games require a smartphone or other mobile device.

WHERE TO FIND LEADS Search online in your mobile device app store.

PAY RANGE $ | Read the terms of service to understand the rules for cashing out any winnings. You may win nothing, a few dollars, or, rarely, $1,000 or more.

DOCUMENT CONVERSION AND FORMATTING

SERVICE PROVIDED Transform documents from one file format to another and style them.

SKILLS AND EXPERIENCE NEEDED ✦✦ | Varies depending on the file formats involved.

SPECIAL EQUIPMENT ✦ | A computer, file conversion software, and a reliable Internet connection.

WHERE TO FIND LEADS People post document conversion and formatting jobs on task-on-demand and freelance platforms.

PAY RANGE $ | A few dollars for common file formats.

ESTIMATOR

SERVICE PROVIDED Estimate the costs of projects, especially in construction, manufacturing, and engineering.

SKILLS AND EXPERIENCE NEEDED ✦✦✦✦ | Depending on the industry, you are likely to need a four-year degree in a construction, engineering, or a math-related field, as well as experience in the job. Some professionals obtain certification.

SPECIAL EQUIPMENT ★ | No special equipment needed. However, you usually need to have experience using estimating software.

WHERE TO FIND LEADS Most estimators work full time; however, you may find part-time work through your professional and personal contacts, on freelance platforms, or advertised openings.

PAY RANGE $$$ | Estimators typically earn around $30 per hour.

FIX SOFTWARE BUGS

SERVICE PROVIDED Correct software errors.

SKILLS AND EXPERIENCE NEEDED ✦✦✦ | Experience as a software developer. A broad knowledge of programming languages and development environments will position you to find the most work.

SPECIAL EQUIPMENT ★ | You'll need a computer and a reliable Internet connection.

WHERE TO FIND LEADS Attend meetups and conferences and network with your friends and colleagues to meet people who need help with projects. You may find work on freelance platforms. Usually bug-fixing is included in a contract for software development, but a busy project team may hire extra hands.

PAY RANGE $$$$ | Bill for your time. Software developers can make $40 per hour or more.

FOREIGN LANGUAGE INTERPRETER

SERVICE PROVIDED Convey the two sides of a conversation between people who speak two different languages, either in person, on the phone, or via video.

SKILLS AND EXPERIENCE NEEDED +++ | Be fluent in both languages you are interpreting, and have a thorough understanding of both cultures. If you work in legal or healthcare settings, your state may require you to be certified.

SPECIAL EQUIPMENT ★ | If you work online, you will need a computer, a reliable Internet connection, and video chat software.

WHERE TO FIND LEADS Find work through your personal and professional contacts, agencies that supply translators, and advertised openings. You may also find some work on freelance platforms.

PAY RANGE $$$ | Most interpreters earn $20–$40 per hour.

HOTEL HOUSEKEEPER

SERVICE PROVIDED Clean hotel rooms and replenish supplies.

SKILLS AND EXPERIENCE NEEDED + | You don't need experience for an entry-level job, though some hotels may prefer you have some.

SPECIAL EQUIPMENT ★ | No special equipment needed, other than what the hotel provides.

WHERE TO FIND LEADS Learn about positions by word of mouth, advertised openings, and inquiring at hotels.

PAY RANGE $ | Hotel housekeepers make an average of $12 per hour.

INVENTOR

SERVICE PROVIDED Create new devices.

SKILLS AND EXPERIENCE NEEDED ++ | Have the ability to observe problems that need solving combined with creativity to imagine solutions. Technology or engineering skills will help you to execute your ideas.

SPECIAL EQUIPMENT ★★ | Tools and materials for building and experimenting with prototypes.

WHERE TO FIND LEADS Ideas can come from anywhere. If you want to sell your invention, do research to determine the market for it and pursue funding to develop it. Crowdfunding platforms offer a way to raise money from the public in small increments to cover your costs.

PAY RANGE $ | A lot of inventions go nowhere, and some inventors make millions.

MARKET RESEARCHER

SERVICE PROVIDED Collect data, interview people, and write reports about product sales, usage, and trends.

SKILLS AND EXPERIENCE NEEDED +++ | A background in marketing, statistics, or related fields. Research and data analysis skills, along with knowledge of the industry you are researching and its products.

SPECIAL EQUIPMENT ★ | You'll need a computer and a reliable Internet connection.

WHERE TO FIND LEADS Network with professional colleagues, and join an online freelance platform.

PAY RANGE $$$ | Market researchers charge anywhere from $25 per hour to more than $100 per hour depending on their experience, education level, and area of expertise.

MEDIATOR

SERVICE PROVIDED Help people resolve disputes instead of going to court.

SKILLS AND EXPERIENCE NEEDED +++ | Have good listening skills, training as a mediator, and get experience working on cases with a mentor and volunteering. To work on court-related mediation cases, you may have to be a lawyer, but states do not place restrictions on private mediation work.

SPECIAL EQUIPMENT ★ | No special equipment needed.

WHERE TO FIND LEADS Get work through mediation associations, your professional and personal contacts, and by promoting your services on social media.

PAY RANGE $$$$ | Mediators' rates vary by location but typically they charge $150–$300 per hour.

MOBILE APP DEVELOPER

SERVICE PROVIDED Create software applications for mobile devices such as smartphones.

SKILLS AND EXPERIENCE NEEDED +++ | Computer programming skills. To be hired as a freelancer, you need some experience developing software and familiarity with mobile app development platforms (which you can get by taking online courses and building your own apps).

SPECIAL EQUIPMENT ★ | You'll need a computer, a reliable Internet connection, a smartphone, and software development tools.

WHERE TO FIND LEADS You can develop your own app and maybe start a company with it. Find freelance work through your friends and colleagues, and by attending meetups and conferences. You may also find work on freelance platforms.

PAY RANGE $$$$ | Mobile app developers in the United States earn close to $50 per hour on average.

MOTION GRAPHICS DESIGNER

SERVICE PROVIDED Create animated graphics for use in videos.

SKILLS AND EXPERIENCE NEEDED +++ | Have artistic ability, graphic design training, animation skills, and experience using graphic design and video editing software. You can take online courses to learn motion graphics skills. Pay attention to visual trends.

SPECIAL EQUIPMENT ★★ | A computer, graphic design and video editing software, and a high-speed Internet connection.

WHERE TO FIND LEADS Tap your professional and personal contacts, join freelance platforms, and look for advertised openings. Have a public portfolio so potential clients can find you.

PAY RANGE $$$ | Motion graphics designers with experience charge rates ranging from $30 to $100 and up.

PACKAGING DESIGNER

SERVICE PROVIDED Create containers and labels for product packages.

SKILLS AND EXPERIENCE NEEDED +++ | Have artistic ability, training as a graphic designer, and work experience.

SPECIAL EQUIPMENT ★ | You need design and prototyping tools, including a computer and software.

WHERE TO FIND LEADS Tap your professional contacts and network in design communities. Join freelance platforms and pitch agencies that create packaging for businesses. Professional associations for graphic designers sponsor directories where members can list their profiles and search for jobs, while online portfolio sites provide another venue to display your work.

PAY RANGE $$$ | Rates vary according to experience, location, and the complexity of the project. For example, packaging designers working directly with business clients may charge anywhere from $30 to $100 per hour for a box.

PHOTOFINISHING LAB WORKER

SERVICE PROVIDED Develop and print photos from film or print digital photos.

SKILLS AND EXPERIENCE NEEDED ✦✦ | Photo labs or studios may want you to have photography or photo finishing experience.

SPECIAL EQUIPMENT ★★★ | Equipment for developing and printing photos, supplied by your employer.

WHERE TO FIND LEADS Photo labs and studios.

PAY RANGE $ | Most jobs in photofinishing labs pay $9–$15 per hour.

PHOTO RETOUCHER OR RESTORER

SERVICE PROVIDED Improve photographs by fixing color, highlights, and shadows and removing blemishes, or returning a photograph to its original condition.

SKILLS AND EXPERIENCE NEEDED ✦✦ | Have photo editing skills, including experience using software. Create a public portfolio of your work that showcases your experience and enables potential clients to find you. You can take classes online to learn retouching and restoration techniques.

SPECIAL EQUIPMENT ★ | A computer and image editing software.

WHERE TO FIND LEADS Get work through photo studios, online retailers, magazine publishers, professional contacts, photography and graphic design communities, and task-on-demand or freelance platforms.

PAY RANGE $$$$ | Freelance photo retouchers with experience typically charge $50–$150 per hour.

PHOTOSHOP EDITOR

SERVICE PROVIDED Use software to modify and manipulate images.

SKILLS AND EXPERIENCE NEEDED +++ | Graphic design training and knowledge of image editing software. Most of these jobs will require you know Photoshop.

SPECIAL EQUIPMENT ★ | A computer and access to Photoshop.

WHERE TO FIND LEADS Sources of work include task-on-demand and freelance platforms, as well as your friends and professional contacts. You can promote your services on social media.

PAY RANGE $$ | Depending on their location and experience, graphic designers get on average $20 per hour for Photoshop work. Some freelancers base their rates according to the number of images in the project.

SLIDE PRESENTATION DESIGNER

SERVICE PROVIDED Create presentation slide decks.

SKILLS AND EXPERIENCE NEEDED ++ | Have design ability; business, marketing, or industry knowledge; storytelling ability; and expertise using presentation software such as PowerPoint.

SPECIAL EQUIPMENT ★ | You need a computer and presentation software.

WHERE TO FIND LEADS Tap your professional and personal contacts, and join freelance platforms. Startup companies may be a good source of work because they need to develop a library of slide decks for presenting to funders and customers, though they may not be willing to pay as much as established businesses.

PAY RANGE $$$ | Rates vary widely, depending on the service you provide. For formatting and basic editing, you might get less than $20 per hour. Someone with proven storytelling and design skills can charge $100 per hour and up.

PRIVATE INVESTIGATOR

SERVICE PROVIDED Conduct surveillance, gather evidence, or run background checks for law firms, individuals, and businesses.

SKILLS AND EXPERIENCE NEEDED ++++ | Most private investigators have a background in law enforcement. State licensing requirements spell out the experience and training you need.

SPECIAL EQUIPMENT ★★ | Equipment appropriate to your assignment, such as surveillance gear.

WHERE TO FIND LEADS Depending on your specialty, law firms, insurance companies, corporate human resources departments, and property owners can be sources of work. Attend events where you can meet potential clients, list yourself in professional directories, get word-of-mouth referrals, and use your personal and professional contacts.

PAY RANGE $$$$ | Private investigator rates typically range from $40 to $100 per hour.

PROOFREADER

SERVICE PROVIDED Read documents and correct typographical, grammatical, punctuation, spelling, and formatting errors.

SKILLS AND EXPERIENCE NEEDED ++ | Expert knowledge of English grammar, punctuation, and style. Obsessive attention to detail.

SPECIAL EQUIPMENT ★ | You need a computer and software (generally the common office productivity applications) for editing documents.

WHERE TO FIND LEADS Tap your professional and personal contacts, and join freelancing and task-on-demand platforms. Publishers, corporate marketing departments, and local small businesses may accept inquiries.

PAY RANGE $$$ | Professional proofreaders charge around $30–$35 per hour or around $3 for a 250-word page.

PSYCHOLOGY STUDY SUBJECT

SERVICE PROVIDED Participate in experiments designed to measure and test thought processes, speech, and behavior.

SKILLS AND EXPERIENCE NEEDED ✦ | You need to qualify for the study. Ask questions to ensure you understand and are comfortable with the research and that you know your rights if you choose to leave the experiment.

SPECIAL EQUIPMENT ★ | You may be asked to use equipment as part of the study.

WHERE TO FIND LEADS Universities. Researchers sometimes conduct studies online, but more often, participants have to appear in person.

PAY RANGE $ | Psychology research studies typically pay $5–$25 per study or per hour, depending on how the study is conducted. Some studies compensate participants with gift cards or in-kind rewards, such as food or products.

Similar Jobs

Brain research subject: participate in sleep studies and other types of research related to brain function.

ROBOTICS ENGINEER

SERVICE PROVIDED Design, build, or program robots.

SKILLS AND EXPERIENCE NEEDED ✦✦✦ | Have an academic background in mechanical or electrical engineering, computer programming, and experience using 3-D modeling software. Projects may have specific technical skill requirements.

SPECIAL EQUIPMENT ★ ★ ★ | If you are building robots in your own lab (or basement), you need the appropriate tools and supplies for your projects.

WHERE TO FIND LEADS Attend meetups and network with your friends and colleagues to meet people who need help with projects. Contribute to open source projects. Because robotics is an emerging technology, university researchers may know of job opportunities. You may also find work on freelance platforms, or by pitching your services directly to robotics companies.

PAY RANGE $$$$ | Depending on their skills and experience, freelancers with robotics, electrical, or mechanical engineering expertise can make anywhere from $40 per hour to more than $100 per hour.

RODEO CLOWN

SERVICE PROVIDED Entertain the rodeo audience between events and protect downed bull riders by distracting the bull (called bullfighting).

SKILLS AND EXPERIENCE NEEDED ++++ | Have experience working with livestock. Learn bullfighting and train at rodeo school and as an apprentice. Create a comedy routine.

SPECIAL EQUIPMENT ★ | A costume and makeup, protective gear, and a barrel.

WHERE TO FIND LEADS Rodeo schools, rodeo personnel can connect you with job opportunities. You may hear about work from friends or rodeo colleagues.

PAY RANGE $$$$ | Most rodeo clowns make up to a few hundred dollars per show.

SOCIAL MEDIA ANALYST

SERVICE PROVIDED Analyze social media and product review data to learn what customers or the public think about a company, product, person, idea, or event.

SKILLS AND EXPERIENCE NEEDED +++ | Knowledge of social media platforms and experience with social media marketing and data analysis.

SPECIAL EQUIPMENT ★ | You need a computer and a smartphone.

WHERE TO FIND LEADS Promote your services and showcase your expertise on social media. Join freelance platforms, and network with your professional and personal contacts.

PAY RANGE $$$ | Social media analysts typically earn $25–$50 per hour.

SOFTWARE DEVELOPER OR ENGINEER

SERVICE PROVIDED Work on computer software applications.

SKILLS AND EXPERIENCE NEEDED +++ | Knowledge of programming languages, development tools, and processes. Although professional developers often have computer science or engineering backgrounds, many are self-taught and hired on the basis of their past work. You have to learn new languages and platforms continuously to maintain and advance your skills; the more you know, the more options you have for work.

SPECIAL EQUIPMENT ★ | You need a computer, a reliable Internet connection, and software development tools that are best for your projects.

WHERE TO FIND LEADS Attend meetups and conferences, and network with your friends and colleagues to meet people who need help with projects. You may find work on freelance platforms.

PAY RANGE $$$$ | Software developers in the United States make $40–$50 per hour on average.

SPEECH RECOGNITION DATA CONTRIBUTOR

SERVICE PROVIDED Help computer software learn to recognize spoken words by making voice recordings.

SKILLS AND EXPERIENCE NEEDED + | No experience needed.

SPECIAL EQUIPMENT ★ | You need a computer with a microphone and a reliable Internet connection.

WHERE TO FIND LEADS Crowdsourcing platforms such as *Amazon Mechanical Turk*. These tasks are not available predictably.

PAY RANGE $ | Tasks typically pay a few cents each.

SPREADSHEET CONSULTANT

SERVICE PROVIDED Set up and format spreadsheets and data.

SKILLS AND EXPERIENCE NEEDED ++ | Expertise using spreadsheet software and some familiarity with data and financial formulas.

SPECIAL EQUIPMENT ★ | You need a computer and spreadsheet software.

WHERE TO FIND LEADS Get work through your professional and personal contacts and on freelance and task-on-demand platforms.

PAY RANGE $ | Freelancers typically charge $10–$30 per hour to create and maintain spreadsheets.

STOCK VIDEOGRAPHER

SERVICE PROVIDED Shoot footage that can be licensed or sold for repeated use.

SKILLS AND EXPERIENCE NEEDED +++ | Have a lot of professional-quality videos.

SPECIAL EQUIPMENT ★ ★ ★ | Your video equipment.

WHERE TO FIND LEADS Stock photography and video agencies purchase footage from videographers who qualify.

PAY RANGE $$ | Earnings vary depending on how stock footage agencies structure payments—you may be able to set your own rates or else get a percentage of every sale.

USER EXPERIENCE (UX) SPECIALIST

SERVICE PROVIDED Recommend ways to make websites and software enjoyable for people to use, which may include making it easy to find information or perform a task such as purchasing or returning a product.

SKILLS AND EXPERIENCE NEEDED +++ | UX specialists should be familiar with the literature about user experience and stay on top of new research. Web design and development skills are essential for creating wireframes (schematics) of website designs and for prototyping.

SPECIAL EQUIPMENT ★★ | You'll need a computer, smartphone, and tablet, as well as a reliable Internet connection.

WHERE TO FIND LEADS Attend meetups and conferences, and network with your friends and colleagues to meet people who need help with projects. You may find work on freelance platforms.

PAY RANGE $$$$ | In the United States, UX specialists can earn $40 per hour or more.

VIDEO EDITOR

SERVICE PROVIDED Edit footage, incorporate special and sound effects, fix color and audio for a film or video.

SKILLS AND EXPERIENCE NEEDED +++ | Have experience in video editing and production, proficiency using video editing software. You'll need a demo reel to get hired.

SPECIAL EQUIPMENT ★★ | Video editing software, a computer, and a high-speed Internet connection.

WHERE TO FIND LEADS Get work through your professional and personal contacts, promote your work on social media, and join freelance platforms (including those specializing in video production services).

PAY RANGE $$$$ | Freelance video editors typically charge $40–$100 per hour.

WEB DESIGNER

SERVICE PROVIDED Create the visual presentation of a website, including the layout, fonts, colors, and navigation.

SKILLS AND EXPERIENCE NEEDED +++ | Graphic design training and experience using web design tools and development platforms.

SPECIAL EQUIPMENT ★ | A computer, a reliable Internet connection, and web design tools. You'll need a portfolio to showcase your capabilities.

WHERE TO FIND LEADS Friends and colleagues can help you find work. Professional associations for graphic designers sponsor directories where members can list their profiles and search for jobs. You may find work on freelance platforms and by promoting your work on social media.

PAY RANGE $$$ | Rates vary according to the experience of the designer and the complexity of the project, but freelancers with greater than basic skills typically charge $30–$80 per hour.

WEB DEVELOPER

SERVICE PROVIDED Build applications for websites.

SKILLS AND EXPERIENCE NEEDED +++ | Experience using web development platforms and programming languages. Full stack developers—software developers who can program or troubleshoot a website's servers and databases as well as the functionality presented to end users (such as buttons, forms, and shopping carts) may find more side hustle opportunities.

SPECIAL EQUIPMENT ★ | You need a computer, a reliable Internet connection, and software development tools.

WHERE TO FIND LEADS Attend meetups and conferences, and network with your friends and colleagues, to find people who may need help with projects. You may find work on freelance platforms. Community organizations or small businesses may need part-time or temporary help with website development and maintenance.

PAY RANGE $$$$ | Software developers in the United States can earn $40 per hour or more.

> *"The first year my laptop was old and it would crash. That was something I didn't realize would be an issue until I was in it."*
> —Linda, spreadsheet consultant

World of Freelance Opportunity

Forty-nine percent of companies have increased their use of contingent workers in the past five years.

Source: EY Global Contingent Workforce Study, 2018

CHAPTER 12
Entertain

Entertainment side hustlers are in a crowded field. Most of the jobs in this category involve performing for an audience, and they're highly competitive. To be successful, you need talent, connections, and a strong reputation. Other entertainment side hustles involve delivering an experience, such as leading tours and hosting social events. Although knowledge and experience in the field is critical, performance skills help in these jobs as well.

KEEPING YOUR HAND IN

Live performers put on a show, such as playing with a band, telling jokes, acting as a movie extra, or doing magic tricks. There can be a fine line between having a side hustle as an entertainer and a career. Many professional actors and musicians do other jobs to pay the bills. If a job with predictable hours and a steady paycheck beckons, an entertainment side hustle means not having to quit the field entirely.

As a performer, your talent and skills are paramount, but ability and a well-honed act aren't enough. You can easily publish your music or launch a video channel, but you have to work to gain a following. And whether you're a rock and roll drummer, a voice actor, or you sing with a wedding band, building an audience and a network of people who will recommend you or hire you takes time. Even veteran entertainers may have to reintroduce themselves if they have been away from the stage for a while. "Back when I was trying to get gigs lined up and nobody knew who I was anymore, I had to take a couple of parade gigs," recalls Russell Bogartz, a trombonist. He had been a member of a rock band during his twenties. Now a product manager for a technology company, he averages two to three music gigs a month.

Delivering an experience may seem to have more in common with teaching a class or planning an event than doing standup. You're organizing and leading people toward a result—in this case, a fun celebration, a thrilling adventure, or an appreciation of the fine points of local cuisine. You have to know your material cold. But putting on an engaging performance—as an emcee at a social event or leading a hiking trip—helps to ensure participants enjoy themselves and recommend you to others.

For people who want an entertainment side hustle with a more predictable paycheck, working for a business that sells party packages (such as a salon or paint-your-own pottery store) or supplies entertainers (such as DJs or costumed characters) may enable you to work a regular shift.

When Russell's children were small, his side-hustle earnings paid for a caregiver during the summer. To ensure the extra income wasn't swallowed by regular expenses, he put it in a separate savings account. "You do the math and you decide you're not going to buy anything else with the money," he says. "There are no bonuses for having a side gig or any other type of earnings when it comes to managing your money."

ENTERTAINMENT SIDE HUSTLES

BALLOON TWISTER

SERVICE PROVIDED Make balloon sculptures on demand at parties or events, or create balloon art as party decorations.

SKILLS AND EXPERIENCE NEEDED +++ | Know how to craft a variety of shapes by twisting balloons together, especially animals, and be able to do it quickly without breaking any balloons. Some artists develop specialties, such as cartoon characters.

SPECIAL EQUIPMENT ★ | You need lots and lots of balloons.

WHERE TO FIND LEADS Your friends, neighbors, colleagues, and local neighborhood or community groups on social media can all be sources for work. You can also list your services on task-on-demand platforms or websites that offer entertainment services.

PAY RANGE $$$$ | Balloon artists typically charge by the hour ($100 per hour is common) or by the piece, factoring in location, the number of guests, and the number of balloons per sculpture.

BUSKER

SERVICE PROVIDED Play music on the street or in public transit stations.

SKILLS AND EXPERIENCE NEEDED ✦✦ | Be proficient at playing your instrument, and have a repertoire of several pieces. Check whether your city requires you to have a permit to perform.

SPECIAL EQUIPMENT ★★★ | Your instrument and its case (set it in front of you to collect contributions).

WHERE TO FIND LEADS Busy locations with pedestrian traffic and space for people to gather are the best venues. In cities, buskers like to play on street corners and in subway stations. While waiting for the light to change or a train to come, people have time to fish out some change.

PAY RANGE $ | Earnings are hard to predict; it depends a lot on where you play, the day of the week, and the time of day. You won't make any money if you aren't good, but even professional performers may collect only a few dollars for a couple of hours of work during weekday morning rush hour.

CELEBRITY IMPERSONATOR

SERVICE PROVIDED Perform as a singer, actor, politician, or other public figure. Put on shows or entertain at parties, events, and festivals.

SKILLS AND EXPERIENCE NEEDED +++ | Resemble the person you're impersonating. Be able to accurately mimic that person's speech and mannerisms while acting, playing music, singing, or dancing. Depending on the celebrity and the venue, you may need a comedy routine, a dramatic monologue, or a set of songs to perform.

SPECIAL EQUIPMENT ★★★ | Costume, makeup, props, or musical instruments where applicable.

WHERE TO FIND LEADS Promote your act on social media, enter contests, go to casting calls, get gigs at local clubs and referrals from event planners. Some entertainment agencies employ impersonators. List your act on task-on-demand platforms or websites that offer entertainment services.

PAY RANGE $$$$ | Depending on how good your act is, the type of events you work at, and your location, you can make anywhere from a few hundred dollars to a few thousand per gig.

Similar Jobs

Impressionist, tribute artist: impressionists perform impressions of celebrities in a comedy act. Tribute artists recreate the sound and performance style of a musician or band.

CHEERLEADER

SERVICE PROVIDED Pump up the crowd and entertain people at professional sports events with dance, tumbling, and acrobatic routines. Some cheerleaders also represent their team at charity and promotional events.

SKILLS AND EXPERIENCE NEEDED +++ | Dance experience, public speaking ability, and other skills, experience, and physical looks sought by the team. Most professional cheerleaders are women.

SPECIAL EQUIPMENT ★ | No special equipment needed, though cheerleaders have to wear uniforms and often conform to strict rules concerning their personal appearance.

WHERE TO FIND LEADS Professional sports teams usually hold tryouts each season for squads of fewer than fifty.

PAY RANGE $ | Cheerleaders are paid $75–$150 per game, on average, and may get $50 to attend events. They may not, however, be paid for rehearsal time and public appearances, which lowers their hourly pay.

CHURCH MUSICIAN

SERVICE PROVIDED Play music during church services.

SKILLS AND EXPERIENCE NEEDED +++ | Know how to play instruments typically used to accompany a church's services (such as an organ, piano, guitar, or other string instruments), and be familiar with the church's music traditions.

SPECIAL EQUIPMENT ★ ★ ★ | The church will have a piano or organ, but you will likely have to supply any other instrument you play.

WHERE TO FIND LEADS Churches in your area, friends and neighbors, and social media are good sources to learn about opportunities.

PAY RANGE $$$ | Many churches don't compensate their musicians, but those that do pay an average of $25 per hour.

CITY TOUR GUIDE

SERVICE PROVIDED Take visitors around a city to see and learn about local historical sites and attractions.

SKILLS AND EXPERIENCE NEEDED +++ | Know about your city, its history, and details about its important sites, neighborhoods, and attractions. Some cities require tour guides to have a license.

SPECIAL EQUIPMENT ★ | No special equipment needed.

WHERE TO FIND LEADS Promote your services with tour companies and hotels, as well as on social media. Some peer-to-peer platforms offer a place for independent guides to list their tours and collect payment from customers.

PAY RANGE $$ | Tour guides working as employees earn an average of $13 per hour, but if you give your own tours, you can make considerably more. You might, for example, offer a three-hour tour for $60 per person: that's $100 per hour if you have a group of five. If you list your tour on a peer-to-peer platform, the platform will take a cut of your earnings.

CLOWN

SERVICE PROVIDED Entertain people, especially children, at parties. Some clowns perform for children in hospitals.

SKILLS AND EXPERIENCE NEEDED ++ | Create a character, costume, and makeup, and develop a funny act. You can learn to be a clown at clown school.

SPECIAL EQUIPMENT ★★ | You'll need a costume, makeup, and props.

WHERE TO FIND LEADS Entertainment companies supply clowns for parties. You might also find openings at theme parks. Your friends and neighbors, social media, and listings on task-on-demand platforms or websites that offer entertainment services are also good sources of work.

PAY RANGE $$$$ | Clowns charge anywhere from $100 to $400 or more per hour depending on factors including their experience, the elements of their act (such as costume changes), and the number of guests. Tips are customary.

COMMERCIALS ACTOR

SERVICE PROVIDED Perform in a video or television ad.

SKILLS AND EXPERIENCE NEEDED ++ | Have acting and improv skills, and develop an image that enables casting directors to determine whether you are the right type for a particular role.

SPECIAL EQUIPMENT ★ | Invest in headshots and a demo reel.

WHERE TO FIND LEADS Attend advertised casting calls. You are more likely to find work if you live in or near a city that supports other types of work for actors. Create profiles for online talent directories and promote yourself using social media.

PAY RANGE $$$$ | Actors are paid to shoot the commercial and again when it is aired. Although many commercials do not pay union rates, the ones that do pay the principal talent or star $84–$168 per hour for a day of shooting.

COMMUNITY THEATER DIRECTOR

SERVICE PROVIDED Oversee mostly volunteer actors and crew to put on a play for the public.

SKILLS AND EXPERIENCE NEEDED +++ | Acting and directing experience, such as unpaid community theater directing work.

SPECIAL EQUIPMENT ★ | No special equipment needed.

WHERE TO FIND LEADS Amateur theater groups. Not every company pays, but if you have been an active participant in local productions, you will learn which groups offer stipends and hear about openings.

PAY RANGE $ | Stipends for community theater directors range from a few hundred dollars to $1,000 or more for several weeks of work.

Similar Jobs

Choreographer, music director, set designer, lighting designer, or box office staff for a community theater: in addition to the director, some amateur theaters pay stipends for other management positions.

COMPOSER

SERVICE PROVIDED Write original instrumental music.

SKILLS AND EXPERIENCE NEEDED +++ | Have musical ability, knowledge of music theory and notation, and experience listening to and playing music. You need to write a lot before you are likely to compose music that anyone wants to buy, and there's a lot of competition.

SPECIAL EQUIPMENT ★★★ | You'll need composing and music production software, as well as a piano or keyboard.

WHERE TO FIND LEADS Network with musicians; they may want to perform your compositions. Query music publishers, or enter competitions. License tracks to stock music agencies for use in advertising, videos, electronic games, or other business uses. License recordings to streaming services. Promote your music on social media.

PAY RANGE $ | Earnings are difficult to predict. Research how the site where you license your music pays you and how much you earn per listen or download. You may earn $10–$20 per sale of a stock music track. If a music publisher wants to buy your work, you will be paid an advance and royalties on sales.

COSTUMED CHARACTER

SERVICE PROVIDED Dress up as a fictional character, such as a princess or superhero, and perform at birthday parties or events.

SKILLS AND EXPERIENCE NEEDED ++ | You don't need specific experience, but you will need a convincing act, including costume and makeup. If you work for an entertainment company, you may need to audition. If you work independently and you are performing as a copyrighted character, research whether you need to get permission from the copyright holder.

SPECIAL EQUIPMENT ★★ | Costume, makeup, and props.

WHERE TO FIND LEADS Entertainment companies supply characters for hire. If you work independently, promote your act to friends and neighbors, and on social media. You may also be able to spread the word by distributing flyers in your community in places where parents of young children gather.

PAY RANGE $ | Pay for costumed characters starts at minimum wage, though how much you earn will depend on where you are performing—whether at a theme park, a business, or a private, event. Tips are customary.

EATING CONTEST PARTICIPANT

SERVICE PROVIDED Compete for prize money by eating a specific food, such as hot dogs or pie. Usually the person who eats the most wins.

SKILLS AND EXPERIENCE NEEDED +++ | You need to train for each event, in part by increasing your stomach capacity. Contestants also develop strategies for consuming the necessary amount of food.

SPECIAL EQUIPMENT ★ | No special equipment needed.

WHERE TO FIND LEADS Look online for competitions.

PAY RANGE $$$$ | Some large competitions pay winners $1,000 or more. The Nathan's Famous Fourth of July International Hot Dog Eating Contest pays winners $20,000.

ENSEMBLE MUSICIAN

SERVICE PROVIDED Perform live with a band onstage, or with a marching band.

SKILLS AND EXPERIENCE NEEDED +++ | Musical ability, training, and experience performing with your instrument.

SPECIAL EQUIPMENT ★ ★ | Your instruments and gear.

WHERE TO FIND LEADS Inquire at clubs, network with other musicians and singers who may have an opening for a performer or be willing to have your band open for them. Look for gigs on websites that post auditions, and in social media groups for musicians.

PAY RANGE $$ | Pay for musicians varies and depends on the type of gig and your location. You might get $50 to march in a parade. If you play at clubs, your earnings may be calculated as a percentage of revenue for the night, meaning you might earn only a few bucks, or $100 and up.

ENSEMBLE SINGER

SERVICE PROVIDED Sing live with a band or group of singers.

SKILLS AND EXPERIENCE NEEDED +++ | Have singing ability, vocal training, and experience performing with your voice.

SPECIAL EQUIPMENT ★ | No special equipment needed.

WHERE TO FIND LEADS Inquire at clubs, and network with other musicians and singers who may have an opening for a performer. Look for opportunities on websites that post auditions, as well as in social media groups for musicians.

PAY RANGE $$ | As with instrumental musicians, earnings vary and depend on the type of gig.

EVENT DJ

SERVICE PROVIDED Play recorded music at parties, dances, or other events.

SKILLS AND EXPERIENCE NEEDED +++ | Detailed knowledge of music, practice assembling playlists and mixing music, proficiency using hardware (such as turntables), software, or both to deliver a performance.

SPECIAL EQUIPMENT ★ ★ ★ | Your music collection and your preferred equipment setup.

WHERE TO FIND LEADS Friends, neighbors, and colleagues may hire or refer you. Promote your act on social media. Entertainment companies also hire DJs to staff parties and corporate events.

PAY RANGE $$$ | DJs may charge $100–$1,000 or more per event, depending on experience, their location, and the type of event.

FACE PAINTER

SERVICE PROVIDED Paint pictures on people's faces, usually at children's parties or events that have entertainment for kids.

SKILLS AND EXPERIENCE NEEDED ++ | Have artistic ability, and practice painting on children's faces. Know basic hygiene and safety. Teach yourself painting techniques and develop a repertoire of designs.

SPECIAL EQUIPMENT ★★ | You'll need nontoxic paints that are approved for use on faces.

WHERE TO FIND LEADS Friends and neighbors may hire or refer you. Promote your services with community groups and on social media. Work for a friend, or at a school or community event for free to get the word out.

PAY RANGE $$$$ | If you have experience as a face painter, you can earn $75–$200 per hour depending on your location.

FISHING GUIDE

SERVICE PROVIDED Take people fishing in freshwater or saltwater.

SKILLS AND EXPERIENCE NEEDED +++ | Fishing and—if you are taking people out on the water—boating expertise. Be trained in first aid. Make sure you have the proper licenses, permits, and insurance.

SPECIAL EQUIPMENT ★★★ | Fishing gear and other necessary equipment, such as a boat.

WHERE TO FIND LEADS List your business on travel review sites and promote it on social media. Get to know local travel agents and hotel concierges who can recommend your outings.

PAY RANGE $ | Most fishing guides make $12–$25 per hour.

> ### Similar Jobs
>
> Hunting guide: if you own land with wildlife that can be hunted, you could establish a hunting guide side hustle. As with fishing, make sure you have the necessary licenses, permits, and insurance.

FOOD TOUR GUIDE

SERVICE PROVIDED Take groups to visit local restaurants and food shops to teach them about local specialties or a type of cuisine.

SKILLS AND EXPERIENCE NEEDED +++ | Know the food, and establish relationships with the local restaurant and food shop owners you visit. Some cities require tour guides to have a license.

SPECIAL EQUIPMENT ★ | No special equipment needed.

WHERE TO FIND LEADS Network with hotel concierges, restaurant managers, specialty food shops, and travel agents who can recommend your tours. Give free tours to generate word-of-mouth referrals and social media posts, and use social media yourself to promote your tours. List your tours on travel and food business review sites. Some peer-to-peer platforms offer a place for independent guides to list their tours and collect payment from customers.

PAY RANGE $$ | Guides who work for tour companies earn $13 per hour on average, but you can earn considerably more operating an independent side hustle. If you charge $25 per person for a two-hour tour, you'll make $50 per hour with a family of four. If you list your tour on a peer-to-peer platform, the platform will take a cut of your earnings.

FORTUNE TELLER

SERVICE PROVIDED Read tarot cards, tea leaves, palms, crystals, give psychic readings, or use another method to make predictions about a person's future.

SKILLS AND EXPERIENCE NEEDED ++ | You can teach yourself fortune-telling methods, but it takes practice to become convincing. Be aware of restrictions on fortune-telling businesses in your state that are designed to protect customers against fraud.

SPECIAL EQUIPMENT ★ | Cards, crystals, or other tools for making your predictions.

WHERE TO FIND LEADS Entertainment agencies supply fortune tellers for parties and events. List your act on websites that offer entertainment services, use social media to promote yourself, and tell fortunes for your friends to generate word of mouth.

PAY RANGE $$$$ | Some fortune teller entertainers charge $150 and up.

GAME SHOW CONTESTANT

SERVICE PROVIDED Compete on a TV show to win prizes.

SKILLS AND EXPERIENCE NEEDED +++ | Watch the show until you're an expert in the game and its rules. If it's a quiz show, study the type of information you need to know to answer the questions, and practice while watching the show or with a board-game version. Reality TV competitions may require that you have a talent or a specific set of skills.

SPECIAL EQUIPMENT ★ | No special equipment needed.

WHERE TO FIND LEADS The shows provide information about how to apply to be a contestant.

PAY RANGE $$$$ | Depending on the show, the lucky winners can take home anywhere from a few thousand dollars to several million. Some game shows also pay contestants a small amount for appearing on the show.

GOSPEL SINGER

SERVICE PROVIDED Perform Christian songs in the gospel style originating in African-American churches.

SKILLS AND EXPERIENCE NEEDED +++ | You need singing ability, vocal training, and experience as a singer, including in the church choir.

SPECIAL EQUIPMENT ★ | No special equipment needed.

WHERE TO FIND LEADS Inquire at local churches, network with other musicians and singers, and look for opportunities on websites that post information about auditions.

PAY RANGE $$$ | Church singers typically earn at least $25 per service.

HISTORICAL INTERPRETER

SERVICE PROVIDED Give tours at a historical site.

SKILLS AND EXPERIENCE NEEDED ++ | Interest in history. Some employers want people in these positions to have a related academic background. For some jobs you will need to know or learn how to use and demonstrate historical trades or crafts.

SPECIAL EQUIPMENT ★ ★ ★ | You may need to wear a period costume.

WHERE TO FIND LEADS Inquire at historical sites. Job openings may be advertised.

PAY RANGE $$ | Historical interpreters typically earn less than $20 per hour.

HOT AIR BALLOON CHASER

SERVICE PROVIDED Set up hot air balloons, then follow them after launch to meet them at their landing place and recover them.

SKILLS AND EXPERIENCE NEEDED +++ | Live near a company that provides balloon tours. You need to be in good physical condition in order to lift equipment, know how to drive (you may need a commercial driver's license), and be able to get up before dawn.

SPECIAL EQUIPMENT * | Employers train crew members to handle balloon equipment.

WHERE TO FIND LEADS Ballooning companies hire crews. Openings may be advertised.

PAY RANGE $ | Crew members make $10–$15 per hour.

JUGGLER

SERVICE PROVIDED Juggle objects as a street performer, onstage, at festivals, or at promotional events. Clowns may include juggling in their acts.

SKILLS AND EXPERIENCE NEEDED +++ | Proficiency in juggling while interacting with your audience. If you perform on the street, check with your city to see whether you need a permit.

SPECIAL EQUIPMENT * | Objects you juggle.

WHERE TO FIND LEADS Friends and neighbors may hire or refer you. Perform for free at a party or event to generate word of mouth. Promote your act on social media and list it on websites that offer entertainment referrals.

PAY RANGE $$$$ | Depending on their experience and location, jugglers charge anywhere from $50 to $100 per hour or more.

LEI GREETER

SERVICE PROVIDED Pass out leis and greet tourists in Hawaii.

SKILLS AND EXPERIENCE NEEDED + | No experience needed.

SPECIAL EQUIPMENT ★ | No special equipment needed.

WHERE TO FIND LEADS Inquire with airport customer service, lei greeting companies, and tour companies. Openings may be advertised openings. You have to live in Hawaii.

PAY RANGE $ | Lei greeters make around $9 per hour.

LUAU DANCER

SERVICE PROVIDED Perform Polynesian dances at events or resorts.

SKILLS AND EXPERIENCE NEEDED ++ | Be trained in Polynesian dance.

SPECIAL EQUIPMENT ★ | No special equipment needed.

WHERE TO FIND LEADS Polynesian dance and entertainment companies nationwide hire dancers to perform at events. In Hawaii, resorts hire dancers to perform in shows for guests.

PAY RANGE $$ | Dancers earn $20 per hour on average.

MAGICIAN

SERVICE PROVIDED Perform magic tricks onstage, or at parties and events.

SKILLS AND EXPERIENCE NEEDED +++ | Learn tricks and be proficient as a performer. Develop an act.

SPECIAL EQUIPMENT ★★ | You'll need props and equipment to perform your tricks.

WHERE TO FIND LEADS Restaurants, bars, entertainment companies, event planners. Do magic for friends to spread the word, promote your act on social media, list your services on a website that provides entertainment referrals.

PAY RANGE $$$$ | Rates vary according to experience, location, venue, and type of performance. You might be able to charge $200–$300 for a birthday party.

MARATHONER

SERVICE PROVIDED Run a marathon or half marathon.

SKILLS AND EXPERIENCE NEEDED +++ | Experience training and racing. You may need a qualifying race or time from another marathon to enter.

SPECIAL EQUIPMENT ★ | You'll need running shoes.

WHERE TO FIND LEADS Learn about races from running clubs, social media, running websites, and other runners. Marathoners can race for prize money around the world.

PAY RANGE $$$$ | Depending on the marathon, winners may receive a few thousand dollars to more than $100,000. Other top finishers may also get prize money.

MASCOT

SERVICE PROVIDED Wear a costume and pump up crowds at sporting or promotional events.

SKILLS AND EXPERIENCE NEEDED + | Mascots don't need special training before getting the job, but acting or dancing experience may be desirable. If you're working for a sports team, you need to be a fan.

SPECIAL EQUIPMENT ★★★ | You'll need a costume, which your employer will provide.

WHERE TO FIND LEADS Inquire at brand ambassador companies and other firms that supply mascots, as well as sports teams and local businesses. Openings may be advertised.

PAY RANGE $ | Mascots earn an average of $10 per hour, although pro-sports mascots can earn $100–$1,000 or more per game.

MIME

SERVICE PROVIDED Perform pantomime onstage, on the street, at events, in schools, or at festivals. Mimes may include juggling or magic in their acts.

SKILLS AND EXPERIENCE NEEDED +++ | Train as a mime (there are programs that specialize in teaching pantomime) and get experience performing as a mime actor.

SPECIAL EQUIPMENT ★ | You'll need a costume, makeup, and props for your act.

WHERE TO FIND LEADS Entertainment companies, event planners, and theme parks may hire mimes. Promote your act on social media, and get friends to spread the word. You may get work by listing on task-on-demand platforms or websites that offer entertainment services. You can also perform on the street if your city allows it.

PAY RANGE $$$$ | Mimes may charge $100–$1,000 or more for a performance, depending on location, venue, and length of the act.

MOVIE OR TV EXTRA

SERVICE PROVIDED Perform a background role in a movie, television show, or video.

SKILLS AND EXPERIENCE NEEDED ++ | You need to have the look required for the role. Have a headshot and resume, as well as biographical data (such as your age, height, and weight), to provide to casting directors.

SPECIAL EQUIPMENT ★ | No special equipment needed.

WHERE TO FIND LEADS Follow local casting agencies on social media to learn of audition opportunities, and create online profiles and search for casting calls on their websites. Help wanted sites for actors also list openings. You are more likely to find work if you live in a city where films and TV shows are frequently shot. Beware of scams: a legitimate production company will not ask you to pay for an opportunity to audition.

PAY RANGE $ | Nonunion actors typically earn around $10 per hour, though you can get more if you have to get wet, or wear extensive makeup, drive, or use props.

MOVIE SERIES OR FILM FESTIVAL DIRECTOR

SERVICE PROVIDED Organize the showing of a series of movies based on a theme.

SKILLS AND EXPERIENCE NEEDED +++ | Have extensive knowledge of movies in a genre, along with project management, marketing, and fundraising experience. You can attend other festivals to observe how they are organized and what makes them successful (you can also cross-promote each other's events). Research any licenses or permits you might need from your city.

SPECIAL EQUIPMENT ★★★ | You will need movies, a venue, and equipment to show them; a way to sell tickets; and other equipment related to showing movies and hosting an audience.

WHERE TO FIND LEADS You need an extensive network of producers, filmmakers, local cinemas, media, cultural institutions, businesses, and government agencies to attract films, gain sponsorships and prizes (some festivals offer winners a distribution deal), get publicity, and line up a venue. Use social media to recruit film makers to submit their films and promote the event.

PAY RANGE $ | To make money from a small film festival, you have to manage it well and it needs to be well attended. You'll do a lot of work for minimal return, so you should love films and the genre you're showing.

MUSIC ARRANGER

SERVICE PROVIDED Adapt a piece of music for performance in a different style, by singers with a particular type of voice, or a specific set of instruments.

SKILLS AND EXPERIENCE NEEDED +++ | You need musical ability, knowledge of music theory and notation, experience listening to and playing music, and familiarity with the work of successful arrangers. Practice by creating arrangements for musicians or bands you know to build a portfolio.

SPECIAL EQUIPMENT ★ ★ ★ | You need a computer and music composition software.

WHERE TO FIND LEADS Use your professional contacts among musicians, music producers, and publishers to find buyers for your work or obtain commissions.

PAY RANGE $$$ | Rates vary, but some freelance arrangers charge $25–$55 per hour.

MUSIC SAMPLER

SERVICE PROVIDED Create sample packs of music for use in other people's recordings.

SKILLS AND EXPERIENCE NEEDED +++ | Musical ability. Know how to record sounds and manipulate them electronically to create original samples. You need permission to license other people's work.

SPECIAL EQUIPMENT ★ ★| You need a computer and sound recording and production software.

WHERE TO FIND LEADS Create a website and license your samples yourself or through a distributor. The market is highly competitive, and you will need to actively promote your work on social media, to your contacts in the music business, by entering contests, and offering freebies.

PAY RANGE $ | Producers license sample packs for prices ranging from $10–$100 or more.

OUTDOOR TOUR GUIDE

SERVICE PROVIDED Lead groups on mountain hikes, bird watching walks, backpacking trips, bicycle tours, snowshoeing, and other adventures.

SKILLS AND EXPERIENCE NEEDED +++ | Have extensive experience in your outdoor sport, become an expert in the flora, fauna, geology, ecosystem, and history of the area where you are guiding. Be trained in first aid and CPR (companies that run outdoor tours often require their guides to have a Wilderness First Aid or First Responder certification). If you are running your own tours, you will need insurance and possibly a license.

SPECIAL EQUIPMENT ★ ★ ★ | Gear and clothing appropriate to your activities.

WHERE TO FIND LEADS Outdoor tour companies hire guides for part-time and seasonal jobs, and openings may be advertised. If you are running your own tours, list your business on travel review sites and promote it on social media, and to hotels, outdoor outfitters, and travel agents.

PAY RANGE $ | Outdoor guides make an average of $12 per hour. You may earn considerably more running tours independently. If you take four people on a three-hour hike for $50 per person, you'll collect more than $60 per hour.

PARTY EMCEE

SERVICE PROVIDED Maintain the party schedule, motivate guests, and lead activities at private parties, including birthday parties and milestone events.

SKILLS AND EXPERIENCE NEEDED ++ | You need experience performing and public speaking.

SPECIAL EQUIPMENT ★ ★ | Depending on the job, you may have to set up, break down, or manage party equipment or supplies.

WHERE TO FIND LEADS Party entertainment companies hire emcees for part-time work. You can also host events for your friends to create word-of-mouth referrals, advertise, promote your business on social media, and list your profile on sites that provide referrals for entertainment services.

PAY RANGE $ | Party emcees typically earn $20–$50 per hour, but experienced emcees may charge more.

PUPPETEER

SERVICE PROVIDED Perform puppet shows at parties, in schools, onstage, at carnivals or festivals.

SKILLS AND EXPERIENCE NEEDED ++ | Practice creating characters and telling stories with puppets. Theater training or experience helps. Some puppeteers are skilled as ventriloquists.

SPECIAL EQUIPMENT ★★ | Puppets. Expert puppeteers make their own.

WHERE TO FIND LEADS Get friends and colleagues to refer you. You can host puppet shows for free to gain word-of-mouth publicity. Pitch your act to schools, libraries, and community centers. List your profile on platforms that offer entertainment referrals.

PAY RANGE $$$$ | Puppeteers' rates are wide ranging and depend on factors such as location, experience, and the types of puppets used in the act. You may be able to charge anywhere from $100 to $500 or more per gig.

RADIO DJ

SERVICE PROVIDED Play music and take calls from listeners on a radio music show.

SKILLS AND EXPERIENCE NEEDED +++ | Experience as an on-air DJ or host.

SPECIAL EQUIPMENT ★★★ | Control board and production equipment provided by the radio station where you work.

WHERE TO FIND LEADS Radio stations. Openings may be advertised.

PAY RANGE $ | Pay varies by location; you can earn more in large cities. DJs make $10 per hour on average.

RIVER RAFTING GUIDE

SERVICE PROVIDED Lead groups down a river, including through whitewater, in rafts.

SKILLS AND EXPERIENCE NEEDED +++ | Have experience leading groups, spend time getting to know the river you want to work on, and train as a guide. Learn about the flora, fauna, geology, ecosystem, and history of the area. Be trained in first aid and CPR, including Wilderness First Responder and Swift Water Rescue certifications. If you are running your own excursions, obtain the necessary insurance and licenses.

SPECIAL EQUIPMENT ★ ★ ★ | Rafts, oars, and related equipment.

WHERE TO FIND LEADS You can learn about openings from rafting companies, training programs, other guides, and on social media. If you run your own tours, promote them with hotel concierges and travel agents. Some peer-to-peer platforms offer a place for independent guides to list their tours and collect payment from customers. In many parts of the United States this work is available only in the summer.

PAY RANGE $ | Outdoor guides earn an average of $12 per hour, and if you work for a rafting company, you may also earn tips. If you run your own tours, you have the opportunity to earn more.

SESSION MUSICIAN

SERVICE PROVIDED Play an instrument during a recording session in a studio.

SKILLS AND EXPERIENCE NEEDED +++ | You need musical ability and training, and experience recording with your instrument or multiple instruments.

SPECIAL EQUIPMENT ★ ★ ★ | Your instruments.

WHERE TO FIND LEADS Network with other musicians, and inquire at recording studios and record labels. You may learn about gigs on social media, or through help wanted listings.

PAY RANGE $$$$ | Rates vary by location, but you may be able to earn $40–$60 per hour without much experience.

SOLO MUSICIAN

SERVICE PROVIDED Play your instrument onstage or make recordings of your own music.

SKILLS AND EXPERIENCE NEEDED +++ | You need musical ability, training, and experience performing with your instrument.

SPECIAL EQUIPMENT ★★★ | Your instrument.

WHERE TO FIND LEADS Inquire at clubs and network with other musicians. You can post your recordings on streaming services.

PAY RANGE $$ | Pay varies and depends on the type of gig. If you play at a club, your earnings will be based on a percentage of the night's revenues. It could be a few dollars, or $100 and up.

SOLO SINGER

SERVICE PROVIDED Sing by yourself or as the featured voice in a band, or make recordings of your songs.

SKILLS AND EXPERIENCE NEEDED +++ | Have musical ability, vocal training, and experience performing as a singer.

SPECIAL EQUIPMENT ★ | No special equipment needed.

WHERE TO FIND LEADS Inquire at clubs, and network with other musicians. You can post your recordings on streaming services.

PAY RANGE $$ | As with musicians, earnings vary and depend on the type of gig. If you play at a club, your earnings will be based on a percentage of the night's revenues. It could be a few dollars, or $100 and up.

> ### *Similar Jobs*
> Children's singer: sing and play guitar for groups of children at birthday parties, schools, or public performances.

SONGWRITER

SERVICE PROVIDED Write original music with lyrics.

SKILLS AND EXPERIENCE NEEDED +++ | You need musical ability, writing ability, knowledge of music theory and notation, and experience listening to and playing music or singing. You need to write a lot before you are likely to compose songs that anyone wants to buy, and there's a lot of competition.

SPECIAL EQUIPMENT ★★★ | You need composing and music production software, and a piano or keyboard.

WHERE TO FIND LEADS Network with other musicians and singers, pitch to music publishers and record labels, or enter competitions. You can record your songs and license them on streaming services. Promote your music on social media.

PAY RANGE $ | Earnings for songwriters are hard to predict. If a music publisher buys your song, you will usually be paid an advance as well as royalties on sales.

SPORTS TEAM OWNER

SERVICE PROVIDED Make top-level business decisions involved in running a professional sports team.

SKILLS AND EXPERIENCE NEEDED +++ | You need business acumen and a few hundred million dollars.

SPECIAL EQUIPMENT ★ | No special equipment needed.

WHERE TO FIND LEADS Network with league executives, investment bankers, and current team owners.

PAY RANGE $$$$ | Owners don't necessarily take a salary but earn millions from their share of the profits. Many own sports teams as an activity apart from their main source of income.

SQUARE DANCE CALLER

SERVICE PROVIDED Run square dances by calling out steps to dancers.

SKILLS AND EXPERIENCE NEEDED +++ | Knowledge of music, singing ability, public-speaking skills. Experience square dancing. Callers typically have training and certification in calling and choreography.

SPECIAL EQUIPMENT ★★ | You'll need audio equipment and music.

WHERE TO FIND LEADS Square dancing clubs need callers for their dances. You can promote your services on social media, get word-of-mouth recommendations, and list on platforms that offer entertainment referrals.

PAY RANGE $$$$ | Square dance callers charge $100 or more per gig, depending on factors that include location and experience.

STANDUP COMIC

SERVICE PROVIDED Make jokes in front of an audience.

SKILLS AND EXPERIENCE NEEDED ++ | It's not enough to be funny; you need to be able to write jokes. You also need an aptitude for reading an audience. Be willing to bomb repeatedly while you hone your set, and have a thick skin for dealing with hecklers.

SPECIAL EQUIPMENT ★ | No special equipment needed.

WHERE TO FIND LEADS Inquire at comedy clubs, and network with other comedians and promoters. After you perform for free at open mic nights (for years, maybe), you may be offered a paying gig. Use social media to build a following. Get friends or colleagues to hire you for parties to gain experience and recommendations. List your profile on platforms that offer entertainment referrals.

PAY RANGE $$$ | Comedy clubs pay $25–$200 depending on whether you're the opening act, the middle act, or the headliner. Party and event comedians charge $100 or more per gig.

STORYTELLER

SERVICE PROVIDED Perform a fictional or nonfictional narrative to an audience.

SKILLS AND EXPERIENCE NEEDED +++ | You need narrative writing ability, public-speaking experience, and knowledge of storytelling traditions and theater.

SPECIAL EQUIPMENT ★ | Sometimes storytellers use props.

WHERE TO FIND LEADS Schools, libraries, coffeehouses, arts organizations, festivals, clubs, and theaters may book you. Network with other storytellers, and promote your act on social media. Volunteer for gigs to generate referrals.

PAY RANGE $$$$ | Storytellers typically change $50 and up for a performance. Experienced professional storytellers sometimes charge $300 per hour.

THEME PARTY HOST

SERVICE PROVIDED Run theme- or activity-based parties for children or adults.

SKILLS AND EXPERIENCE NEEDED + | No experience needed.

SPECIAL EQUIPMENT ★★ | Equipment or materials needed to conduct party activities.

WHERE TO FIND LEADS Businesses that offer party packages for customers—such as a spa party at a salon, or a kids' gymnastics party at a gym—sometimes hire people to run these events. If you offer a party package through your own business, get customers by advertising, promoting events on social media, and listing them on a platform that offers entertainment referrals.

PAY RANGE $ | Party hosts typically earn minimum wage or slightly more.

TRIATHLETE

SERVICE PROVIDED Compete in triathlons.

SKILLS AND EXPERIENCE NEEDED +++ | Train and race running, cycling, and swimming in open water. Triathletes compete at four different levels of difficulty, based on distances. Races may have qualifying rules.

SPECIAL EQUIPMENT ★ ★ | You need running shoes, a bicycle, and a swimsuit.

WHERE TO FIND LEADS Learn about races through triathlon clubs, social media, triathlon websites, other triathletes. Triathletes can compete around the world.

PAY RANGE $$$$ | Prize money ranges from less than $100 to more than $100,000. Top finishers other than winners may get awards.

VLOGGER

SERVICE PROVIDED Create and perform in an online video show.

SKILLS AND EXPERIENCE NEEDED +++ | Know how to perform in front of a camera, be able to write, and be an expert at whatever your show is about. Learn from studying successful vloggers.

SPECIAL EQUIPMENT ★ ★ ★ | You'll need video recording and editing equipment (you can start with your smartphone or laptop).

WHERE TO FIND LEADS Use social media to promote your channel.

PAY RANGE $ | If you vlog on *YouTube*, your channel needs to meet an eligibility threshold of viewers and subscribers in order to make money from advertising. You need a lot of daily views, or a lot of viewers watching the ads, to make more than a couple hundred dollars a year.

VOICE ACTOR

SERVICE PROVIDED Narrate, provide information, or speak the lines of a character in a film, television show, commercial, or video without appearing onscreen.

SKILLS AND EXPERIENCE NEEDED +++ | Know how to act, and have performance and live reading experience, as well as familiarity with recording technology. Work with a voice coach is helpful.

SPECIAL EQUIPMENT ★★ | You'll need gear for a home studio, including a computer, microphone, audio-recording and editing software, and sound proofing.

WHERE TO FIND LEADS Look for gigs on voice casting websites and freelance platforms.

PAY RANGE $$$$ | Rates are per recording depending on factors such as its length, and how or where it will be used.

WEDDING BAND MUSICIAN

SERVICE PROVIDED Perform as a singer or instrumentalist with a band playing popular songs at weddings and other social events.

SKILLS AND EXPERIENCE NEEDED +++ | Have musical ability, as well as training and experience performing with your instrument or singing.

SPECIAL EQUIPMENT ★★★ | You need your instruments and gear.

WHERE TO FIND LEADS Other musicians, friends and colleagues, event planners, social media. List a profile on a platform that provides entertainment referrals.

PAY RANGE $$$ | Wedding bands can earn $150 or more per gig.

> ### *Similar Jobs*
> Cover band musician: play popular songs at bars, parades, or community events.

WINE TOUR GUIDE

SERVICE PROVIDED Take people to a series of restaurants, bars, or vineyards to taste and learn about wine.

SKILLS AND EXPERIENCE NEEDED +++ | Know about wine and, if you run your own tours, establish relationships with the local restaurants, bars, wine shops, or vineyards you visit (experience as a bartender or wine shop employee helps). Some cities require tour guides to have a license.

SPECIAL EQUIPMENT ★ | If your tour involves driving, you'll need a vehicle, along with the necessary permits and insurance.

WHERE TO FIND LEADS Inquire at vineyards and with tour companies. If you run your own tours, network with hotel concierges, travel agents, restaurant and bar owners, wine shops, and vineyards. Promote your tours on social media. Some peer-to-peer platforms offer a place for independent guides to list their tours and collect payment from customers in exchange for a cut.

PAY RANGE $$ | Guides who work for tour companies earn $13 per hour on average. If you run independent tours, you can make considerably more.

> *"You do the math and you decide you're not going to buy anything else with the money."*
> —Russell Bogartz, trombonist

Entertain Us
Spotify adds 20,000 new recordings daily.

Source: *Spotify*

CHAPTER 13
Communicate

Communications side hustles include writing, editing, video production, public speaking, and related work that require skill at telling a story and shaping a message. Jobs in this category cover original work such as blogs, books, essays, reviews, and articles for which the author gets the credit, as well as corporate products such as marketing copy, grant proposals, white papers, and anything you ghostwrite for someone else. They're appealing because, unlike with other types of jobs, the work can often be done anywhere, at any time.

DEVELOP AND WIDEN YOUR SKILL SET

You need strong writing skills, but for most communications side hustles, that ability is only a starting point. To produce engaging work, especially for public consumption, you need curiosity, enthusiasm for your subject, and attentiveness to detail. Furthermore, all writing, editing, or producing isn't the same. Whether you're blogging, writing fan fiction, crafting business plans, producing a how-to video, or podcasting, you need to master both your material and your genre so you can communicate with authority. If you don't have experience, you may have to practice a lot in order to build enough knowledge and experience to attract a following and develop a convincing portfolio of work.

Building your side hustle around a topic or a genre you know well will enable you to generate income more quickly than if you're diving into a completely new area. For example, if you're an expert in any field, you can write or speak about your work to provide advice or educate readers. Readers may buy your ebook, textbook, or a work based on your academic or business research. You could get paid for speaking at an industry event. If your book, articles, or speeches are related to a business, you may be able to generate leads that provide more income.

Commissioned assignments can provide a steady source of work. If you have a journalism background, online or print newspapers and magazines offer a market for researched articles, interviews, and news items. With business knowledge, you can find jobs creating a wide variety of internal and external communications. These include crafting website copy, press releases, white papers, or sales scripts, as well as editing articles, marketing materials, books, or promotional videos. Many professionals who do creative work—for example, writing fiction or creative nonfiction, or making short films—support that work with commissions. Others earn their living exclusively this way.

Your network will be your best source for commissioned assignments. Articles, blogs, and other communications are often time sensitive; it's often easier for editors and marketing directors to hire someone they already know or who they meet by referral.

All writing and editing jobs described in this chapter require that you have a computer and a reliable Internet connection to interact with clients and work on assignments.

Kevin Lindstrom, a lawyer with a solo practice in Dallas, landed a two-year gig covering the FC Dallas soccer team for Major League Soccer, thanks in part to his college journalism major, a prior job selling tickets for the club, and his reputation for fairness as an active participant in the local fan community. "If I compare the time I put into it versus the money, I don't think I got paid more than $10 per hour," he says. But as with his other side hustles, mostly soccer related, "If I can find something to be productive from a financial standpoint that I enjoy, there's value to it."

COMMUNICATIONS SIDE HUSTLES

BLOGGER

SERVICE PROVIDED Write blog posts for your own blog or for hire.

SKILLS AND EXPERIENCE NEEDED ✦✦ | You need writing and storytelling ability, research skills, and knowledge of the subject you are blogging about.

SPECIAL EQUIPMENT ✦ | No special equipment needed.

WHERE TO FIND LEADS To blog for hire, tap professional and personal contacts, join freelance platforms, pitch corporate marketing departments and content agencies, and use social media. Businesses often need regular blog posts for their websites, while content agencies license topical posts to business and publishing clients.

PAY RANGE $$$ | Rates for blog posts vary. Content agencies may pay around $60 for a 600–700-word post, but if you have experience, and you are writing exclusive content, rates of up to $500 per post are possible. On your own blog, you can earn money from advertising by joining an ad network (a few cents per page view), promoting affiliate marketing links (see Chapter 8), or selling ads.

BOOK DESIGNER

SERVICE PROVIDED Create covers, typography design, and layout for books.

SKILLS AND EXPERIENCE NEEDED ✦✦✦ | You need to have artistic ability and graphic design training. Publishers or self-publishing authors who hire you will want you to have work experience. You should enjoy reading books.

SPECIAL EQUIPMENT ✦ | You'll need graphic design and publishing software.

WHERE TO FIND LEADS Tap your professional and personal contacts. Join freelance platforms. List your profile in professional directories and network with writers and editors by attending conferences and participating in writer communities. Promote your work on social media.

PAY RANGE $$ | Freelance graphic designers typically charge anywhere from $20 to $150 per hour but may charge more depending on the project.

BOOK EDITOR

SERVICE PROVIDED Edit book manuscripts.

SKILLS AND EXPERIENCE NEEDED +++ | You need writing and editing experience, and familiarity with the genre of books you're editing as well as the different levels of book editing.

SPECIAL EQUIPMENT ★ | No special equipment needed.

WHERE TO FIND LEADS Your professional and personal contacts may hire you or provide referrals. Join freelance platforms and list your profile in professional directories. Network with writers at conferences and participating in writer communities. Promote your work on social media.

PAY RANGE $$ | Depending on the level of editing, experience and the type of project, freelance book editors typically charge $20–$125 per hour.

BUSINESS PLAN WRITER

SERVICE PROVIDED Write business plans for companies to present to investors or bankers.

SKILLS AND EXPERIENCE NEEDED +++ | Have writing ability and experience writing business plans. Be familiar with investor, lender, or stakeholder requirements. Expertise in a specific industry may help you differentiate your services.

SPECIAL EQUIPMENT ★ | No special equipment needed.

WHERE TO FIND LEADS Get work and referrals from your professional and personal contacts and join freelance platforms. Startups that need new rounds of financing and small businesses that are expanding can be good sources of work. Promote your services using social media.

PAY RANGE $$$$ | Writers charge $50-$150 per hour to write a business plan, with a typical project earning around $6,000.

CLOSED CAPTIONER

SERVICE PROVIDED Transcribe spoken text to create subtitles for TV broadcasts and video recordings.

SKILLS AND EXPERIENCE NEEDED +++ | You need training to learn how to do live transcription. If you have been a court reporter, you're qualified.

SPECIAL EQUIPMENT ★★★ | Stenographic keyboard for live captioning, software for video closed captioning.

WHERE TO FIND LEADS Apply to work for captioning services, and look for opportunities on freelance platforms. You may find advertised openings on help wanted sites.

PAY RANGE $$$$ | Pay for closed captioners ranges from $50 to $75 per hour.

> ### Similar Jobs
> Subtitler: use software to insert translated text into a video.

COPY EDITOR

SERVICE PROVIDED Review written material to improve readability, correct grammar, style, and usage, and perfect accuracy.

SKILLS AND EXPERIENCE NEEDED ++ | You need writing ability, editing experience, and knowledge of English grammar, style, and usage. Industry-specific knowledge, including understanding of its terminology, will make you effective at copyediting business documents and marketing materials. Many companies have their own style guides, and becoming familiar with some of them may help you get repeated work.

SPECIAL EQUIPMENT ★ | No special equipment needed.

WHERE TO FIND LEADS Tap professional contacts who are editors or who create marketing content: they can hire you or provide word-of-mouth referrals. Join freelance platforms and use social media to promote your work.

PAY RANGE $$ | Depending on experience and whether the project is for a publisher, advertising agency, or a business, copyeditors typically charge $20–$125 per hour.

COPYWRITER

SERVICE PROVIDED Write advertising copy, product descriptions, emails, and other marketing materials.

SKILLS AND EXPERIENCE NEEDED ++ | You need to be able to write. Creativity, sales and marketing knowledge, awareness of social trends, and familiarity with your clients' industry will help you get hired.

SPECIAL EQUIPMENT ★ | No special equipment needed.

WHERE TO FIND LEADS Professional contacts, including editors, other writers, and people with marketing or advertising responsibilities. Join freelance platforms and social media to promote your work.

PAY RANGE $$ | Depending on experience and the type of project, copywriters make $20–$150 or more per hour.

EBOOK WRITER

SERVICE PROVIDED Write and publish short books to promote your expert knowledge about a topic that interests your current or potential business customers.

SKILLS AND EXPERIENCE NEEDED ✦ | Be able to write. Have in-depth knowledge of your topic and your customers' interests.

SPECIAL EQUIPMENT ★ | No special equipment needed.

WHERE TO FIND LEADS Offer your book from your own website or through an electronic publishing platform. Promote your book to your customers on your website and using direct email and social media.

PAY RANGE $ | Self-published ebooks typically retail for less than $10. You may also decide to offer the book for free as a way to promote your professional services and gain extra revenue that way.

ESSAYIST

SERVICE PROVIDED Write literary nonfiction articles expressing a thought process and a point of view about a current problem or a question.

SKILLS AND EXPERIENCE NEEDED ✦✦✦ | You need writing and storytelling ability, creativity, and familiarity with the essay form.

SPECIAL EQUIPMENT ★ | No special equipment needed.

WHERE TO FIND LEADS Make contacts with editors at websites and magazines that publish essays. Enter contests (research them to learn about their reputation, judging process, and benefits for the winners) and make cold submissions (research writers' guidelines first).

PAY RANGE $$ | Rates vary widely, from around $25 to a few hundred dollars.

FAN FICTION WRITER

SERVICE PROVIDED Write a novel or short stories inspired by famous people or characters in a book or movie created by someone else.

SKILLS AND EXPERIENCE NEEDED ✦✦ | You need creative writing and storytelling ability, and you have to be a super fan. Learn about copyright law regarding fan fiction to ensure your work does not infringe on an original work; it's illegal to sell written works featuring copyrighted characters, stories or settings.

SPECIAL EQUIPMENT ★ | No special equipment needed.

WHERE TO FIND LEADS Self-publish your stories or novels and promote them to other fans and the public through social media and fan communities.

PAY RANGE $ | Although some fan fiction writers have become wealthy, most don't make much money. Many fan fiction ebooks sell for $5 or less and don't get mainstream attention.

FOOD WRITER

SERVICE PROVIDED Write about recipes, ingredients, chefs, food producers, restaurants, and culinary trends.

SKILLS AND EXPERIENCE NEEDED +++ | You need writing and storytelling ability, creativity, and experience cooking and exploring food trends.

SPECIAL EQUIPMENT ★ | No special equipment needed.

WHERE TO FIND LEADS Start a blog, post about food on social media, and pitch ideas to websites and magazines that publish recipes, articles, or essays about food. Network with other food writers, editors, and chefs who might want writing help.

PAY RANGE $$ | Rates vary, but 20 cents per word is common for web articles.

FREELANCE JOURNALIST

SERVICE PROVIDED Write researched and reported nonfiction articles for a news organization or magazine.

SKILLS AND EXPERIENCE NEEDED +++ | You need writing and storytelling ability, creativity, and journalism training or related experience producing stories involving a combination of interviews and research. Focus on one or a few topics.

SPECIAL EQUIPMENT ★ | No special equipment needed.

WHERE TO FIND LEADS Network with editors and other writers. Join freelance platforms. Pitch ideas to websites and magazines in your subject area.

PAY RANGE $$ | Rates vary, but a range of 20 cents–$1 per word is typical.

Similar Jobs

Brand journalist: use the techniques of journalism to write marketing content.

GHOSTWRITER

SERVICE PROVIDED Write articles and blogs for someone else who will be credited as the author.

SKILLS AND EXPERIENCE NEEDED ✦✦✦ | You need writing ability, creativity, and the aptitude for eliciting and refining your client's ideas. Good interviewing and research skills are essential.

SPECIAL EQUIPMENT ★ | No special equipment needed.

WHERE TO FIND LEADS Content marketing agencies and corporate marketing departments hire ghostwriters to work with business experts. Your writer and editor contacts may provide referrals to clients. You may also get work from freelance platforms.

PAY RANGE $$$ | Article and blog ghostwriters earn $25–$125 per hour or more.

GRANT WRITER

SERVICE PROVIDED Write applications for nonprofits seeking funding from foundations and public agencies.

SKILLS AND EXPERIENCE NEEDED ✦✦✦ | You need writing and editing experience and storytelling ability. Knowledge of your clients' business, an aptitude for blending contributions from different sources into a consistent voice, and familiarity with different funders' expectations for proposals will help you succeed.

SPECIAL EQUIPMENT ★ | No special equipment needed.

WHERE TO FIND LEADS Pitch your services to nonprofit organizations. Find opportunities on help wanted websites that focus on nonprofit and philanthropy jobs. Practice writing grant proposals for free to prove your work is successful.

PAY RANGE $$ | Rates range from $20 to $150 or more per hour, depending on experience.

GREETING CARD WRITER

SERVICE PROVIDED Write messages for printed greeting cards.

SKILLS AND EXPERIENCE NEEDED ++ | You need writing ability and skill at crafting short poems or witty quips.

SPECIAL EQUIPMENT ★ | No special equipment needed.

WHERE TO FIND LEADS Some greeting card companies accept unsolicited submissions (look for writer guidelines) and sometimes hold contests. If you are an illustrator or know someone who is, you can produce and sell your own cards.

PAY RANGE $$$ | Publishers typically pay $25–$150 per submission.

JINGLE WRITER

SERVICE PROVIDED Write short songs for use in advertising.

SKILLS AND EXPERIENCE NEEDED +++ | You need musical ability, experience writing songs, and knowledge of the jingle genre. You also need to be able to understand your client's ideas and goals for the jingle.

SPECIAL EQUIPMENT ★★ | A computer and software for composing and producing music.

WHERE TO FIND LEADS Join freelance platforms and pitch your services to ad agencies and jingle houses. Local small businesses may be a source of work. Professional colleagues may provide referrals, and you can promote your services on social media.

PAY RANGE $$$$ | Jingle writers typically charge $100 or more per composition.

MUSIC REVIEWER

SERVICE PROVIDED Provide opinions about recorded music or performances.

SKILLS AND EXPERIENCE NEEDED +++ | To be published as a music journalist, you need to know your genre in depth and be able to write engaging stories. At the other end of the reviewing spectrum, a few crowdsourcing websites that collect opinions from listeners about unpublished songs are primarily interested in what you think as a consumer.

SPECIAL EQUIPMENT ★ | If video or audio is your medium, you will need a camera or recording equipment and editing software.

WHERE TO FIND LEADS For music journalism, start a blog, use social media, network with editors and other writers, submit to websites and magazines that accept submissions (look for writer guidelines). To participate in crowdsourcing websites, you need only sign up.

PAY RANGE $$ | Websites and magazines may pay by the word (expect less than $1 per) or offer a flat rate (say $50 for a blog post). Research the fine print on crowdsourcing sites: some require you to earn a minimum amount to get paid, while others award points and pay in gift cards.

NONFICTION AUTHOR

SERVICE PROVIDED Research and write a book to document, explain, or analyze facts or real-life events.

SKILLS AND EXPERIENCE NEEDED +++ | You need writing ability and experience, strong research skills, and in-depth knowledge of your topic or genre. If you are writing to give advice or make recommendations, have practical experience. Read a lot of books in your genre to learn what editors and readers expect.

SPECIAL EQUIPMENT ★ | No special equipment needed.

WHERE TO FIND LEADS Attend writers' conferences to meet agents and editors. Book authors who want to be traditionally published usually need an agent to query editors on their behalf. You can also self-publish your book.

PAY RANGE $$ | For a first book, traditionally published authors typically get an advance of a few thousand dollars. The publisher has to recover the advance from book sales before paying royalties (typically 10 percent for physical books and 25 percent for electronic copies). Self-published authors get higher royalties (*Amazon* advertises up to 70 percent on electronic copies). Most book authors earn no more than a few thousand dollars in royalties over the life of the book.

NOVELIST

SERVICE PROVIDED Write a book about fictional characters and events.

SKILLS AND EXPERIENCE NEEDED +++ | You need creative writing and storytelling ability, as well as practice writing fiction. To craft believable characters, scenes, and plots, you need excellent observation and research skills. Read a lot of books in your genre.

SPECIAL EQUIPMENT ★ | No special equipment needed.

WHERE TO FIND LEADS Attend writers' conferences to meet agents and editors. Book authors who want to be traditionally published usually need an agent to query editors on their behalf. You can also self-publish your book.

PAY RANGE $$ | As with nonfiction, traditionally published authors typically get an advance of a few thousand dollars. The publisher has to recover the advance from book sales before paying royalties (typically 10 percent for physical books and 25 percent for electronic copies). Self-published authors get higher royalties (*Amazon* advertises up to 70 percent on electronic copies). Most book authors earn no more than a few thousand dollars in royalties over the life of the book.

Similar Jobs

Short story writer: submit to e-zines and journals that publish short stories (research writer's guidelines) and enter contests (research them to learn about their reputation, judging process, and benefits for the winners).

PODCASTER

SERVICE PROVIDED Write and deliver an audio show with regular episodes.

SKILLS AND EXPERIENCE NEEDED ++ | You need writing and public-speaking experience, and in-depth knowledge of your podcast subject matter. Be familiar with how to use audio production software and equipment, and be disciplined to produce material on a regular schedule. Research podcasting platforms to choose one to host your show.

SPECIAL EQUIPMENT ★ | Audio production software and equipment (such as a microphone).

WHERE TO FIND LEADS Get listeners and subscribers by promoting your podcast to your customers if you have a related business, on social media, and to podcast review sites. To make money, you can sell sponsorships (if your podcast is high quality and you have good listener data), charge for back episodes, join affiliate marketing programs (see Chapter 8), crowdfund it, or use it to promote your other products or services to increase sales.

PAY RANGE $$ | Average advertising rates for a podcast range from $15 to $25 per 1,000 listeners for ads of 10–60 seconds.

POET

SERVICE PROVIDED Write poetry.

SKILLS AND EXPERIENCE NEEDED +++ | You need creative writing ability, keen observational skills, emotional perceptiveness, and willingness to plumb your own feelings. As for writing in other genres, to write good poetry you have to read it too.

SPECIAL EQUIPMENT ★ | No special equipment needed.

WHERE TO FIND LEADS Submit to literary magazines and journals that accept unsolicited material, enter contests, publish your own work, submit to greeting card companies. Some poets have attempted businesses writing poems on demand.

PAY RANGE $ | Most journals pay writers with copies. If they pay cash, it's a small honorarium: $5–$50 is typical. Legitimate publishers will not ask for payment to publish your work. Contests may have entry fees; you can research them to learn about their reputation, judging process, and benefits for the winners.

PRESS RELEASE WRITER

SERVICE PROVIDED Write public announcements for businesses, nonprofits, and public agencies.

SKILLS AND EXPERIENCE NEEDED ++ | Writing ability, public relations experience.

SPECIAL EQUIPMENT ★ | No special equipment needed.

WHERE TO FIND LEADS Tap your professional contacts, especially people with connections to PR agencies. Join freelance platforms. Small and growing businesses, including startups, may be good sources of work.

PAY RANGE $$$$ | On average, writers earn around $100 per hour to write press releases, although they may charge per project.

PROPOSAL WRITER

SERVICE PROVIDED Write documents to persuade a business to engage another company or an individual to buy its products or services.

SKILLS AND EXPERIENCE NEEDED +++ | You need writing and editing experience and familiarity with potential customers' expectations for proposals. Knowledge of clients' business and their industry will give you credibility and enable you to write effective proposals.

SPECIAL EQUIPMENT * | No special equipment needed.

WHERE TO FIND LEADS Reach out to your professional and personal contacts, including other writers who work on proposals, and business development or sales managers who may be interested in having help. Join freelance platforms.

PAY RANGE $$$$ | Freelance proposal writers may earn $40–$120 per hour.

PUBLIC SPEAKER

SERVICE PROVIDED Give speeches to audiences at conferences, training sessions, and other public or private events, or present webinars.

SKILLS AND EXPERIENCE NEEDED +++ | You need writing and public-speaking experience and in-depth knowledge of the topics you're presenting. If you want to improve your public-speaking skills, you can join a group to learn new techniques and practice.

SPECIAL EQUIPMENT * | No special equipment needed.

WHERE TO FIND LEADS Do some free gigs to gain experience while becoming known to audiences. Write and get published in places where event organizers can learn about your expertise.

Work your professional and personal contacts to provide referrals. Identify yourself as a public speaker in your social media profiles.

PAY RANGE $$$$ | Public speakers who are not famous typically charge at least $1,500 for an event. Experienced speakers may get $10,000 or more.

SALES SCRIPTWRITER

SERVICE PROVIDED Create pitches for direct marketing or for sales people to use when presenting products or services to potential customers.

SKILLS AND EXPERIENCE NEEDED +++ | You need writing ability, sales or marketing experience, and familiarity with your clients' industry and customer needs.

SPECIAL EQUIPMENT ★ | No special equipment needed.

WHERE TO FIND LEADS Network with your friends and colleagues in marketing or sales roles, or who run small businesses. You may find work on freelance platforms.

PAY RANGE $$$$ | Writers charge an average of $80–$90 per hour, or $1–$2 per word, for sales letters or scripts.

SLOGAN WRITER

SERVICE PROVIDED Create a catchphrase or tagline to represent a brand or incorporate into a product.

SKILLS AND EXPERIENCE NEEDED ++ | You need writing ability and creativity. Be skilled at capturing a mood or message in a few words. As with creating brand names (see Chapter 8), writing slogans is usually part of a larger branding and advertising effort. If you have relevant experience, you could offer slogans along with other branding services.

SPECIAL EQUIPMENT ★ | No special equipment needed.

WHERE TO FIND LEADS Network with advertising, public relations, and marketing professionals. Join freelance platforms and register with contest sites: sometimes brands use these to run competitions.

PAY RANGE $$ | Some contests pay winners $30 and up. Copywriters make $20–$150 or more per hour.

TEXTBOOK AUTHOR

SERVICE PROVIDED Write or contribute to textbooks.

SKILLS AND EXPERIENCE NEEDED ++++ | You need experience as a writer, extensive knowledge of the field covered in the book, and a related academic degree.

SPECIAL EQUIPMENT ★ | No special equipment needed.

WHERE TO FIND LEADS The ideas for textbooks (and their electronic equivalents) and related materials are often developed by publishers and assigned to writers. To get work, you need to identify publishers you want to work for and develop contacts at those companies. If you have your own idea for a textbook, you need to submit a query.

PAY RANGE $ | Textbook contributors are typically paid in royalties on book sales. The size of the royalty depends in large part on how many authors contribute to the textbook.

TV AND MOVIE REVIEWER

SERVICE PROVIDED Critique television shows and movies.

SKILLS AND EXPERIENCE NEEDED +++ | You need in-depth knowledge of TV shows and movies, including television and film history, along with writing ability and experience.

SPECIAL EQUIPMENT ★ | If video or audio is your medium, you will need a camera or recording equipment and editing software.

WHERE TO FIND LEADS Start a blog (see "Blogger" in this chapter), tap professional or personal contacts at websites and magazines, or pitch to print or online publications that accept reviews by freelancers (research writers' guidelines).

PAY RANGE $$ | If you publish reviews on your own blog, how much you earn will depend on how many visitors you have. Website and magazine rates vary, but top out at $100 per review.

> ### *Similar Jobs*
> Book reviewer, video game reviewer: some websites that specialize in book reviews pay freelance writers $5–$100 per review. Others pay instead in free books. Video game review sites are likely to pay between 15 cents and 35 cents per word ($75–$175 for a 500-word article). As with other freelance journalism work, get writers' guidelines from the site you want to pitch.

VIDEOGRAPHER

SERVICE PROVIDED Film events on video for live broadcast or later editing.

SKILLS AND EXPERIENCE NEEDED +++ | Know how to use video equipment (including editing software) and have experience shooting in different environments. Be able to read the scene in order to capture unanticipated action or details.

SPECIAL EQUIPMENT ★★★ | Cameras and video-editing and production software.

WHERE TO FIND LEADS Develop contacts with marketers, public relations professionals, and producers. Pitch your services to video production companies. Promote your work on social media, your own video channel, and profiles in professional directories. You may find work on freelance platforms.

PAY RANGE $$$ | Videographers typically charge anywhere from $30 to $250 per hour, depending on experience and whether they also include editing services.

VIDEO PRODUCER

SERVICE PROVIDED Create and develop audio and video content for product marketing, education, training, testimonials, and announcements.

SKILLS AND EXPERIENCE NEEDED +++ | You need experience shooting and editing video, storyboarding, and creating scripts. Project management experience is essential.

SPECIAL EQUIPMENT ★ ★ ★ | Video editing and production software.

WHERE TO FIND LEADS Cultivate contacts with marketers, public relations professionals, and video production companies. Promote your work on social media, your own video channel, and profiles in professional directories. Startups and small businesses may be good sources of work, and you may find opportunities on freelance platforms.

PAY RANGE $$$ | Video producers typically charge anywhere from $30 to $250 per hour.

WEB EDITOR

SERVICE PROVIDED Plan, edit, and organize content for a website.

SKILLS AND EXPERIENCE NEEDED +++ | You need writing and editing experience, familiarity with online navigation and search engine optimization practices, and subject matter expertise.

SPECIAL EQUIPMENT ★ | No special equipment needed.

WHERE TO FIND LEADS Network with writers, editors, and website managers. Corporate marketing departments and content marketing agencies can be good sources of work, especially if you have contacts at a company. Promote your services on social media. You may find work on freelance platforms.

PAY RANGE $$$ | Web editors typically charge $25–$100 per hour.

WHITE PAPER WRITER

SERVICE PROVIDED Write reports for a company describing or explaining an aspect of a product or service to educate potential and current customers.

SKILLS AND EXPERIENCE NEEDED +++ | You need writing experience, research and interviewing skills, knowledge of the subject matter, and familiarity with your clients' industry and its customers.

SPECIAL EQUIPMENT ✶ | No special equipment needed.

WHERE TO FIND LEADS Network with other writers and editors. Corporate marketing departments, content marketing agencies, and publishers that create custom content for advertisers can be good sources of work. You may find opportunities on freelance platforms. Promote your services on social media.

PAY RANGE $$$$ | Rates vary. Writers typically charge anywhere from $2,500 to $10,000 depending on the project.

"If I can find something to be productive from a financial standpoint that I enjoy, there's value to it."
—Kevin Lindstrom, soccer fan

Writers on the Rise
Jobs for writers and authors are projected to grow 8 percent by 2026, compared to 2016.

Source: US Bureau of Labor Statistics

CHAPTER 14
Serve

Service side hustles include a diverse set of jobs that ensure safety, security, a fair playing field, and enjoyment of public places and events. Many jobs in this category involve working directly for the federal, state, or local government in part-time or temporary positions. Others involve fulfilling an official role or contributing to a public process as a private citizen, and lend themselves to flexible freelance work. When performing these jobs, people frequently witness or have direct impact on important events in others' lives.

JOB REQUIREMENTS

Because service side hustles often require carrying out a legal process, enforcing rules, or performing effectively in dangerous situations, most of these jobs have formal training requirements. How extensive the training, and how you get it, depends on the role. You may be able to train on the job, or you may have to become qualified before you can begin your work.

The armed forces reserves and National Guard provide basic and ongoing training to soldiers. The US Census Bureau instructs census takers how to administer door-to-door surveys for the decennial population count. Local police train school crossing guards. Sports leagues sponsor training for referees and scorekeepers. To fill other service roles, such as a notary, process server, or building inspector, you need to complete state certification or licensing requirements.

Because of these requirements for some service side hustles, they're well suited for people who have full-time experience on the job. Bail bondspeople, bounty hunters, and process servers are more likely to succeed at a side hustle if they have worked at the job full time. A professional engineer needs several years of work experience just to be eligible for the qualifying exam.

As with many side hustles that involve giving advice (Chapter 5) and caring for people (Chapter 6), you can also parlay your work experience into a related side hustle. Veteran building contractors, plumbers, and electricians may already have the professional training and practical work experience they need to be qualified as inspectors. Banks and law firms are among the biggest users of notary services; they may sponsor any required training for employees, who can also get extra work independently. The National Guard and armed forces reserves have roles for service members who leave active duty. Ordained clergy—already a part-time position at some houses of worship—are licensed to perform any wedding ceremony. The best sports referees are passionate fans with playing experience.

Theresa Carey, a writer in California, decided to train as a volleyball referee after years of playing and coaching. She officiates up to five college matches per week in the fall, winter, and spring. "I didn't ref this intensely when I had kids at home," she says. "It would be hard to do this with little kids because there are some weird hours—Saturdays, and dinner time during weekdays."

She chose the job primarily to stay connected to the sport, but she was also motivated by her experiences with bad referees who made playing and coaching frustrating. Now she encourages young players to train. "For a college student it's good money," she observes, and the availability of work can help fill gaps in the household budget for anyone who is short of funds. "During economic downturns, people go into reffing because they can't get other work."

SERVICE SIDE HUSTLES

ARMY RESERVIST

SERVICE PROVIDED Serve part time in the army reserves.

SKILLS AND EXPERIENCE NEEDED ++++ | Meet qualifications for service and complete training, or convert from active duty. For new recruits, the entry requirements include taking a vocational aptitude test that helps identify the army jobs for which enlistees are best suited. To be an officer, you need to have a college degree.

SPECIAL EQUIPMENT ★ | The army trains reservists for their jobs, including how to use any equipment they need.

WHERE TO FIND LEADS New recruits need to visit their local recruiting office. To be hired, you have to qualify for and be willing to fill an open position.

PAY RANGE $$ | Base pay for a private is more than $3,000 for two weeks of training each year and a weekend per month, plus applicable allowances and bonuses. Pay increases with rank and years of service.

> ### Similar Jobs
> Navy, marine corps, coast guard, or air force reservist: each military branch maintains reserve units.

BAIL BONDSPERSON

SERVICE PROVIDED Enable defendants who don't have cash to post bail by providing a bond—backed by the defendant's assets—to cover bail costs.

SKILLS AND EXPERIENCE NEEDED +++ | Complete training and obtain a license as required by state law. A background in business or finance helps.

SPECIAL EQUIPMENT ★ | No special equipment needed.

WHERE TO FIND LEADS Courts.

PAY RANGE $ | Bail bondspeople charge defendants 10–20 percent of the bail bond amount, as allowed by state law. On a $10,000 bond—a typical price for bail—a bail bondsperson would make $1,000 or more.

BOUNTY HUNTER

SERVICE PROVIDED Work for bail bondspeople to track down fugitives.

SKILLS AND EXPERIENCE NEEDED ++++ | Complete training and obtain a license as required by state law, including weapons training, self-defense, and law. A few states do not allow bounty hunting.

SPECIAL EQUIPMENT ★★★ | Bounty hunters sometimes use surveillance equipment and carry firearms.

WHERE TO FIND LEADS Bail bondspeople.

PAY RANGE $ | Bounty hunters typically earn 10–20 percent of the value of the bond. On a $10,000 bond—a typical price for bail—a bounty hunter would make $1,000 or more.

BUILDING INSPECTOR

SERVICE PROVIDED Inspect buildings to determine if they comply with building codes.

SKILLS AND EXPERIENCE NEEDED +++ | Experience in construction trades and a license or certification required by state or local law.

SPECIAL EQUIPMENT ★★ | You need a ladder, flashlight, measurement tools, safety goggles, and other equipment for inspecting the building site and making observations safely.

WHERE TO FIND LEADS Though they typically work full time, local governments may hire part-time building inspectors.

PAY RANGE $$$ | Most building inspectors earn $25 per hour or more.

CENSUS TAKER OR ENUMERATOR

SERVICE PROVIDED Go door to door collecting information from residents for the decennial census, and other surveys.

SKILLS AND EXPERIENCE NEEDED ✦✦ | Pass a test and complete a short training course.

SPECIAL EQUIPMENT ★ | No special equipment needed.

WHERE TO FIND LEADS The US Census Bureau will begin recruiting field workers for the 2020 census in January 2019. The agency takes applications for enumerators on an ongoing basis.

PAY RANGE $$ | Compensation varies by location, but it averages around $15 per hour.

CITY COUNCILOR

SERVICE PROVIDED Serve as an elected member of a local government legislative body.

SKILLS AND EXPERIENCE NEEDED ✦✦ | Be an adult resident of the city where you serve and be elected to represent a district or precinct. Many city councilors prepare for the role by participating in community organizations, working for a municipal agency, or interacting with the city government through their primary jobs. Successful candidates often develop ideas about specific policies they want to promote or a vision for the community.

SPECIAL EQUIPMENT ★ | No special equipment needed.

WHERE TO FIND LEADS City councilors serve defined terms and have to run for reelection when their terms are up. Any city resident who is eligible to run can campaign for the office.

PAY RANGE $ | Varies. Being a city council member in a large city is often a full-time job. In a small town, it is often a volunteer position. In between, elected representatives may receive a few dollars, a few hundred, or several thousand.

CLERGY

SERVICE PROVIDED Lead religious services, perform religious ceremonies, and attend to congregants' spiritual needs.

SKILLS AND EXPERIENCE NEEDED ✦✦✦✦ | Be ordained in your faith. Most clergy have advanced degrees.

SPECIAL EQUIPMENT ★ | No special equipment needed.

WHERE TO FIND LEADS Religious denominations vary in how they appoint their clergy, but part-time positions are becoming more common.

PAY RANGE $$$ | Pay varies. Guidelines published by the United Church of Christ recommend paying $15,250–$21,250 annually to a pastor working 10–13 hours per week.

CROSSING GUARD

SERVICE PROVIDED Manage traffic at crosswalks so school-children can cross busy streets safely.

SKILLS AND EXPERIENCE NEEDED ✦✦ | No experience needed. Local police departments typically train crossing guards.

SPECIAL EQUIPMENT ★ | No special equipment needed. Crossing guards wear a uniform supplied by the police department or school district.

WHERE TO FIND LEADS Apply at local police departments. You may hear of openings by word of mouth or find them advertised.

PAY RANGE $ | School crossing guards make an average of $11 per hour.

EXPERT WITNESS

SERVICE PROVIDED Provide opinions during a legal proceeding about technical evidence in your field, such as a medical specialty, accounting, or computer forensics.

SKILLS AND EXPERIENCE NEEDED ++++ | You need in-depth expertise in your specialty area, and you will have to prepare for delivering testimony. Excellent communication and interpersonal skills are essential to working with clients; you must also be comfortable explaining and defending your conclusions in depositions and, if necessary, in court.

SPECIAL EQUIPMENT ★ | No special equipment needed.

WHERE TO FIND LEADS Network with your professional and personal contacts, and get to know lawyers. Insurance companies often hire expert witnesses, and you can promote yourself to potential clients by listing a profile in expert witness directories.

PAY RANGE $$$$ | It depends on your field and your reputation as an expert. Rates range from $100 to $1,000 or more per hour.

FUNERAL OFFICIANT

SERVICE PROVIDED Conduct funeral services.

SKILLS AND EXPERIENCE NEEDED +++ | Ordained clergy commonly conduct funeral services. You can also train as a nondenominational or nonreligious funeral celebrant.

SPECIAL EQUIPMENT ★ | No special equipment needed.

WHERE TO FIND LEADS Sources of work include your own and colleagues' congregations, funeral homes, and your personal and professional contacts. List your profile in a professional directory to help potential clients find you.

PAY RANGE $$$$ | Funeral officiants may get $50–$500 as an honorarium. For a religious service, the amount may be determined by local custom. In some churches, it's expected that congregants will give a donation to the church for services you perform.

GRANT REVIEWER

SERVICE PROVIDED Evaluate grant applications for US federal agencies as a peer reviewer.

SKILLS AND EXPERIENCE NEEDED ++++ | Be an experienced researcher in your field. Some agencies also look for reviewers who have related experience outside academia.

SPECIAL EQUIPMENT ★ | No special equipment needed.

WHERE TO FIND LEADS Federal agency websites post calls for reviewers.

PAY RANGE $$$$ | A few agencies pay an honorarium, cover travel expenses, or both. For example, the Bureau of Justice Assistance pays $125 per application. The National Institutes of Health pays $100–$200 per review meeting for written critiques and $200 per day for in-person meetings or teleconferences.

JUSTICE OF THE PEACE

SERVICE PROVIDED In the few states that have them, a justice of the peace performs civil marriages and may preside over minor court proceedings and administer oaths and other duties according to state law.

SKILLS AND EXPERIENCE NEEDED +++ | Unlike other judicial officials, a justice of the peace does not always have to be a licensed attorney, though they may have to meet other qualifications to hold office.

SPECIAL EQUIPMENT ★ | No special equipment needed.

WHERE TO FIND LEADS Depending on the state, a justice of the peace is either elected or applies for an appointment.

PAY RANGE $$$$ | For a wedding ceremony, a typical rate is $50-$100.

MOCK JUROR

SERVICE PROVIDED Give online survey feedback to attorneys about their cases before trial.

SKILLS AND EXPERIENCE NEEDED + | No experience needed, but you have to meet minimal qualifications. Attorneys may look for jurors with specific demographics.

SPECIAL EQUIPMENT ★ | No special equipment needed.

WHERE TO FIND LEADS Sign up on a mock jury site.

PAY RANGE $ | Jurors are paid $10–$60, depending on the site.

NATIONAL GUARD SERVICE MEMBER

SERVICE PROVIDED Serve in a military unit under the jurisdiction of state governors. Though the National Guard may be called for national defense, units more typically respond to state and local emergencies, such as natural disasters.

SKILLS AND EXPERIENCE NEEDED + | Meet eligibility requirements and complete training. New recruits take a vocational aptitude test that helps to identify the types of jobs in the National Guard they would be best at.

SPECIAL EQUIPMENT ★ | Service members are trained to use equipment they need to perform their duties.

WHERE TO FIND LEADS Local recruiting offices. To be hired, you have to qualify for and be willing to fill an open position.

PAY RANGE $$ | Base pay for an enlisted private is more than $3,000 for two weeks of training each year and a weekend per month.

NOTARY

SERVICE PROVIDED Witness signatures on government or business documents, administer oaths, verify authenticity, and other tasks to prevent fraud. In some states, notaries are called upon to swear in witnesses when depositions are taken by phone or video.

SKILLS AND EXPERIENCE NEEDED ✦ | Each state has eligibility requirements, and a few require training or suggest taking a course.

SPECIAL EQUIPMENT ★ ★ ★ | Notary seal, certificates, and a journal for keeping records. You may be required to carry insurance.

WHERE TO FIND LEADS Professional and personal contacts can help you find work, and you may find opportunities with banks, law offices, and title companies. You can promote your services on social media and list your profile in a professional directory.

PAY RANGE $ | Notary rates are set by state law in most states and typically range from $2 to $10 per signature.

PARK RANGER

SERVICE PROVIDED Work in a local, state, or national park, or at a site with historic, cultural, or environmental significance, such as a battlefield or scenic river. Jobs include enforcing rules and regulations, helping visitors, giving tours, and running interpretive programs.

SKILLS AND EXPERIENCE NEEDED ✦✦✦ | The variety of park ranger roles require different types of training. The National Park Service, states, and localities publish their requirements.

SPECIAL EQUIPMENT ★ ★ | The equipment you need depends on the job and the agency you work for.

WHERE TO FIND LEADS Talk with park staff, and inquire at local or state agencies that run parks, as well as the National Park Service. Agencies will post available jobs and may advertise openings. Many park ranger jobs are seasonal.

PAY RANGE $$ | Pay varies by position, experience, the size of the park, and jurisdiction. Hourly rates for seasonal workers are typically less than $20 per hour.

PROCESS SERVER

SERVICE PROVIDED Serve subpoenas and other legal documents to people involved in court cases.

SKILLS AND EXPERIENCE NEEDED ++ | Each state sets eligibility requirements for obtaining a license; some may require you to take a class. You may need accreditation to work on financial cases.

SPECIAL EQUIPMENT ★ | No special equipment needed.

WHERE TO FIND LEADS Process-serving companies, training programs, law offices, and court offices may be sources of job opportunities. You can list your profile in professional directories.

PAY RANGE $$$$ | Process servers typically charge $45–$75 per document served.

PROFESSIONAL ENGINEER

SERVICE PROVIDED Sign, seal, and submit engineering plans or drawings for regulatory approval. Due to the extensive education and training required for this work, it's most suitable as a side hustle for people who already do it professionally and who either want to earn extra money or need to work part time.

SKILLS AND EXPERIENCE NEEDED ++++ | To become a licensed professional engineer, you need a four-year engineering degree, four years of experience working for a professional engineer, and to pass two exams. You need a professional engineer license to work as a consultant or in private practice, and in some states to teach engineering.

SPECIAL EQUIPMENT ★★ | Tools, including software, needed for your projects.

WHERE TO FIND LEADS Tap your professional and personal contacts, inquire at engineering firms, and participate in professional associations. Job openings may be advertised.

PAY RANGE $$$$ | Most engineering consultants charge more than $160 per hour.

REFEREE

SERVICE PROVIDED Enforce rules on the field, court, or rink during team sporting events.

SKILLS AND EXPERIENCE NEEDED +++ | Know your sport (ideally from having played it) and take the necessary training courses. Be able to handle heckling and irate fans—and parents if you referee games for high school or younger students.

SPECIAL EQUIPMENT ✭ ✭ | A whistle and necessary protective gear.

WHERE TO FIND LEADS Learn about opportunities from state or local referee associations, other referees, and coaches. Because sports leagues run dozens of games a season, and there are many levels of play, it can be easy to find work.

PAY RANGE $$$ | Varies by sport and level. High school referees in Texas typically earn $30–$125 per game.

Similar Jobs
Umpire: call balls, strikes, outs, and errors during baseball games.

SCOREKEEPER

SERVICE PROVIDED Record scores at sports events, including games and tournaments.

SKILLS AND EXPERIENCE NEEDED ++ | Knowledge of scoring and rules for the sport you are recording. For league games or tournaments, experience playing the sport is usually preferred and sometimes required.

SPECIAL EQUIPMENT ✭ | Scorekeeping tools, which may include score sheets, the scoreboard, and a time clock.

WHERE TO FIND LEADS Get work through local recreational programs, sports leagues, or clubs, and coaches, referees, or other scorekeepers you know, as well as your personal or professional contacts. Some openings may be advertised.

PAY RANGE $ | Scorekeepers may be paid per hour or per game, and the amount depends on the sport, the level, and the league. You may get $10 per hour to score recreation league softball games, and $30 or more to score a college basketball game.

SECURITY GUARD

SERVICE PROVIDED Control building entrances, monitor building security measures, and patrol property to protect it against theft and other illegal activity.

SKILLS AND EXPERIENCE NEEDED + | Employers usually provide training. Most states require security guards to be registered, especially if they carry weapons (in which case you also need weapons training). You may need a driver's license.

SPECIAL EQUIPMENT ★★ | You may need to drive or use surveillance equipment. Armed guards have weapons.

WHERE TO FIND LEADS Property management companies, security services companies, and local businesses may hire security guards. You may also learn of opportunities through social media and your professional and personal contacts.

PAY RANGE $$ | Security guards make an average of $14 per hour.

STATE LEGISLATOR

SERVICE PROVIDED Serve as a state senator or representative making laws for your state.

SKILLS AND EXPERIENCE NEEDED ++ | While formal experience isn't required, many people who run for state legislator have other public-service experience. They may have held elected local government positions, worked as a government employee, interacted with state agencies through their primary jobs, held appointed government positions, or been involved with organizations that work to influence state policies. Successful candidates usually develop ideas for policies they would like to implement or have a vision for the future of the state.

SPECIAL EQUIPMENT ★ | No special equipment needed.

WHERE TO FIND LEADS Anyone who meets state eligibility requirements—usually concerning age, citizenship, and district residency—can run for office. Some states require you to pay a filing fee or collect a certain number of signatures to get on the ballot.

PAY RANGE $$ | All fifty states pay their legislators, but only ten pay a full-time salary. Among the rest, twenty-six states pay an average of $41,110 for three-fourths time, and fourteen pay an average of $18,449 for a little more than half time.

WEDDING OFFICIANT

SERVICE PROVIDED Perform marriage ceremonies.

SKILLS AND EXPERIENCE NEEDED +++ | Be licensed in your state to perform marriages. You can be an ordained religious leader, a justice of the peace, a judge, or a professional celebrant.

SPECIAL EQUIPMENT ★ | No special equipment needed.

WHERE TO FIND LEADS Promote your services among your personal and professional contacts, and on social media. List your profile on wedding planning websites and professional directories. If you are a religious leader, you will likely perform wedding ceremonies for your congregation.

PAY RANGE $$$$ | Wedding officiants' fees range from $50 to $400 or more.

"During economic downturns, people go into reffing because they can't get other work."
—Theresa Carey, volleyball referee

Index

About the Author

Elana Varon began her career with a side hustle: writing documentation for a software startup. A business writer and editor, she has spent more than two decades chronicling the ways that advances in technology change how people work.

From 2006 to 2011, Elana was the executive editor of *CIO*, where she directed the magazine's monthly coverage of business technology, leadership, and innovation. In 2011, she founded Cochituate Media, where she provides editorial services to corporate and nonprofit clients. She lives in Massachusetts with her husband, two teenagers, and a Siberian kitten.

Printed in the USA
CPSIA information can be obtained
at www.ICGtesting.com
CBHW020710050524
7986CB00005B/207